CONSTITUTIONAL STUDIES

CONSTITUTIONAL STUDIES

Contemporary Issues and Controversies

Edited by

ROBERT BLACKBURN

MANSELL

First published in 1992 by
Mansell Publishing Limited, A Cassell Imprint
Villiers House, 41/47 Strand, London WC2N 5JE,
England
387 Park Avenue South, New York, NY 10016-8810,
USA

Reprinted in paperback 1994

© Robert Blackburn and the contributors, 1992

All rights reserved. No part of this publication may be
reproduced or transmitted in any form or by any means,
electronic or mechanical including photocopying,
recording or any information storage or retrieval system,
without prior permission in writing from the publishers
or their appointed agents.

British Library Cataloguing-in-Publication Data
A catalogue record for this book is available from the
British Library.
ISBN 0-7201-2125-6 (Hardback)
ISBN 0-7201-2204-X (Paperback)

Library of Congress Cataloging-in-Publication Data
Constitutional studies: contemporary issues and
controversies / edited by Robert Blackburn.
  p.   cm.
Includes bibliographical references and index.
ISBN 0-7201-2125-6 (Hardback)
ISBN 0-7201-2204-X (Paperback)
  1. Great Britain—Constitutional law. 2. Great
Britain—Politics and government—1979–
I. Blackburn, Robert, 1952–
KD3989.C66   1992
342.41—dc20
[344.102]   92-1345
                                                CIP

Typeset by Colset Private Limited, Singapore
Printed and bound in Great Britain by
Biddles Ltd, Guildford and King's Lynn

Contents

	The Contributors	vii
	Introduction ROBERT BLACKBURN	ix
1	The Future of the British Monarchy ROBERT BLACKBURN	1
2	Cabinet Government since Bagehot G. W. JONES	14
3	Margaret Thatcher's Resignation as Prime Minister ROBERT BLACKBURN	32
4	The Nationalization Legislation of the 1940s and the Privatization Legislation of the 1980s: A Constitutional Perspective JOHN McELDOWNEY	42
5	Administrative Law: Is the System Now in Place? ANTHONY BRADLEY	65
6	Political Parties: Conservative Political and Constitutional Ideology JOHN RAMSDEN	79
7	Political Parties: The Constitution of the Social and Liberal Democrats CHARLES RADCLIFFE BEALE	92

CONTENTS

8   Fairness and Political Finance: The Case of Election Campaigns   120
     DAWN OLIVER

9   Does Britain Need Proportional Representation?   136
     PHILIP NORTON

10   Judicial Independence in Britain: Challenges Real and Threats Imagined   148
     GAVIN DREWRY

11   By Law Established: The Church of England and its Place in the Constitution   168
     DOMINIC GRANT

    Index   187

Contributors

ROBERT BLACKBURN is Senior Lecturer in Law and Director of the Centre of British Constitutional Law and History at King's College London.

GEORGE W. JONES is Professor of Government at the London School of Economics and Political Science.

JOHN McELDOWNEY is Senior Lecturer in Law at the University of Warwick.

ANTHONY BRADLEY is a practising barrister, and Emeritus Professor of Constitutional Law in the University of Edinburgh.

JOHN RAMSDEN is Reader in Modern History at Queen Mary and Westfield College, University of London.

CHARLES RADCLIFFE BEALE is a policy adviser to the New South Wales government in Australia and a former political researcher to Robert Maclennan MP.

DAWN OLIVER is Reader in Public Law at University College London.

PHILIP NORTON is Professor of Politics at the University of Hull.

GAVIN DREWRY is Professor of Public Administration at Royal Holloway and Bedford New College, University of London.

DOMINIC GRANT is an administrative officer in the parish of St Mary-at-Finchley.

Introduction

This book contains a selection of studies on the constitutional affairs of the UK. The initiative behind the book came from the work of the Centre of British Constitutional Law and History, which was founded at King's College London in 1987, and which over the period since has rapidly established itself as one of the UK's leading academic institutions devoted to the promotion of scholarship and research into constitutional matters. All but two of the chapters in this collection were prepared for publication by each author out of material first delivered as a public lecture or seminar in one of the Centre's annual programmes between 1988 and 1991. The other two chapters are the product of research undertaken in the Law School at King's College under the supervision of the Director of the Centre.[1] The book is an interdisciplinary work, in that the contributors to it include lawyers, historians and political scientists, and it was the editor's request to each of them to avoid so far as possible the use of technical jargon belonging to one particular discipline. It is hoped therefore that the book will be of use to all readers who have a special interest in the constitution of the UK. Each chapter contains an independent analysis of some important subject or controversy in recent years, and collectively the book aims to provide a balance of the broad range of inquiries that are involved in developing an understanding of the constitutional process in Britain.

Most of the chapters in this book are concerned with questions of constitutional change. Of those which consider existing arrangements with possible future improvements in mind, Chapter 1 by Robert Blackburn addresses some of the problems which now confront the British monarchy and makes some suggestions for reform. In Chapter 5 Anthony Bradley questions whether Britain has now reached the stage of a coherent system of administrative justice, and considers what is

INTRODUCTION

still to be done. In Chapter 9 Philip Norton discusses the issues posed by the proposal for changing the British system of elections to the House of Commons to one of greater representative proportionality. The reform issue of disestablishment of the Church of England is dealt with in Dominic Grant's account of the Anglican Church and its place in the British constitution. Chapters in the collection giving consideration to matters in our recent past and the contemporary lessons to be drawn, include John McEldowney's analysis in Chapter 4 of the Conservative government's privatization legislation in the 1980s. He draws comparisons with the form of the nationalization Acts in the 1940s, and assesses the quality of political accountability and regulation to protect the public interest within the legal framework of the newly privatized public utility companies. In Chapter 2 George Jones considers the evolution of the cabinet since the nineteenth century, and gives his views on the conflicting theories of whether cabinet government or prime ministerial government is the most appropriate description of the contemporary political executive in Britain. Charles Beale in Chapter 7 gives an account of the demise of the old Liberal Party in 1987–1988 and its permanent merger with members of the SDP to form the Social and Liberal Democrats. While this was not directly a constitutional issue, the story has important implications for the British party system which colour and explain the constitutional process of government and opposition. Another historical episode of major political importance, that of Margaret Thatcher's resignation as prime minister in November 1990, is explored from a constitutional perspective by Robert Blackburn in Chapter 3. In Chapter 10 Gavin Drewry provides an analysis of the theory and practice of judicial independence over the twentieth century, and in Chapter 6 John Ramsden provides a highly topical historical analysis of conservative theory on our political and constitutional structure. This is written at a time when major constitutional challenges are facing the UK, and the Conservative leadership remains loyal to the notion of 'rolling constitutional change' (to use the words of cabinet minister John Patten),[2] in preference to the radical reform programmes of the opposition parties.

This then brings us to the heart of what has become a central preoccupation of constitutional writing in the 1990s. The period since the 1960s has witnessed a sustained, critical re-examination of British political institutions, and how they might be made more effective, encompassing, for example, the reforms establishing the modern House of Commons select committees and the Parliamentary Commissioner for Administration, and the restructuring of local government, in the 1960s and 1970s, and the attempts at reforming the House of Lords in 1969 and at devolution of government to Scotland and Wales in 1978. A new stage was reached when in the latter years of the 1970s

INTRODUCTION

the former Lord Chancellor, Lord Hailsham, issued warnings of 'elective dictatorship' in Britain and called for a new constitution which would be committed into legal, written form.[3] If Lord Hailsham found little support for his views within the Conservative leadership between 1979 and 1987 when he returned to government office, the years since 1988 have seen an extraordinary development of interest and a proliferation of reform programmes in the subject emanating from the Labour and Liberal Democrat political parties, Charter 88, research institutes such as the Institute for Public Policy Research, and individual writers such as, most recently, Rodney Brazier.[4] In the past 18 months alone, there have been published no fewer than four written constitution proposals.[5] In 1993 Mansell Publishing is launching a major new list of titles called The Constitutional Reform Series. If ever there was a time for a series of in-depth inquiries into particular components of the constitutional structure, giving a fresh appraisal and evaluation of its present working along with analysis of current proposals for improvement and reform, then that time is now.

It is important for readers to know that the chapters in this book were written at different times over the period 1989–91: Chapter 2 in 1989; Chapters 4, 6, 7, 9 and 10 in 1990; and Chapters 1, 3, 5, 8 and 11 in 1991.

It has been a pleasure for the editor to work with all the contributors to the book, and he thanks each of them for their support and helpful co-operation in publication.

R.B.
King's College London
December 1991

NOTES AND REFERENCES

1 Chapters 7 and 11.
2 *Political Culture, Conservatism and Rolling Constitutional Change*, The 1991 Swinton Lecture.
3 See: *Elective Dictatorship* (1976); and *The Dilemma of Democracy* (1978).
4 Rodney Brazier, *Constitutional Reform* (1991).
5 Liberal Democrats, Federal Green Paper No. 13, *We the People: Towards a Written Constitution* (1990); Institute for Economic Affairs, *Constitutional Reform in the United Kingdom* (1990); the *Commonwealth of Britain Bill* [1990–91] HC 161 (presented by Tony Benn MP); Institute for Public Policy Research, *The Constitution of the United Kingdom* (1991).

1

The Future of the British Monarchy

ROBERT BLACKBURN

One of the greatest fallacies in contemporary British politics is the assumption of the durability of the monarchy. Its ancient history, its wealth and splendour, and the seemingly inexhaustible curiosity and affection of the British people towards the royal family, all serve to disguise the fact that the monarchy is now facing a greater crisis of accommodating social and political change than ever before. The reality is that far from resting upon a solid foundation, built up over many hundreds of years, the British Crown is a fragile institution that in many fundamental respects either contradicts or fits awkwardly into a modern democratic system of government.

The lesson is that supporters of royalty must wake up to the fact that the monarchy will require careful nurturing if it is to survive long into the twenty-first century. One hundred and twenty years ago the Grand Old Man of Victorian politics, William Gladstone, doubted that the monarchy would survive for much longer.[1] That it has done so, and indeed adapted with success to the post-universal-suffrage era, despite many potential flashpoints such as the constitutional crisis over the House of Lords in 1909–1911 and the Abdication crisis in 1936, is a tribute to the personal characters and diplomacy of King George V, King George VI and Queen Elizabeth II. In this chapter I intend to explore some of the central issues which confront the British monarchy at the end of the twentieth century, and I put forward some suggestions concerning the future for consideration by readers of this book, and also by the politicians at Westminster whose responsibility it is to safeguard and keep under constant review the workings of the parliamentary system of government to which they belong.

ROBERT BLACKBURN
THE CONSTITUTIONAL OFFICE OF MONARCH

The monarch is the UK's head of state, whereas the prime minister is the head of 'Her Majesty's Government'. Legally and ceremonially the Queen is vested with the executive powers necessary to govern the country, but the principal convention of 'limited' or 'constitutional' monarchy is that the powers of the monarch are exercised upon the advice of ministers who sit in and are responsible to Parliament. These executive powers are known collectively as 'the royal prerogative', and include powers exercised directly by the Queen such as the appointment of ministers or the calling of a general election, and those exercised indirectly on her behalf by civil servants or ministers such as treaty negotiations and international diplomacy.

The structure of British government into which the monarchy is embedded is a jumble of contradictory legal theory and political practice. The common law has it that the monarch has an absolute discretion to withhold assent to legislation passed by both Houses of Parliament, but the royal veto by convention has not been exercised since 1704. Again, in law the Queen has an absolute discretionary power to appoint whomsoever she pleases as prime minister, but by convention she does not: constitutionally she had to appoint John Major in November 1990, following the resignation of Margaret Thatcher, by virtue of his being leader of a majority party in the House of Commons. Constitutional commentators in Britain have tended to side-step these contradictions in the basic law affecting the monarchy, to the considerable bemusement of other Europeans and of Americans, who, in their own countries, have traditionally been anxious to commit fundamental rights and obligations into clear, intelligible legal form, generally incorporated in a written constitution. British politicians and commentators have instead described the whole executive structure as subject to a constitutional theory called 'ministerial responsibility'. So far as the monarchy is concerned, its general principles may be summarized as follows: (1) ministers, not the monarch, are responsible for the government of the country; (2) the monarch exercises her prerogative powers and duties in accordance with the advice of ministers; (3) the monarch will not make public speeches or utterances on matters of a party political nature independent of ministerial advice; (4) the monarch should not be personally criticized for her acts of state and, if she is, will not reply; and (5) ministers will answer questions and criticisms of the public acts of the monarch. The rationale of avoiding criticism of, and reply by, the Queen is to sustain the monarch's political neutrality, which might otherwise lower public regard for the institution of monarchy itself. In the words of Sir Ivor Jennings, 'the Queen never takes responsibility'.[2]

The political influence of the monarchy is more subtle. Walter Bagehot struck the right chord in 1867 when he wrote that 'the Sovereign has, under a Constitutional Monarchy such as ours, three rights – the right to be consulted, the right to encourage, the right to warn'.[3] The Queen may express her opinions privately to ministers, and by custom she is kept informed of matters of national policy by way of the prime minister visiting her for weekly audiences at Buckingham Palace and her right to receive cabinet papers and minutes. Her private secretary has said she spends two or three hours each day reading various state papers.[4] It may be impossible to imagine a prime minister being swayed by royal views on central questions of social or economic policy, but we know from political memoirs that King George V and King George VI exerted pressure leading to certain changes of mind by prime ministers, such as King George VI directing Sir Winston Churchill to cancel his intention to visit Normandy with the invasion force in 1944, and in the following year contributing to Clement Attlee's reconsideration of placing Hugh Dalton in charge of the Foreign Office.[5] No doubt the influence, or force of expression of opinion, by a monarch will vary according to the personality on the throne, and Queen Elizabeth II, like her father, is generally regarded as being of a reserved, introverted disposition. It is fascinating to conjecture how her more outward-going eldest son will fare when he becomes King Charles III. But the fact is that the institution of monarchy has a positive vested interest in *not* being associated with particular items of public or social policy, for it knows that therein lies the political danger of falling foul of one or more of the political parties.

TITLES AND SUCCESSION TO THE THRONE

As a result of Britain's past empire, Queen Elizabeth II is monarch not only of the UK but also of Antigua and Barbuda, Australia, the Bahamas, Barbados, Belize, Canada, Grenada, Jamaica, Mauritius, New Zealand, Papua New Guinea, Saint Lucia, St Christopher and Nevis, St Vincent and the Grenadines, the Solomon Islands, and Tuvalu. She is also 'Head of the Commonwealth', a title acquired in 1949 as a result of India's desire on independence to become a self-governing republic but to remain within the Commonwealth. The Queen acts upon the advice of UK ministers on all occasions and wherever she is travelling, except when she is within one of those Commonwealth states where she is retained as monarch, when she will act upon the advice of that country's prime minister. In her absence from those countries apart from Britain where she is queen, her legal and ceremonial powers are delegated to a governor-general to perform. It is interesting to note that when she is delivering her Christmas broadcast and Commonwealth Day message in March, she acts solely in her capacity as Head of the Commonwealth, free from any ministerial advice, and the speeches represent at least 60 or 70 per cent her own personal work, including choice of topic and the writing of the first and final drafts.[6] This contrasts sharply with, say, the Queen's Speech at the opening of each annual parliamentary session in the House of Lords, each syllable of which is prepared for her by 10 Downing Street.

In theory 'the monarch never dies'. At the moment that King George died, Elizabeth II automatically became Queen, and her accession was formally recognized by an Accession Council consisting of Privy Councillors and other leading citizens. A coronation is not necessary for succession to the Crown (indeed, King Edward VIII was never crowned), but takes place several months afterwards in a spectacular ceremony that consecrates and confirms the new monarch. A series of historic statutes exclude Roman Catholics and persons marrying Roman Catholics from the succession because, as head of the Anglican Church since King Henry VIII, the monarch must be in communion with the Church of England and swear to uphold the Established Church. The rules of succession to the throne are hereditary according to the feudal law of primogeniture, sons before daughters, with the eldest son (or, if deceased at the death of the monarch, his own children) preferred. Thus Queen Elizabeth's children in order of birth are Prince Charles, Princess Anne (the Princess Royal), Prince Andrew and Prince Edward; and the order of succession at present is Prince Charles, then his sons Prince William and Prince Henry, Prince Andrew, then his daughters Princess Beatrice and Princess Eugenie, Prince Edward, the Princess Royal, then her children Peter Phillips and Zara Phillips. Strictly speaking, according to feudal law affecting the nobility, if there are no sons and more than one daughter of the departing monarch, the daughters are considered equal in law regardless of age and succeed jointly. This combination arose for the first time in 1952, King George VI leaving the two Princesses Elizabeth and Margaret, but Parliament rightly rejected this nonsense and confirmed the order of succession to Queen Elizabeth alone.

Is it right that the law should discriminate against female succession? No one today can seriously imagine that a man is better fitted to be monarch than a woman. The example of Queen Elizabeth in itself is the living refutation of such an absurd proposition, and it might be noted also that two of the other seven European monarchies have female occupants of the throne, Queen Beatrix of the Netherlands and Queen Margrethe II of Denmark. The issue is not a pressing one in Britain, since Prince Charles is in any event older than Princess Anne, and Prince Charles's first two children are both boys. Nonetheless any review or codification of the legal principles affecting succession to the throne must surely remove this sex discrimination and simply provide for the eldest child to succeed.

Consideration should also be given to formalizing the means of quitting the throne, or disclaiming rights of succession by reluctant persons. The idea that the monarch holds office until death is deeply ingrained in historical practice and the ideology of the British Crown. There is a statutory framework for a regency in the case of mental or physical infirmity such as old age might bring, in the Regency Act 1937 passed as a direct result of the painful experience of King George V frequently being too ill in the 1930s even to sign state papers. However, either tradition or the law might be further changed to permit the Queen to retire in favour of Prince Charles at any time from now on, given that she has passed her 65th birthday. The pressures on and work of a contemporary monarch are enormous, and few would blame her if she wished to pass on the mantle to her son whilst she was still alive, indeed active and healthy and able to enjoy a normal retirement.

MONARCH AND PRIME MINISTER

Those who followed the dramatic events whereby John Major succeeded Margaret Thatcher as prime minister in November 1990 might be forgiven for believing that a British prime minister is appointed by the largest party in the House of Commons. Constitutionally this is of course incorrect, for it is the Queen who possesses the prerogative to appoint prime ministers. There are no legal requirements to guide the Queen's choice, only the custom that the prime minister should be an MP, the party processes which make it clear who are the party leaders and therefore candidates for being premier, and the rather vague maxim that she or he must be able 'to command the confidence' of the House of Commons.

This is fine so long as a general election produces an overall majority for one party, whose leader will automatically be appointed prime minister by the Queen, but problems arise if no such single party domination of the Commons exists. Even under the existing 'first past the post' electoral system hung parliaments occur from time to time, and it seemed quite likely that the 1992 general election would produce one, with Labour and the Conservatives running so closely in the opinion polls throughout the fifth year of the last parliament. Under proportional representation of any variety, hung parliaments would become more likely and possibly the norm. The general rule is that the prime minister has the first claim on attempting to form a government, either as a minority in the Commons or in a governing coalition. But if he fails, either by his own admission as with Edward Heath in

February 1974, or by way of a no-confidence motion being carried against his government at the opening of Parliament as with Stanley Baldwin in 1923, then he must resign and allow the leader of the opposition into 10 Downing Street.

The office of prime minister derives immense power and authority from effectively being able to utilize all the Crown prerogatives as he or she wishes. In practice it is the prime minister personally who tenders advice on all the most important matters, and by convention the crucial powers of cabinet appointments and dissolution of Parliament are solely the responsibility of the premier. It is this arrangement above all that has led many commentators, including R. H. S. Crossman, J. P. Mackintosh and Tony Benn, to deny that there is any real system of 'cabinet government' at all in Britain any more, but one of 'prime ministerial government' instead.[7] Many people would have dearly wished to be a fly on the wall at the weekly meetings of Queen Elizabeth and Margaret Thatcher, upon which there was much speculation about personal difficulties and jokes about whether they both employed the royal 'we' in conversation together. It does seem to be the case that over the past 25 years, the Labour prime ministers Harold Wilson and James Callaghan enjoyed a far warmer relationship with the Queen than that with the Conservatives Edward Heath and Margaret Thatcher.[8] For John Major it is early days.

DISSOLUTION OF PARLIAMENT

Apart from the power to control the composition of cabinet (and by November 1990 there was not a single original member of Margaret Thatcher's 1979 cabinet left, apart from herself), the most precious Crown prerogative at the disposal of the prime minister is the dissolution of Parliament and freedom to set the date of a general election. This power is derived historically from the feudal theory that Parliament is the personal creature of the Crown, to be summoned and dismissed for advice and consent to taxation whenever the monarch pleased.[9] It is now employed by a prime minister to select an election date on which he thinks he is most likely to win. It is a source of tremendous political advantage over the opposition.

Are there no limits to what the prime minister can advise the Queen over dissolution? Over the past 150 years there has been a great deal of theorizing about some 'reserve' or 'personal' discretion which a monarch possesses to rebut prime ministerial advice. Thus in 1858 Lord Aberdeen, premier between 1852 and 1855, told Queen Victoria that 'there is no doubt of the power and prerogative of the Sovereign to refuse a dissolution – it [is] one of the very few acts which the Queen of England [can] do without responsible advice'.[10] Fifty years later the leading constitutional historian Sir Sidney Low said, 'It is well within the prerogative of the Sovereign to refuse his assent to a dissolution of Parliament, if advised on inadequate or frivolous grounds'.[11] In the 1950s, the most respected constitutional lawyer this century, Sir Ivor Jennings, classified dissolution as one of the 'personal prerogatives' of the Crown,[12] and as recently as the summer of 1991 Lord Armstrong, the former Cabinet Secretary, publicly stated that 'It is not just theoretically correct, but common sense, that the Sovereign should have the right to withold consent to a request for a dissolution'.[13] The reality is that no monarch has rejected a prime minister's advice on dissolution since 1832. Certainly insofar as a prime minister's advice might be actually unconstitutional (for example if a prime minister who lost an election ever refused to resign and instead requested a second election, hoping to improve his party's results), then the Queen would be both entitled and obliged to dismiss him or her and appoint the leader of the opposition as the new prime minister. But for the Queen to intervene in circumstances where there are no clear constitutional rules poses grave dangers to the monarchy, for the rebuttal of the prime minister's advice would almost certainly lead to the resignation of the government, and the Crown would have incurred the anger of one of the main political parties who one day would be returned to office. As Lord Hailsham has said, 'the Monarch who ventured to use the prerogative against either of the two main parties of the state would risk either enforced abdication or republicanism'.[14]

The way forward is for Britain to adopt a fixed-term parliament as is common elsewhere around the world. A set period of four years between each general election would fit closely with existing practice, and it would have the democratic advantage of all parties and the electorate knowing the election date in advance, whereas at present a prime minister gives less than six weeks' notice for a general election.[15] Fixed arrangements normally provide prescribed conditions when an earlier election may take place, and in Britain this might be where the government loses a confidence motion in the Commons. No question of mediation by the monarch of a dispute between the parties on the legitimacy of an early dissolution could therefore arise, and the monarchy would be protected from any embroilment in political controversy.

CROWN FINANCE

The fabulous wealth of the British monarchy has again recently been in the news as a result of the Liberal Democrat MP Simon Hughes' Bill in the House of Commons to tax the Queen in the same way as an ordinary citizen.[16] This issue is more complex than it may seem, and is further confused by regular press speculation on the value of the Queen's property, often wildly inaccurate. Simply to say that the Queen has enormous houses at Buckingham Palace, Windsor Castle or Balmoral is by itself not much more helpful than saying John Major has big houses in Downing Street and Chequers. The great majority of the Queen's wealth goes with the job and cannot be personally disposed of or sold.

The extent of the royal fortune is undeniably huge. Estimates loosely bandied about, because there is no official accounting, are anything up to £7 billion. The royal jewellery, and art and antiques collection, is nothing less than fantastic, and again, although there is no official study of the royal holding, many books have been published on the subject identifying individual items, for example those well known, or known to have been given as gifts by visiting heads of state, or jewels worn at public occasions.[17] Huge Crown estates of land stretch across Great Britain, and include Sandringham, Windsor Great Park, holdings in London, and the properties contained within the Duchies of Lancaster and Cornwall. The value of the Queen's personal assets, such as her stocks and shares portfolio, can only be guessed at as the Queen's holdings are exempted from disclosure in published company accounts under the 1976 Companies Act.

About three-quarters of the cost of running the British monarchy, including the palaces, travelling and state visits overseas, is financed by public departments. So, for example, the Department of the Environment spend £25.7 million on the upkeep of royal palaces last year, the Ministry of Transport £2.3 million on the royal train, and the Ministry of Defence £6.7 million on the Queen's Flight. The remaining expenditure is covered by the Civil List, the Privy Purse and the Queen's personal resources. The Civil List is a payment from the Treasury, covering mainly staff salaries and household expenses, and from January 1991 is set at £7.9 million. This is a scheme dating back to the accession of King George III in 1760, whereby each monarch has surrendered to the Exchequer for life the hereditary revenues from the Crown estates, excepting the Duchies of Lancaster and Cornwall, in return for an annual sum. Last year the Treasury made a notional 'profit' of £5 million from this arrangement.[18]

A perennial problem of the British monarchy is the absence of any clear distinction between its public and private affairs. At present there is still some difficulty in determining what belongs to the nation on the one hand, and what are the Queen's personal assets on the other; and by the same token, between what expenses are incurred by her in the performance of her public duties, and those which are entirely for her own personal benefit. If, as Simon Hughes maintains, it is impossible to 'justify to people who have low incomes just above the poverty line and who pay tax as they are required to do, that the woman who by common consent is the richest woman in the country is at the same time exempt',[19] then this can only be answered by a proper account of Crown finance, with the Palace being completely open, undertaken by a Commons' select committee or a Home Office inquiry that lays down a legal framework for distinguishing between what is to be regarded as national, and what is to be regarded as personal, Crown property. There may be a moral case for subjecting the Queen's personal income from financial investments to tax, but few will want to see the monarchy carrying out its ceremonial functions in anything less than a splendid fashion, or the Exchequer taking away with one hand what it then needs to give back with the other. The royal family itself will be acutely aware of the historical financial difficulties it suffered into the early part of this century, following Queen Victoria's inheritance in 1837 of a debt position of £50,000.

PALACE AND PRESS

From much of the media's point of view the royal family represent the greatest soap opera of all. If there is no other news to be had, or even if there is, an 'exclusive' piece of gossip or unusual photograph of a leading member of the royal family is guaranteed to sell the newspaper. The fierce circulation war amongst the tabloids in the 1980s has caused a relentless hounding of the royal family, causing the Queen upon occasion to summon editors to Buckingham Palace and plead with them to desist. In July 1991 one paper had a huge 'exclusive' photograph of Prince Andrew bathing in the nude ('Get set to grab glimpse of the cheeky clown prince' read the front page). Another paper in the same month had an 'exclusive' story on how Prince Charles had not paid his tailor's bill for a year ('Pay up Charles – You've had your trousers "on loan" for over a year' ran the front-page headlines). Princess Diana is hardly ever out of the newspapers and magazines, and nor are rumours that her marriage to Prince Charles is collapsing (even if, in the opinion of one writer for *The Independent*, which itself follows a policy of minimal royal reporting, 'they are about as likely to get divorced as is the Archbishop of Canterbury').[20] An early excess of zeal by the media affecting Princess Diana was a published photograph of her on a private beach on holiday in the Caribbean, taken in secret from a long distance using a 1200 metre lens, when she was five months pregnant and dressed only in her bikini.[21] That was in 1982, the same year in which the Queen made her complaint known publicly that her daughter-in-law, the future Queen, felt 'totally beleaguered'.

It seems that whatever members of the royal family do, however mundane, is of interest to the public; but is it really in the public interest that their private lives are treated in this way, exposed to such a glare of publicity, and often trivialized to the point of humiliation? Their position is different from, say, that of a politician or pop star, both of whom make a free personal decision on a career in the public eye. The Queen and Prince Charles, together with their spouses and children, have no choice in the matter by accident of birth. The Queen's father, King George VI, a shy man with a stammer, found the strain of public speeches and ceremonies alone, without today's pressures, emotionally and physically exhausting, and it may have contributed to his early death; his wife, now Queen Elizabeth the Queen Mother, never forgave the Duke and Duchess of Windsor for thrusting these responsibilities upon them in 1936 through the Abdication. Clearly, a high level of intrusion into the personal lives of monarchs is an essential, unavoidable element of the office: there are restrictions over whom the monarch may marry – something King Edward VIII found intolerable; as the nation's figurehead and symbol, not to mention head of the Church of England, a moral, idealized way of life is looked for in the Queen and her family; the clothes the Queen wears and how she looks is part of the ceremonial function she performs. But there is a danger to the institution of monarchy if the media constantly pursues the royal family in similar fashion to that of the past ten years, often demeaning them and giving offence through unwarranted invasion of their domestic lives. According to the former MP Lord Deedes, 'Such mendacity cumulatively has damaged the Royal Family, and is intended to do so. It seems a mistake to dismiss the press onslaught upon the Royal Family as mere harmless, circulation-building fun. Cumulatively its impact is substantial.'[22]

For not only may the public image of the monarchy suffer (some believe the quality of press coverage in the 1980s is the reason for the significantly lower esteem in which the monarchy is held by young persons under 25 years, recently revealed in a Gallup opinion poll),[23] but it becomes increasingly likely that the Windsor family themselves may become disenchanted with the institution, and the holder or prospective holder of the Crown may be unwilling to make the necessary sacrifice of any semblance of a normal, private life for him or herself, spouse and children. The proper balance between press freedom and any citizen's right to respect for their private and family life is always a difficult one, and English law is no help in this respect because, unlike virtually every other European country, it possesses no common-law or statutory right of privacy. So far as the monarchy is concerned, parliamentarians should consider whether some specially formulated guidelines are now necessary, within which the media can operate, to help distinguish between legitimate news coverage and unfair invasion of the royal family's private life.

REPUBLICANISM AND MONARCHY

In Britain 'the appendages of a Monarchy have been converted into the essence of a Republic', to use Walter Bagehot's well-known, approving expression.[24] If a formal British republic was to be established, it would continue to be founded upon the British system of parliamentary government, with ministers and the chief executive, the prime minister, continuing to sit in the legislature, Parliament, and be directly answerable to it. This basic political structure is quite different from, for example, the American model of separation of powers, where the president exercises the executive power conferred upon him by the Constitution and the people independent of Congress. A British president would perform a ceremonial function similar in character to that now exercised by the Queen. However, insofar as the president might be directly elected by the population for a prescribed term of office, he or she could justify making independent public speeches or utilizing any 'reserve' powers (for example over prime ministerial appointment or dissolution affairs) in an overtly political fashion by virtue of his or her own mandate from the electorate. Under a British republic the head of state would be far less likely to be as impartial or politically neutral as a hereditary monarch, who would be only too well aware that the monarchy lacks any ostensible democratic authority for political autonomy of its own.

Of course, Britain once had a *de facto* republic in the 11 interregnum years of 1649–1660, under Oliver Cromwell, serving as head of state or 'Lord Protector' as he was called. But in legal doctrine today that constitutional era is deemed never to have existed: all Acts passed in those years were null and void, and although King Charles II was not ceremonially installed on the throne until the 1660 Restoration, technically he succeeded as monarch at the very moment his father King Charles I was beheaded in Whitehall on 30 January 1649.

Today, republican sentiment is rousing itself in parts of the Commonwealth, particularly Australia, where last July the 'Australian Republican Movement' was launched with more than 100 prominent citizens signing as founding members, setting the goal of a referendum on the issue and the institution of a republic in Australia by the year 2001. In Britain, Tony Benn, the Labour MP and former cabinet minister, introduced a Commonwealth of Britain Bill[25] into the House of Commons in May 1991, proposing abolition of the Crown and its replacement by a president, who would be a Member of Parliament, elected by two-thirds majority of both Houses of Parliament sitting together. In Benn's view, 'the Crown is a totally insupportable basis for a Constitution'.[26]

But abolition of the monarchy has never been a seriously live political issue in twentieth-century Britain. Despite Tony Benn's recent public espousal of abolition, the republican-minded MPs in the Commons in our recent history are easily counted, such as William Hamilton, who in the 1960s and 1970s enjoyed making rude comments about Princess Anne and other members of the royal family,[27] and James Maxton in the 1930s, whose contribution to the otherwise deeply solemn parliamentary debates on the royal abdication was to recite a version of Humpty Dumpty as wishful thinking that the monarchy 'could not be put together again'.[28] The fact is that a major public opinion poll on the monarchy showed that in 1990 only 6 per cent of British people thought the country would be better off if the Crown was abolished.[29] Another poll taken in July 1991 showed that 75 per cent of the public thought Britain needed a royal family, 89 per cent believed they were good for tourism and a revenue earner for the country, 68 per cent thought they filled an important constitutional role, and 78 per cent wanted to see the royal family survive into the next century.[30] The consistently high level of support for the monarchy in Britain does not mean that the institution itself is not in need of certain modifications to equip itself better for the twenty-first century. Indeed, it makes those changes all the more necessary. For ultimately the future of the British monarchy depends upon a carefully trodden course of mutual acceptance.

NOTES AND REFERENCES

A shortened version of this paper appeared in the November 1991 issue of *Politics Review*.

1 Letter to Earl Granville, 3 December 1870. See: H.J. Hanham, *The Nineteenth Century Constitution* (1969), pp. 33–34.
2 *Cabinet Government* (3rd edn, 1959), p. 341.
3 *The English Constitution* (1867, Fontana edn 1963), p. 111.
4 Memorandum of the Queen's Private Secretary to the Select Committee on the Civil List: HC [1971–72] 29, Minutes of Evidence, App. 13.
5 See: Sir Winston Churchill, *The Second World War* (1948–1953), Vol. 5 (Penguin edn, 1985), pp. 546–554; B. Pimlott, *Hugh Dalton* (1985), p. 415.
6 See: R. Blackburn, 'The Queen and Ministerial Responsibility', *Public Law* (1985), 361.
7 See: R.H.S. Crossman, *Inside View* (1972); J.P. Mackintosh, *The British*

Cabinet (3rd edn, 1977); T. Benn, *Arguments for Democracy* (1981), Ch. 2.
8 See: A. Morrow, *The Queen* (1983), Ch. 16.
9 See: R. Blackburn, *The Meeting of Parliament* (1990).
10 *Letters of Queen Victoria* (1st Series, III), pp. 363-365.
11 *The Governance of England* (2nd edn, 1914), p. 109.
12 *Cabinet Government* (3rd edn, 1959), Ch. XIII.
13 BBC Radio 4, 'Analysis' programme, 20 June 1991.
14 *The Dilemma of Democracy* (1978), p. 193.
15 See: R. Blackburn, 'The Public Announcement of General Elections', *Electoral Studies* (1990), 226.
16 Constitutional Reform Bill, HC [1990-91] 204, which proceeded no further than a First Reading.
17 For an account of the royal wealth see: A. Morton, *Theirs is the Kingdom* (1989).
18 Figures from departmental and Crown Estate accounts from 1990-1991 reported in *The Independent*, 10 July and 27 June 1991.
19 House of Commons Debates, 3 July 1991.
20 *The Independent*, 13 July 1991.
21 See: D. Keay, *Royal Pursuit* (1983).
22 *The Daily Telegraph*, 25 June 1991. Lord Deedes is also a former editor of *The Daily Telegraph*.
23 Gallup Poll commissioned for *The Daily Telegraph*, 24 July 1991.
24 Ibid., p. 262.
25 HC [1990-91] 161, which proceeded no further than a formal First Reading.
26 House of Commons Debates, 17 May 1991.
27 W. Hamilton, *My Queen and I* (1975).
28 House of Commons Debates, 10 December 1936.
29 MORI Poll, January 1990.
30 Gallup Poll, *supra* (note 23).

2
Cabinet Government since Bagehot

G. W. JONES

PARK, PRECURSOR OF BAGEHOT

J.J. Park was an early political scientist. He saw himself as a 'disciple' and 'promoter' of 'the nascent school of *inductive politics*, or *observational* political science', which sought to penetrate behind theories and accepted wisdom to discover what actually happened.[1] His lectures on *The Dogmas of the Constitution*, written in the early 1830s, around the time of the first great parliamentary reform Act, not only foreshadow much of what Walter Bagehot wrote in the 1860s and 1870s around the time of the second great parliamentary reform Act,[2] but also reveal the operation of a governmental system remarkably modern in its essential characteristics. Or perhaps one should say that today's governmental system has not changed significantly in its basic features from the 1830s or even, if one accepts J.J. Park's analysis, from the 1690s.

For his contemporary aptness take this passage:

> We find, that no sooner is an administration formed, than it immediately takes upon itself not only what is properly called the *executive* government, but another and much more important function . . . the management, control, and direction, of the whole mass of political legislation, according to its own views of political science and civil economy; – that, although some scattered portions of legislation are gladly left by this over-burdened administration to private individuals, who are desirous, either through vanity or public spirit, of signalizing themselves as legislators, – yet even this is done, as it were, by the connivance of the administration, or *government*, as it is emphatically called; and that it follows as

a necessary consequence, from government being always in the majority of the House of Commons, that no private individual could carry any measure through parliament which government should see reason to oppose . . .; finally, that as soon as, from any circumstances whatever, government, or the administration, shall be deprived of the power of so managing, controlling, and directing the course of political legislation, by a change of the majority into the minority, or find sufficient reason to apprehend that they *shall* be deprived of that power, they do, according to the actual course of the constitution, resign office, upon the express ground that *they* can no longer carry on the government . . .[3]

Here we see important aspects of cabinet government, still very much relevant today.

In Park's view 'the exercise of the prerogative and of the general government' had in the seventeenth century been 'virtually transferred from the Crown to the party constituting the majority for the time being in the House of Commons . . .' He deplored the way this majority was put together, through 'the help of that mass of corruption, and political prostitution', and wished there was some other 'mechanism' to perform that task, as do many today who wish that parties, the modern equivalents of corruption and political prostitution, were not so dominant in the Commons or among voters. But so far no one has come up with an effective substitute.

His approach in many respects was similar to Bagehot's. Where Bagehot distinguished the 'dignified' from the 'efficient' parts of the constitution,[4] Park contrasted the theoretical and formal; the 'artificial mechanism', as he called it, with the real and practical, which he called 'the living agency'. The former, he noted, 'serves rather to *conceal* than to *declare* the real agency which is employed'.[5] His interest, like Bagehot's, was to explain the real. He rejected the view that 'the real principles and machinery of practical government' should be kept secret, 'as a sort of arcana, or hidden knowledge . . . as if it were something that it was unsafe to let the public look into.'[6] Bagehot took Park's insight further, explaining the value of the 'dignified' elements as a means to encourage deference by the people towards the governing elites.[7]

Like Bagehot,[8] Park saw that the essence of the British constitution was not separation of powers but their combination. He took issue with such authorities as Montesquieu, Blackstone, De Lolme and Paley, who proclaimed that law-making was the responsibility of the legislative assembly and law-executing of the executive, and that in the legislature the three branches of king, Lords and Commons were independent and checked each other.[9] Instead, Park saw a 'commixture'[10] or an 'intermixture',[11] a merging of executive and legislature.[12] This 'infusion'[13] of the executive into the legislature was to avoid a collision between the two by enabling the executive to influence it in the early stages, even 'anticipating its operation'.[14] (Here Park was expressing the modern political-science notion of the law of anticipated reactions.) Thus there was no need for the executive to deploy a veto against a Commons' decision; it used its preventive check among them to stop such a decision being taken.[15] It had to avoid being put in the position of explicitly turning down popular measures emanating from the Commons for fear of provoking insurrection outside. So important was the House of Commons that the executive had to control it. Instead of opposing it, the executive sought ways to influence it from within.

This merging of executive and legislature was not just to the advantage of the executive. The legislature benefited too. The executive was drawn from the majority in the Commons and was dependent on it to continue in office. Government was conducted 'in the face of day, namely in the House of Commons', which secured to the people 'a degree of freedom and participation in the government . . . which no system of checks could have given them, if that government had been carried on, as before the Revolution, in the dark conclaves of the Court and the Privy Council,'[16]: *out* of parliament'.[17] Park's view was that 'the powers of government, which were previously carried on principally by force of the prerogative, have been essentially and substantially exercised and carried on in the House of Commons, as the great public council,[18] and thence in the face of the country; which has come to take a part, and exercise a voice, in every act of the cabinet . . .' (the only mention of cabinet in Park's lectures).[19]

BAGEHOT AND THE CABINET

Bagehot's great insight was into the cabinet. He saw it as the means through which the executive and legislature were linked. Like Park he asserted that: 'The efficient secret of the English Constitution may be described as the close union, the nearly complete fusion, of the executive and legislative powers.'[20] This fusion was achieved by the cabinet. 'A cabinet is a combining committee – a *hyphen* which joins, a *buckle* which fastens, the legislative part of the state to the executive part of the state. In its origin it belongs to the one, in its functions it belongs to the other.'[21] But unlike Park he saw the cabinet as a committee of the legislature. Park saw ministers, rightly, as *officers of the Crown*,[22] and thus the cabinet was, from his perspective, a committee of the executive, an offshoot of the Privy Council as later historians have shown.[23] Bagehot, nevertheless, was uneasy about designating the cabinet as a legislative committee since he observed it had a power no assembly was likely to entrust to it, the power to dissolve the assembly. In any case, as the later development of select committees has revealed, they are more truly the committees of the legislative assembly and they can come into conflict with the cabinet. The cabinet should more appropriately be seen as a hybrid, a committee of the executive but composed of parliamentarians, overwhelmingly from the Commons. As its members are chiefs of the majority party they can normally guarantee that the Commons will support the government and its measures.

Bagehot recognized that three characteristics were essential for cabinet government: party discipline, collective responsibility and secrecy. 'Without the discipline of parties', wrote Bagehot in 1875, there would be 'government by incoherent public meetings'. Parliament had to be 'disciplined and regimented so as to be, for all practical purposes, under the control of a few minds': otherwise 'government by a miscellaneous assembly would be hopeless'. For the party in the Commons to continue to have confidence in the cabinet, and stay united behind it, the cabinet itself had to act as a united entity: collectively responsible. And secrecy was necessary for the 'confidential cooperation' of cabinet members: to assist the cabinet to reach those compromises on which it could unite. He recognized that a cabinet was always divided into various factions, but that its members had in the end to agree, or the government would collapse because its party supporters in the Commons would themselves be divided, and would no longer be able to provide a majority to sustain it in office.[24]

The purpose of the cabinet in Bagehot's eyes was to act as 'a board of control . . . to rule the nation': that is, as Britain's supreme political directorate. He did not analyse the sorts of decisions taken by cabinet, but his notion of a central 'board of control' was encompassed in the description of cabinet functions given in the Haldane Report of 1918 on the Machinery of Government: 'the final determination of policy to be submitted to Parliament; the supreme control of the national executive in accordance with the policy prescribed by Parliament; and the continuous co-ordination and delimitation of the authorities of the various departments of state.'[25] What these statements of the Haldane Committee fail to capture is the vital political role performed by cabinet, which Bagehot had recognized: it is the place where contentious issues that have been unable to be decided earlier are finally resolved in an authoritative decision binding on all members.[26]

G. W. JONES
BAGEHOT AND THE PRIME MINISTER

So far in this chapter I have focused on the views of J.J. Park and of Walter Bagehot in the nineteenth century. In turning to survey cabinet government since then, I am struck by how relevant their views are not only for the years that immediately followed but even for the operation of cabinet government today. Their judgements, however, are not today's conventional wisdom. Now we are increasingly told that cabinet government has been supplanted by prime-ministerial government, and in the tenth year of Margaret Thatcher as prime minister the accepted wisdom is that our system is as good as presidential. It is one-woman rule, by she who must be obeyed.

It is worth considering Bagehot's view of the prime minister. It was not of someone who just expressed the consensus of the cabinet or was simply *primus inter pares*. He noted that the prime minister has 'a sort of authority which none of his colleagues share . . . He is the acknowledged chief of his party, and links his colleagues together.'[27] He has 'the responsibility of controlling all the other ministers, and is, in a special sense, answerable for their shortcomings, and credited with the merit of their successes'. But, aware of the constraints under which a prime minister operated, Bagehot observed 'he is in no sense exempted from that necessity of carrying his colleagues with him . . .' He stated that the prime minister 'is quite as unable to override his colleagues with a high hand, month after month, as they would be to override him. Joint responsibility is the rule of English cabinets.'[28]

In *The English Constitution* he wrote that: 'We have in England an elective first magistrate as truly as the Americans have an elective first magistrate.' But the British prime minister differed from the American president because the latter was elected directly by the people while the former was elected by the representatives of the people.[29] The prime minister depended on acquiring and retaining the support of the majority in the Commons. Once in office he had to choose his associates in cabinet, but his choice was limited. Bagehot recognized that the prime minister had to select some from a 'charmed circle'; that is, those who had made political reputations for themselves and commanded considerable support in their party. He had more leeway in allocating 'the division of cabinet offices' among them. Bagehot's conclusion was that the 'highest patronage of a Prime Minister' is 'a considerable power, though it is exercised under close and imperative restrictions'.[30]

He wrote that Sir Robert Peel was the last prime minister 'who gave a real supervision to the general business of the country', but that since then the business had so grown that it was impossible for a prime minister to exercise 'such general supervision'.[31] This 'augmenting' of the tasks of the prime minister had gone on from 1850 until Bagehot reckoned it must make 'the miscellaneous work of a Prime Minister most teasing and vexing'. He referred to the other work: leading in the Commons;[32] consulting with and often controlling colleagues; composing quarrels of the cabinet; writing to the Queen; dispensing patronage; forming legislative plans; and generally acting as 'the head of our business'. He observed: 'we shall wonder how any man can be equal to so much'.[33]

DECLINE OF THE CABINET?

Since Bagehot wrote, it has often been asserted that the power of the cabinet has been supplanted by that of the prime minister. For instance, he ascribed to cabinet the power to request from the monarch a dissolution of Parliament. But from 1918 the prime minister alone came to exercise that power, which, it is argued, enhanced the sway of the prime minister over the cabinet. However, there is considerable doubt whether the prime minister's power is always strengthened by being able to request a dissolution, and in any case recent prime ministers, including Margaret Thatcher, have taken care to consult their cabinet colleagues about possible dates of a general election: a prudent move, both to take soundings from other specialists in politics and to spread responsibility in case of defeat.[34]

Many commentators have drawn attention to other developments alleged to elevate the prime minister over the cabinet, to such an extent that they believe that cabinet government has been replaced by prime-ministerial government. Debate about the respective powers of the prime minister and cabinet has flourished for over 25 years, since John Mackintosh and his disciple Richard Crossman resurrected the argument that cabinet government was a myth, and had become Bagehot's 'dignified' and not the 'efficient' part of the constitution.[35] In recent years, especially in Margaret Thatcher's third term of office, new protagonists have joined in, including some who previously had recognized that prime ministers were constrained by political and administrative checks, and by what can be called the structural pressures of collegial decision-making. For instance, the latest, Professor Anthony King of Essex University, sees her as very different from earlier prime ministers.[36] Not only has she enjoyed unprecedented electoral success and has thus been prime minister for a longer continuous period than any other since the mid-nineteenth century, but also she has her own broad policy which she is determined to impose on the government. She leads from the front in an assertive style, bullying,[37] cajoling and wrongfooting her opponents, exploiting her sex to disconcert her colleagues, and above all deploying her patronage, appointing and sacking, to produce a cabinet loyal to her agenda.

However, all these features are contingent, political and specific, matters of style not structure, highly likely to be changed with another prime minister with a different style.[38] And Professor King notes that Margaret Thatcher's power has sometimes slipped during her ten years in office, as during the months before the invasion of the Falkland Islands in the spring of 1982, when she was probably defeated more times in cabinet than any previous prime minister and had to accede to her colleagues' demand that cabinet have a general discussion on economic policy, and in the aftermath of the Westland affair in 1986, when she again suffered defeats in cabinet, for example over the proposed sale of Austin Rover to Americans, when it was reported that she was seriously considering resignation.[39]

FOUR SUPPOSED THREATS TO CABINET GOVERNMENT

Cabinet committees and *ad hoc* meetings

Some also point to more structural changes that Margaret Thatcher has made to the process of governing which are said to erode cabinet government. First, as Peter Hennessy has pointed out, she has reduced the number of cabinet and cabinet comittee meetings and relies on more informal meetings of a few ministers and their advisers with herself and her advisers. In such bilaterals or trilaterals she is thought to be able to infiltrate her views into the policy-making process more effectively: stitching up decisions before cabinet meets.[40] Cabinet committees and *ad hoc* meetings are depicted as fragmenting the cabinet, devaluing it, so that it is either not involved or merely notes decisions taken earlier in a smaller group. However, cabinet committees and meetings of the prime minister with a few other ministers are not new.[41] Both occurred during the nineteenth century, as can be seen from the diaries of Gladstone, and in the years before the First World War, as can be seen from Asquith's letters to Venetia Stanley.[42] Cabinet committees were common in the 1920s and 1930s and became more systematized during and immediately after the Second World War.[43]

An important distinction can be made between cabinet committees and ministerial meetings serviced by the Cabinet Office, and the more informal *ad hoc* ministerial meetings. They differ in function. Cabinet committees are more part of the decision-*taking* process, *ad hoc* meetings more part of the decision-*making* process. In cabinet committees decisions may be taken with the full authority of cabinet itself, while in *ad hoc* meetings discussions can take place preparatory to later decision by a minister, cabinet committee or cabinet itself. In *ad hoc* meetings much preliminary work can be cleared away, early soundings can occur and the ground can be prepared: sifting out matters on which agreement can be reached and highlighting issues in dispute between ministers on which further work is needed. They enable ministers, including the prime minister, to be better informed about topics on the government's agenda: indeed, they strengthen ministers' collective involvement in policy-making by enabling them to participate at an early stage in the process, perhaps at a point previously left to civil servants.[44] Margaret Thatcher's use of such meetings, far from presidentializing the system, increases the contribution of her ministerial colleagues, both individually and collectively.

The other critical point to note is the composition of such meetings and of cabinet committees. *Ad hoc* meetings will involve the departmental minister responsible, who will have to implement the eventual decision. If he disagrees, the matter will wend its way through the more formal procedures. Cabinet committees invariably consist of two types of minister: those with a departmental interest in the subject under consideration, the functional ministers most directly concerned, who cannot be excluded, and who would take the lead in full cabinet and be listened to with most deference by their colleagues; and some other ministers not so closely involved but with weight in cabinet, 'who will be important when it comes to selling it in Cabinet'.[45] Thus such gatherings are, in Gordon Walker's words, 'partial cabinets', composed of those who would carry the cabinet if it had itself decided on the matter.[46] They are in effect mini-cabinets in which all members are virtually represented, and operate as if they were the full cabinet, but with the proviso that the minister most directly concerned with the topic, and the chairman, have the right to take the issue to full cabinet if unhappy with the sense of the committee. These cabinet committees anticipate the likely reactions of their colleagues in full cabinet, whose views they know well from close working acquaintance over many years in party and Parliament, and from current Whitehall networks of information. Thus *ad hoc* meetings and cabinet committees do not damage cabinet government: they enhance it. They have enabled the cabinet to survive as the 'central board of control' in the face of the great increase in governmental business which has occurred since the days of Bagehot.[47]

Margaret Thatcher's approach to cabinet government can be seen as making cabinet more efficient, especially in its main task of resolving disputes unable to be settled earlier. Without prior sieving cabinet might have become clogged. Instead it is able to concentrate on divisive issues. Margaret Thatcher has streamlined cabinet government without losing its essential collective nature.

This streamlining is welcome to ministers, since it not only saves time but also helps to keep cabinet together. Two types of matter can be handled at cabinet committees: those not very contentious which can be easily dealt with; and those very divisive which ministers may be pleased to avoid. Ministers may not want to experience gruelling arguments over sensitive issues in full cabinet, such as over defence in Labour cabinets or over public expenditure for all governments. They may be happy to leave their resolution to the ministers most concerned together with others to look after wider aspects, who include the prime minister herself.

She has the function of acting as guardian of collective government, since the prime minister has the essential task to perform of maintaining cabinet unity.[48] Her assertiveness is not necessarily to promote her own personal policy predilections: it can advance a collective view from cabinet. In committees and meetings she can ensure that cabinet as a whole is not forgotten. Thus cabinet committees and ministerial meetings are not necessarily evidence of presidential government, but can bear witness to the continued vitality of cabinet government, and since ministers are also parliamentarians, pre-eminently from the House of Commons, they bear witness also to the continued vigour of parliamentary government, as both Park and Bagehot would have regarded it.

Prime-ministerial dominance of the media

The second recent development said to be making Britain more presidential is the prime minister's increasingly direct appeal to the public, and the centralization of her relationships with the media through her Chief Press Adviser. But, for a long time, prime ministers have made direct appeals to the public, personalizing their governments to the electorate, as did Gladstone and Disraeli in the time of Bagehot. In the nineteenth and early twentieth centuries prime ministers personally maintained close contact with proprietors, editors and reporters, and sought to ensure that a favourable line was presented, even distributing honours as rewards for helpfulness.[49] Until 1931 one of the prime minister's secretarial staff usually kept the press informed day-to-day about the prime minister's views. In 1931 the first press adviser to the prime minister was appointed, and since then 10 Downing Street has housed a press or public relations adviser, sometimes a former journalist, sometimes a member of the government information service, and sometimes a civil servant from a line position. His role has been to project the prime minister through the media, and to advise him on how to conduct himself to gain good reports.[50] The staff of the adviser have grown, and from time to time attempts have been made to bring the information and press offices of departmental ministers under closer supervision from 10 Downing Street.

Margaret Thatcher's chief press adviser, Bernard Ingham, is an ebullient and assertive character, devoted to pushing the prime minister's case.[51] He came to 10 Downing Street in late 1979 and is the longest-serving official there after the prime minister herself. When he speaks to the media he is taken to be acting on her behalf. For some time he tried to unify the government information service under his leadership and to exert control over the activities of departmental press offices, at last achieving his goal in February 1989 when he was appointed head of profession for government information officers, a position previously held by the director-general of the Central Office of Information.[52] Departmental press and information offices are increasingly staffed by officials who have served for a time in his office.

However, his influence should not be exaggerated. Ministers and their departmental officials are eager to preserve their autonomy and, although efforts are made to co-ordinate the timing of departmental statements, they have not accepted subservience to Ingham. They keep open their own lines to the media, and ensure that their case is purveyed, even to counter that of the prime minister. Reports in the press and broadcasting do not rely only on prime-ministerial guidance or a steer from Ingham. Veteran *Times* reporter Geoffrey Smith has stated that his judgements are much influenced by talks with ministers, and that his assessment of the government comes from the impression that ministers create as a team.[53]

The prime minister does not indulge in anything like the presidential press conference. Margaret Thatcher gives occasional interviews on television and radio, often on popular programmes and not just serious broadcasts about public affairs; she gives occasional interviews to the press, often again popular journals; and she exploits travels around the country to provide 'photo opportunities' for media coverage. She also gives in the course of a year a number of major speeches or lectures at formal gatherings of her party or of national institutions, and she makes some set-piece speeches at events abroad. Her main channels of communication to the nation remain Parliament, especially question time, where she comes under constant attack, and regular daily briefings by her press staff. But other ministers use the same means. The way they perform in Parliament and their briefings to the media have an important effect on the standing of the government. The media do not simply focus on the prime minister. Their reporting shapes the reputations of her colleagues, building up some as counterweights to her. She is not able to dominate news management.

Politicization of the civil service

The third development said to contribute to presidentialization is the politicization of the civil service by Margaret Thatcher through appointments to its top ranks. Prime ministers since the 1920s have had to approve appointments to the leading civil-service positions, the most important of which are permanent secretaries, the official heads of the departments. She is reputed to ask of names put before her: 'Is he one of us?' More than earlier prime ministers, she has taken an interest in these appointments and not only of those at the very top, and because of her longevity in office she has been responsible for the appointment of most leading civil servants, including all permanent secretaries. Some of them were not thought to be the favourite candidates of the official hierarchy. They had often served in her private secretariat at 10 Downing Street or had come to her attention at meetings she attended. Since Park and Bagehot wrote, the civil service has evolved as a formidable estate of the realm. Crossman regarded it as a buttress of prime-ministerial power. However, a recent study by a working group of the Royal Institute of Public Administration, *Top Jobs In Whitehall*, concluded that there was no evidence that appointments were made on party-political grounds,[54] and there is no sign that any opposition party would insist on the removal of any of the prime minister's appointees, if it became the government.[55]

The prime minister is seeking to change the culture of the civil service to a more business-like style. She is doing it partly by appointing to leading positions officials oriented to action, constructive problem-solvers, who will energetically find ways to achieve the political objectives of the government and display managerial capacity in handling resources and implementing government policies.[56] Margaret Thatcher does not favour the traditional style of urbane scepticism, which focused on pointing out to ministers difficulties and pitfalls that lay ahead as the consequences of following particular policies, and found problems to every solution. She prefers doers to snag-hunters. She wants the civil service to be less a policy adviser and general administrator and more a policy implementer.

Her approach is in fact likely to lead to a reduction of political, including prime-ministerial, interference in the civil service. She has supported a series of reforms which involve devolving to line managers, organized in executive agencies, responsibility for achieving set objectives within specified budgets. The emphasis is on the setting of clearer goals for civil servants and devising performance indicators to measure their output so that their pay can be more closely linked to their success or failure. The implication of this change is that ministers will set strategic policy guidance and leave civil servants to manage, thus diminishing political intrusion into departmental activities. The end result, if it succeeds, will not reinforce a presidential system. This fragmentation of the bureaucracy is likely to lead to a dispersion of policy actors into policy communities and networks where the main gainers will be the bureaucracy and those interest groups with whom it comes into close contact during the course of its work, not the prime minister.

A prime minister's department

The fourth development said to be sustaining a presidential system is the building up of the prime minister's own staff at Downing Street, both in her Policy Unit and through individual special advisers, coupled with the abolition in 1983 of the Central Policy Review Staff, located in the Cabinet Office, which acted as a 'think tank' for the cabinet as a whole.[57] Through these personal advisers she is said to be able to penetrate the policy-making process earlier and deeper than have previous prime ministers, and to be able more effectively to question departmental proposals and even to propose alternative policies.

However, her team of advisers are small-scale, not more than about ten in all; fluctuating in composition, rarely staying for more than two to three years; comparatively young and inexperienced when set alongside the staff in departments serving ministers; in no way matching in expertise and weight departmental resources. They may raise questions about departmental proposals but are unlikely to prevail in promoting a whim of the prime minister against a determined minister. She has not at her personal disposal the staff available to help presidents, or even prime ministers in other parliamentary systems.[58] Pressure for the establishment of a Prime Minister's Department was defeated largely on the grounds that it would stimulate antagonism from ministers and their departments, and would signify a change in the British constitution from cabinet to prime-ministerial government. That Britain still has no Prime Minister's Department is a sign that it is not under prime-ministerial government.[59]

The central co-ordinating department in Britain is the Cabinet Office, located in Whitehall but connected to 10 Downing Street by an internal corridor whose door is symbolically locked, thus signifying that the Cabinet Office is not the personal staff of the prime minister but serves the cabinet as a whole. It sustains collective government, ensuring that all departments whose business is before cabinet make their contributions to its proceedings, and that cabinet decisions, not the instructions of the prime minister, are issued as the marching orders for departments. As its name shows, the Cabinet Office underpins collective decision-making through cabinet, not the prime minister alone.[60]

The role played by her personal advisers may in fact also strengthen collective government. The danger to policy-making in British central government is departmentalism. Powers are allocated not to the prime minister nor to cabinet but to ministers. They feel personally, that is individually, responsible, and their political ambitions mean that the collective perspective is continually menaced by pressures of fragmentation. The prime minister as chairman of cabinet has the key responsibility to keep ministers together, forging consensus and constraining maverick tendencies. Her staff can help her in this task, briefing her so that she can keep up with them, monitor their activities and participate in meetings with them. Otherwise, in pursuit of their personal, political and departmental goals, ministers would roll over both her and cabinet.[61]

CONCLUDING OBSERVATIONS

Margaret Thatcher is the most assertive and interventionist prime minister since Lloyd George. She brings to government a missionary, evangelical approach, combined with great and persistent energy.[62] She brings a distinctive *style* to government, but she has not changed the *structure* of central government. The basic features of parliamentary and cabinet government, as recognized by J.J. Park and Walter Bagehot, remain intact. In 1979 she came to power following a defeat of the Labour government on a Commons vote of confidence, and her own government suffered a defeat at second reading in 1986 of the Shops Bill, which had to be dropped.[63] Parliament certainly still matters.[64] Cabinet has been streamlined and made more efficient, but without losing its essential capacity to determine those issues which could not be settled earlier and to set guidelines within which ministers, *ad hoc* meetings and cabinet committees have to operate. She is not the sole channel of communication to the public about the government; she does not monopolize the public relations of the government. The civil service has not been transformed into her personal fiefdom. She has not created a Prime Minister's Department, but continues to rely on a small and frequently changing group of advisers who do not match the resources available to her ministerial colleagues. They have their own followings in their party. Their activities help to shape the reputation of the government. And because they know that they must all agree with cabinet decisions they have a great incentive to ensure that their views are expressed at cabinet, to avoid having to implement a decision they cannot accept and possibly having to resign.

The office of prime minister is like a piece of elastic: it can be stretched to accommodate an interventionist prime minister like Margaret Thatcher, but it can also contract to contain a more passive prime minister. She has so far not operated outside the confines of cabinet and parliamentary government. She has been constrained by their structures and political pressures. Like all prime ministers, she has to engineer consensus out of a fissiparous group of colleagues with their own power bases in Parliament and the party. She is only as strong as they let her be. Her style is not to seek the lowest common denominator of agreement between them, but the highest to accord with her assessment of party policy. As long as her style brings success to her party it will be accepted, but if times change and her luck runs out and she appears a liability, she will be dropped and another leader with a different style will emerge. Then the elastic will reshape to fit a new prime minister.

NOTES AND REFERENCES

This chapter was delivered as The J.J. Park Memorial Lecture at King's College London on 6 February 1989. The author wishes to thank John Barnes, Alan Beattie and June Burnham for their help in its preparation.

1 J.J. Park, *The Dogmas of the Constitution* (London: B. Fellowes, 1832), pp. xvi–xvii.
2 Bagehot never mentions Park's work in his writings.
3 Park, *The Dogmas*, pp. 39–40.
4 W. Bagehot, *The English Constitution* (1872 edn), reprinted in N. St John-Stevas (ed.), *The Collected Works of Walter Bagehot*, Vol. V (London: The Economist, 1974), pp. 205–210.
5 Park, *The Dogmas*, p. 31.
6 *Ibid.*, p. 11.
7 Bagehot, *The English Constitution*, pp. 208–210, 367, 376–383.
8 *Ibid.*, pp. 204–205. Sir William Holdsworth noted that Park 'anticipates Bagehot in his criticism of the theory that the powers of government are divided, and that its excellence consists in a system of checks and balances . . . But he fails to bring out the fact, so clearly emphasised by Bagehot, that the most impressive feature of the constitution is the system of Cabinet government' (Sir William Holdsworth, *A History of English Law*, Vol. XII, edited by A.L. Goodhart and H.G. Hanbury (London: Methuen, 1952), p. 445). Together Park and Bagehot put in place of the separation of powers an idea central to the British political tradition, 'balance': that is, that, while legislative power is shared between government (cabinet) and Parliament (House of Lords and pre-eminently the House of Commons), executive power is concentrated in the government (cabinet).

9 Park, *The Dogmas*, pp. xiv and 33-34.
10 *Ibid.*, pp. 8-9.
11 *Ibid.*, p. 24.
12 *Ibid.*, p. 41.
13 *Ibid.*, p. 49.
14 *Ibid.*, p. 44.
15 *Ibid.*, pp. 44 and 46.
16 *Ibid.*, pp. 61-62.
17 *Ibid.*, p. 41.
18 He quoted with approval from an article in the *Edinburgh Review* the phrase referring to the Commons as 'the great depository of the political power of the nation' (Park, *The Dogmas*, p. 48).
19 Park, *The Dogmas*, p. 8. He also wrote: 'down to the period of the Revolution at least, the government of this country was mainly carried on by force of the prerogative; namely, upon the actual discretion and responsibility of ministers, out of parliament; and not as now, with the concurrence, at every step, and previous participation, of the legislature' (p. 101).
20 Bagehot, *The English Constitution*, p. 210.
21 *Ibid.*, p. 212.
22 Park, *The Dogmas*, p. 11.
23 See: J.P. Mackintosh, *The British Cabinet* (London: Stevens, 3rd edn, 1977), pp. 35-72.
24 Bagehot, *The English Constitution*, p. 213. See also: W. Bagehot, *The State of the Parties* (1876), reprinted in N. St John-Stevas (ed.), *The Collected Works of Walter Bagehot*, Vol. VII (London: The Economist, 1974), pp. 222-223; W. Bagehot, *Prince Bismarck on Cabinets* (1875), reprinted in N. St John-Stevas (ed.), *The Collected Works of Walter Bagehot*, Vol. VIII (London: The Economist, 1974), pp. 279 and 281; and W. Bagehot, *The Character of Sir Robert Peel* (1856), reprinted in N. St John-Stevas (ed.), *Bagehot's Historical Essays* (New York: Doubleday, 1965), pp. 199-201.
25 *Report of the Machinery of Government Committee* (London: HMSO, 1918), Cd 9230.
26 See: G.W. Jones, 'Development of the Cabinet', in W. Thornhill (ed.), *The Modernization of British Government* (London: Pitman, 1975), pp. 31-62; and M. Burch, 'The United Kingdom', in J. Blondel and F. Müller-Rommel (eds), *Cabinets in Western Europe* (London: Macmillan, 1988), pp. 17-32.
27 W. Bagehot, *Prince Bismarck on Cabinets* (1875), reprinted in N. St John-Stevas (ed.) *The Collected Works of Walter Bagehot*, Vol. VIII (London: The Economist, 1974), p. 280.
28 *Ibid.*, p. 279.
29 Bagehot, *The English Constitution*, p. 211.
30 *Ibid.*, pp. 211-212.
31 W. Bagehot, *The Structure of the New Government* (1874), reprinted in N. St John-Stevas (ed.), *The Collected Works of Walter Bagehot*, vol. XIV (London: The Economist, 1986), p. 168.
32 In the 1940s the prime minister gave up that role to another minister, so Margaret Thatcher does not have that daily chore.
33 W. Bagehot, *The Premiership* (1875), reprinted in N. St John-Stevas (ed.), *The*

Collected Works of Walter Bagehot, Vol. VI (London: The Economist, 1974), pp. 66–67.
34 See: W. G. Andrews, 'Some Thoughts on the Power of Dissolution', *Parliamentary Affairs*, 13 (1960), 286–296.
35 J. P. Mackintosh, *The British Cabinet* (London: Stevens, 1962); R. H. S. Crossman, 'Introduction' to Walter Bagehot, *The English Constitution* (London: Fontana, 1963); R. Crossman, *Inside View* (London: Jonathan Cape, 1972). Mackintosh's role in the drafting of these Godkin lectures delivered by Crossman is shown in R. Crossman, *The Diaries of a Cabinet Minister*: Vol. 3, *Secretary of State for Social Services, 1968-70* (London: Hamish Hamilton and Jonathan Cape, 1977). The debate on prime-ministerial power can be followed in A. King (ed.), *The British Prime Minister* (London: Macmillan, 2nd edn, 1985), pp. 175–241, and in A. H. Brown, 'Prime Ministerial Power', Parts I and II, *Public Law* (Spring and Summer 1968), 28–51 and 96–118. Two recent proponents of prime-ministerial power are M. Burch, 'The British Cabinet: A Residual Executive', and M. Doherty, 'Prime Ministerial Power and Ministerial Responsibility', in *Parliamentary Affairs*, 41 (1988), 34–67.
36 A. King, 'Mrs Thatcher as a Political Leader', in R. Skidelsky (ed.), *Thatcherism* (London: Chatto and Windus, 1988), pp. 51–64.
37 So did Edward Heath and James Callaghan, but they still had to carry their cabinets with them.
38 But the more the possibilities of the office have been exploited, the greater the repertoire of styles open to a prime minister and the greater the range of expectations about his behaviour.
39 A good review of the Thatcher period of government, and a valuable bibliography, can be found in the symposium, 'The Thatcher Years', *Contemporary Record*, I (1987), No. 3, pp. 1–31. See also: P. Jenkins, *Mrs Thatcher's Revolution* (London: Jonathan Cape, 1987); and K. Harris, *Thatcher* (London: Weidenfeld and Nicolson, 1988).
40 See: P. Hennessy, *Cabinet* (Oxford: Blackwell, 1986).
41 Cabinet committees are examined in comparative perspective in T. T. Mackie and B. W. Hogwood (eds), *Unlocking the Cabinet* (London: Sage, 1985).
42 H. C. G. Matthew (ed.), *The Gladstone Diaries*, Vols 7 and 8 (Oxford: Clarendon Press, 1982), covering the years 1869 to 1871. M. and E. Brock, *H. H. Asquith: Letters to Venetia Stanley* (Oxford: Oxford University Press, 1982).
43 S. S. Wilson, *The Cabinet Office to 1945* (London: HMSO, 1975); R. K. Mosley, *The Story of the Cabinet Office* (London: Routledge and Kegan Paul, 1969).
44 As with James Callaghan's 'economic seminar'. See: B. Donoughue, *Prime Minister* (London: Jonathan Cape, 1987), pp. 101–102.
45 P. Hennessy, 'The Prime Minister, the Cabinet and the Thatcher Personality', in K. Minogue and M. Biddiss (eds), *Thatcherism: Personality and Politics* (London: Macmillan, 1987), p. 63.
46 P. Gordon Walker, *The Cabinet* (London: Fontana, 1972), pp. 87–91.
47 It could be argued that the prime minister is stronger in full cabinet where she can usually rely on the support of ministers not directly involved to give her the benefit of the doubt than in the smaller gatherings where she is up against the ministers most involved, most informed and most likely to resist her interventions.
48 The important distinction between what a prime minister *has* to do and *may* do is

explored in R. Rose 'British Government: The Job at the Top', in R. Rose and E. N. Suleiman (eds), *Presidents and Prime Ministers* (Washington, DC: American Enterprise Institute, 1980), pp. 1–49.

49 See: S. Koss, *The Rise and Fall of the Political Press*, Vol. 1, *The Nineteenth Century*; and Vol. 2, *The Twentieth Century* (London: Hamish Hamilton, 1981 and 1984).

50 See: G. W. Jones, 'The Prime Ministers' Secretaries: Politicians or Administrators?', in J. A. G. Griffith (ed.), *From Policy to Administration* (London: Allen and Unwin, 1976). For the period from Lloyd George to James Callaghan see: J. Margach, *The Abuse of Power* (London: W. H. Allen, 1978).

51 M. Cockerell, P. Hennessy and D. Walker, *Sources Close to the Prime Minister* (London: Macmillan, 1985); M. Cockerell, *Live from Number 10* (London: Faber and Faber, 1988).

52 C. Brown, 'Critics mock new job for Ingham', *The Independent*, 10 February 1989. Bernard Ingham had been carrying out the duties of head of government information officers during the illness of the Director-General of the COI.

53 G. Smith, 'The Prime Minister and the Press', in K. W. Thompson (ed.), *Presidents, Prime Ministers and the Press* (Lanham: University Press of America, 1986).

54 RIPA Working Group, *Top Jobs in Whitehall* (London: RIPA, 1987). See also: P. Hennessy, 'Mrs Thatcher's Poodle? The Civil Service since 1979', *Contemporary Record*, 2 (1988), No. 2, 2–4.

55 A sign did appear a few days after this sentence was written in remarks attributed to John Cunningham, the Labour Party's Environment spokesman, who was reported as saying that because of 'politicisation of the civil service' under Margaret Thatcher 'there must be a number of people in Whitehall now in senior positions who are, frankly, compromised by that – and they'd have to go' (P. Hennessy, 'Why New Masters Could Mean Wholesale Change', *The Independent*, 9 January 1989). However, he did not say he would ask for a change and he was making a personal not a party statement.

56 See: L. Metcalfe and S. Richards, *Improving Public Management* (London: Sage, 1987): A. Harrison and J. Gretton, *Reshaping Central Government* (Oxford: Policy Journals, 1987); and The Efficiency Unit, *Improving Management in Government: The Next Steps* (London: HMSO, 1988).

57 See: T. Blackstone and W. Plowden, *Inside the Think Tank* (London: Heinemann, 1988).

58 See: P. Weller, *First among Equals* (Sydney: Allen and Unwin, 1985); and W. Plowden (ed.), *Advising the Rulers* (Oxford: Blackwell, 1987).

59 On the Policy Unit and advisers of prime ministers, see: G. W. Jones, 'The United Kingdom', in W. Plowden (ed.), *Advising the Rulers* (Oxford: Blackwell, 1987); and D. Willetts, 'The Role of the Prime Minister's Policy Unit', *Public Administration*, 65 (1987), 443–454.

60 On the Cabinet Office see: G. W. Jones, 'Development of the Cabinet', in W. Thornhill (ed.), *The Modernization of British Government* (London: Pitman, 1975), pp. 50–53; P. Hennessy, 'A Magnificent Piece of Powerful Bureaucratic Machinery', *The Times*, 8 March 1976; Lord Hunt of Tanworth, 'Cabinet Strategy and Management', *CIPFA/RIPA Conference*, Eastbourne, 9 June 1983; and C. Campbell, *Governments under Stress* (Toronto: University of Toronto Press, 1983), pp. 55–67.

61 Whether the analytical capacity of the centre of British central government is adequate, and where it should be located, are frequently discussed. See the exchange between P. Weller and G. W. Jones in *Public Administration*, **61** (1983), pp. 59–84; and K. Berrill, 'Strength at the Centre – The Case for a Prime Minister's Department', in A. King (ed.), *The British Prime Minister* (London: Macmillan, 2nd edn, 1985), pp. 242–257.
62 See G. W. Jones, 'Cabinet Government and Mrs Thatcher', *Contemporary Record*, **1** (1987), No. 2, 8–12.
63 P. Regan, 'The 1986 Shops Bill', *Parliamentary Affairs*, **41** (1988), 380–401.
64 See M. Ryle and P. G. Richards (eds), *The Commons under Scrutiny* (London: Routledge, 1988); and the symposium 'Parliament – Does It Still Matter?' in *Contemporary Record*, **2** (1988), No. 3, 2–17 and 27–28.

3

Margaret Thatcher's Resignation as Prime Minister

ROBERT BLACKBURN

The news of Margaret Thatcher's forced resignation as prime minister, announced to the world at precisely 9.33 a.m. on 22 November 1990, astounded the British public and world opinion alike. 'It is an awesome event.' 'She has been stabbed in the back.' 'It is a hell of a way to go.' These were some of the reactions given to the press that day by stunned Conservative MPs, who, together with their Labour and Liberal Democrat opponents, now had to re-adjust their whole political focus to accommodate the reality of post-Thatcherite Conservatism. The Americans looked on in even greater disbelief than when the British voted Sir Winston Churchill out of office in 1945 just after victory in the Second World War. Since Friday 4 May 1979 when Margaret Thatcher had entered 10 Downing Street as the first ever woman prime minister, she had dominated the British political scene in a fashion unparalleled this century in peace-time. Her record of 11 continuous years in office was the longest period of any prime minister since Lord Liverpool in 1812–1827, outdoing even Gladstone, Disraeli, Lloyd George and Churchill. She had been leader of the Conservative Party for 16 years, taking them to three successive electoral triumphs in 1979, 1983 and 1987. Yet that November, plotting and manoeuvring in the parliamentary Conservative Party manifested itself in a party leadership contest, which while failing to defeat her, destabilized her position sufficiently to allow cabinet colleagues to deliver the final *coup de grâce*, by telling her in her office at the House of Commons on the evening of 21 November that it would be best if she now stood down.

MARGARET THATCHER'S RESIGNATION
THE CONSERVATIVE PARTY LEADERSHIP ELECTION

It was perhaps surprising that Margaret Thatcher had not chosen to go voluntarily for personal reasons in the summer of 1989, having completed two years of her third administration, to allow herself and her husband, Sir Denis Thatcher, to enjoy a normal retirement after passing the major achievement of ten years in office, and in a job which is one of enormous physical and mental stress. This would have been the natural time for her to resign and permit a successor to establish himself in place with a comfortable amount of time before a general election need be called. However, as is considered below (pp. 35–36), the political tendency in Britain is very much for prime ministers to choose to remain in power for as long as they can, and Margaret Thatcher succumbed to this pattern of political behaviour. In several interviews given towards the end of 1989 and the beginning of 1990, she made it plain that she intended to stay on and fight for a fourth term of office. For example, on 18 March 1990 in a long interview with the *Sunday Express*, she informed that newspaper's political editor that she would fight 'every inch of the way' to stay in power at the next general election. This privately dismayed many members of the Conservative Party and galvanized the minds of those who were not among her personal supporters as to how the party might be released from her grip. Their opportunity to mount any sort of credible challenge for the leadership at all, unlike Sir Anthony Meyer's disastrous attempt the previous year, came in the autumn of 1990 through a chance combination of political factors highly unfavourable to Margaret Thatcher. The annual party conference in Bournemouth at the end of September had done little to calm Tory jitters over the sustained Labour Party lead in the public opinion polls; the poll tax remained deeply unpopular in the country, and divisive and controversial within the Conservative Party itself; on 18 October the party suffered a disastrous by-election defeat at Eastbourne, shortly followed on 8 November by humiliation in the Bradford North by-election by coming third; and finally, Sir Geoffrey Howe delivered a devastating critique of Margaret Thatcher's attitude towards Europe and her style of government in his resignation speech in the House of Commons on 13 November.

The Conservative Party rules for electing a leader date from 1965, and followed the recommendations of a party committee chaired by the former leader and prime minister Sir Alec Douglas-Home.[1] Before then, there had been no formal rules, and hence there could have been no party challenge to the position of the leader in office as prime minister as befell Margaret Thatcher in 1990. The rules in force in 1990 provided for annual elections, although the current leader would be automatically declared elected if there is no other valid nomination put forward, as is generally the case each year. Following Mrs Thatcher's defeat, in 1991 the rules were amended so that today an election to challenge an incumbent leader will be held only if 10% of the party's MPs notify the chairman of the 1992 Committee in writing that they believe one to be necessary. Unlike the Labour and Liberal Democrat Parties, which permit party members outside the parliamentary party to cast votes, the Conservative Party gives only its MPs the right to vote. The timing of the election is to be within 28 days of the beginning of each new parliamentary session, and any ballots necessary will be organized by the chairman of the 1922 Committee.[2] A system of three ballots is provided for, with a prescribed threshold to be reached upon each occasion by the winner. On the first ballot, a winner must receive both an overall majority of those entitled to vote and 15 per cent more of those entitled to vote than any other candidate. On the second ballot only an overall majority is needed. If this is still not attained, then the three candidates with the most votes in the second ballot are carried over to a third ballot, where a system of preferential voting is employed to ensure that one of the three candidates is assured of an overall majority.

On the ballot held on 20 November, following Michael Heseltine's candidature being put forward on 15 November, the day after Sir Geoffrey Howe's resignation speech and the last day for receipt of nominations, the result from votes cast by 372 Conservative MPs was: Margaret Thatcher 204 (54.8 per cent), Michael Heseltine 152 (40.9 per cent), abstentions 16 (4.3 per cent). Margaret Thatcher had therefore gained an overall majority but failed to clear the 15 per cent margin of victory – by a mere 1.1 per cent or, effectively, two votes. In Paris at a conference when she heard the results, she immediately told the press awaiting outside her residence that she would allow her name to go through to the second ballot. The following day, she made a further statement to the press outside 10 Downing Street, saying 'I fight on, I fight to win', which was later confirmed in a press release from her office, and indeed under the rules had the same result from the first ballot been duplicated in the second, her victory would have been assured. However, it had immediately become clear that a significant number of Conservative MPs who had voted for Margaret Thatcher in the first round would have switched their support to Michael Heseltine in the second, having seen his degree of support and having voted for the prime minister out of loyalty in the first round. In the evening of 21 November, Margaret Thatcher sat in her office at the House of Commons and saw her cabinet colleagues one by one to hear their views on the situation: by a clear majority, reported to be 12 to 7, they advised her that they believed she would be defeated in the second ballot, and some bluntly delivered the conclusion that she should resign now.[3]

THE PRIME-MINISTERIAL RESIGNATION

Early the next morning, a press notice was issued from 10 Downing Street in the following terms: 'The Prime Minister, the Right Honourable Margaret Thatcher FRS MP, has informed The Queen that she does not intend to contest the second ballot of the election for leadership of the Conservative Party and intends to resign as Prime Minister as soon as a new leader of the Conservative Party has been elected. The Prime Minister will seek an Audience of The Queen later this morning to convey her decision formally. The Prime Minister has issued the following statement:

> 'Having consulted widely among colleagues, I have concluded that the unity of the Party and the prospects of victory in a General Election would be better served if I stood down to enable Cabinet colleagues to enter the ballot for the leadership. I should like to thank all those in Cabinet and outside who have given me such dedicated support.'

John Major, then Chancellor of the Exchequer, and Douglas Hurd, the Foreign Secretary, then declared their candidacies, and in the second ballot held on 27 November, Major achieved 185 votes to Heseltine's 131 and Hurd's 56. Although Major had failed to score the overall majority required for outright victory, in the face of his substantial lead Heseltine and Hurd immediately withdrew, allowing the chairman of the 1922 Committee to declare Major the newly elected leader of the Conservative Party.

The manner of Margaret Thatcher's departure as prime minister, by way of removal as party leader while still serving in office, is unique in British twentieth-century history. There were before her 17 other premiers, and of them in fact only two chose to retire for purely voluntary reasons – Stanley Baldwin in 1937 and Harold Wilson in 1976. Perhaps more surprising is that only four prime ministers have left office for the last time following defeat at a general election – Clement Attlee in 1951, Sir Alec Douglas-Home in 1964, Edward Heath in 1974 and James Callaghan in 1979. Stanley Baldwin, Ramsay MacDonald, Sir Winston Churchill and Harold Wilson all withstood electoral defeats as prime minister but returned to 10 Downing Street at a later date. Coalition government has been more common this century than is now generally remembered, embracing the years 1915–1916, 1916–1918, 1918–1922, 1931–1935, 1935–1940, 1940–1945, totalling 23 years, almost a quarter of the entire century. Three prime ministers were obliged to resign either as a result of the breaking up of a coalition government, as with Lloyd George in 1922, or owing to the formation of a coalition and the requirement for a leader acceptable to all parties, as with Herbert Asquith in 1916 being replaced by Lloyd George, and Neville Chamberlain in 1940 being replaced by Sir Winston Churchill. The greatest number of the century's prime ministers, seven, reluctantly resigned office owing to illness or old age: Lord Salisbury in 1902, Sir Henry Campbell-Bannerman in 1908, Bonar Law in 1923, Ramsay MacDonald in 1935, Sir Winston Churchill in 1955, Sir Anthony Eden in 1957, and Harold Macmillan in 1963. History certainly discloses a powerful tendency for prime ministers to cling to power for as long as possible, and in a system which imposes no maximum duration upon the term of their tenure.

THE PRIME MINISTER AND THE CONSTITUTION

Several important constitutional questions arose from the events of November 1990. There was often evident in public discussion some confusion about the constitutionality of what was going on, which is hardly surprising, of course, given the fact that Britain does not possess a constitution that is codified in writing and therefore readily accessible and understood. In fact there is no written, legal provision for the office of prime minister at all; it is purely a creature of *de facto* political practice exercising the ancient powers of the Crown.[4] The office of prime minister together with matters of appointment and dismissal are regulated instead by historical precedent and non-legal conventions. The first and most important query that arose was whether the prime minister was in fact bound to resign government office if she lost the party leadership. The legal answer to this is 'no', for, as stated, there is no law on the appointment and dismissal of prime ministers apart from the anachronism of the royal prerogative. The constitutional answer is also 'no', for the convention is that prime ministers are only obliged to resign following a no-confidence motion on their administration being carried in the House of Commons.[5] Since constitutional conventions are also not codified or committed to writing in Britain, they are to be discovered in authoritative texts on the constitution such as *Erskine May* or that of Wade and Bradley,[6] or in the verbal or written opinions of acknowledged consitutional experts such as Lord St John of Fawsley (formerly Norman St John-Stevas, the former cabinet minister and Leader of the House of Commons), Lord Blake (the Oxford University constitutional historian, and adviser to Buckingham Palace), and Lord Hailsham (the former Lord Chancellor and Chairman of the Conservative Party). These three peers were regularly consulted by the media and the press around the time of the election contest and Margaret Thatcher's resignation. Lord St John stated the convention in forthright terms:

> The constitutional position is of crystal clarity. Reigning Prime Ministers cannot be removed from office against their will save by one thing – the carrying of a vote of No Confidence on the floor of the Commons. No amount of secret hugger-mugger in upstairs Commons committee rooms with all the paraphernalia of counting secret ballot papers . . . can alter that central principle.[7]

The political reality, however, is that Margaret Thatcher was obliged to resign because the loss of the leadership removed her political authority to command and depend upon the Conservative Party majority in the Commons. There is a fine line between constitutional and political considerations in terms of legitimacy to hold office. What distinguishes a breach of constitutional convention, however, is the role of the Queen. Only if and when Margaret Thatcher might be voted down in a no-confidence motion in the Commons, and then refused to resign, would the Queen be expected to intervene and dismiss her; not before, and not by reason alone of the loss of the party leadership. The distinction between constitutional and political considerations was of sufficient significance, it transpired later on, for Margaret Thatcher to give thought to staying on as prime minister despite the loss of the party leadership. Commenting on the result of the first ballot, when she won 204 votes to Heseltine's 152, she revealed in an interview:

> I could have said, 'I got the majority – as a matter of fact I got more than my successor – and I will go on to a second ballot'. Or I could have said, 'Well it is only the Leadership of the Party, it is not for Prime Minister, therefore I will continue as Prime Minister, because I was elected as Prime Minister and I have never been defeated by the people and I have never been defeated by Parliament as a whole'. I could have divided the two. It would have been possible. Yes, I considered that quickly. But I have known for some time that when you have been there for twelve years the time will come when you will soon have to go.[8]

CONSTITUTIONAL QUESTIONS

What would have happened if Margaret Thatcher had resigned in disgust as prime minister straight away on 22 November before a new Conservative Party leader had been elected in the following week or fortnight in the second or third ballot? A similar issue arose again in 1991 when the mortar attack on 10 Downing Street in February led constitutionalists to ponder who, if John Major had perished, would run the country until a new Conservative leader was elected. The constitutional answer is that cabinet collectively would continue to govern the country, electing one of their number to be interim chairman, or the Queen would be entitled to appoint an interim prime minister who could command Commons support if she was advised that special political circumstances either at home or abroad made it necessary. Lord Blake's view was that 'the Government could manage without a Prime Minister because the office holds no specific departmental responsibilities'.[9]

Some commentators at the time found the secrecy with which Conservative MPs cast their votes in the leadership ballot improper and undemocratic,[10] especially since party rules required extensive consultation with constituency party members before casting their vote[11] but then precluded the local parties from actually knowing how their MP cast his or her vote. Many Conservatives, including John Lee MP and Lords St John, Blake and Hailsham, condemned the party rules for allowing a leadership challenge when in government, and expressly or by implication criticized those MPs who voted against Margaret Thatcher. Lee argued at the time that it was 'wrong in principle to vote against a sitting Prime Minister'.[12] Lord St John said the operation of the rules when the leader was prime minister was 'a constitutional monstrosity'.[13] However, none went so far as to maintain that the party rules were actually unconstitutional in themselves, although in Lord St John's opinion, 'if not technically unconstitutional, [they] are certainly against the spirit of the Constitution and flout the deepest and best values of the Conservative Party, such as loyalty, respect for office and recognition of authority'.[14]

Another issue affecting the legitimacy with which a prime minister holds office arose from claims, coming especially from members of the Labour and Liberal Democrat Parties, that a change in the leader of the party in power should automatically cause a general election to take place. This was influenced no doubt by political opportunism as much as constitutional principle. Nonetheless the argument that an election should take place as a consequence of Margaret Thatcher's resignation reflected a highly presidential view of the office of prime minister. It implied that a prime minister's authority flowed directly from the electorate, whereas in Britain the electoral process is a parliamentary one. Referring to the change of Conservative leader and prime minister as an 'electoral *coup d'état*' which undermined the strength and clarity of government, the then Labour leader Neil Kinnock said, 'I believe and my colleagues believe that the sovereign right to do that rests with the British people'.[15] Labour's campaign co-ordinator at that time, John Cunningham, said, 'a change of government should be decided by the electorate'.[16] Allies in this viewpoint came from unexpected quarters, including the former Conservative cabinet minister Nicholas Ridley, who said he regarded Michael Heseltine's challenge to Margaret Thatcher as 'breathtaking' in its implications for a change in government policy, especially over closer European economic and monetary union, without a general election or a referendum.[17] However, when the arguments for an election were put to Margaret Thatcher by Neil Kinnock at prime minister's question time in the Commons on the day she formally announced her intention to resign, her response did not need to be addressed in terms of constitutional or political theory, for the last period of Labour government had experienced a change of prime minister halfway through in 1976. Neil Kinnock said:

> May I pay tribute to you on your decision this morning. You showed by that you amount to more than those who have turned against you in recent days. You consider the principle of choice to be extremely important, and that is rightly so. Do you agree that the people of Britain should have the power of choice in a General Election?

Margaret Thatcher replied, 'No. No more than we had an election when Mr Wilson changed to Mr Callaghan.'[18]

CONCLUSION

It is characteristic of the British system of parliamentary government that there is no constitutional mechanism in existence for removing a prime minister which is otherwise than politically damaging to the governing party itself. In present circumstances no party is going to censure its own leader by a formal motion in the House of Commons, which would be tantamount to political suicide. Recent proposals for constitutional reform by the Institute for Public Policy Research have suggested a mandatory, legal requirement for a Commons resolution to appoint and dismiss prime ministers.[19] This is intended to operate under another of its proposals, for a different electoral system which incorporates a closer proportionality between national votes cast at a general election and party representation in the Commons.[20] In the absence of an overall majority for one party, which is a more likely scenario under either the additional member or single transferable vote systems, the House of Commons would be compelled to act more in the fashion of a genuine electoral college.[21] For traditional constitutionalists, however, the key to constitutional accountability of the considerable power now exercised by a prime minister in office is already evident in the *status quo* and is illustrated precisely by the events of November 1990. Whether or not constitutional reform of the prerogative powers of the prime minister, or the terms upon which prime ministers hold office, is likely in the foreseeable future, undoubtedly the manner of Margaret Thatcher's resignation must cause serious re-examination of the Richard Crossman–John Mackintosh[22] thesis which has dominated constitutional thinking for the past three decades, that 'the post-war epoch has seen the final transformation of Cabinet Government into Prime Ministerial Government'.[23] For there is now a contemporary, dramatic example of party, and ultimately cabinet, loss of confidence as the process by which a prime minister may be deposed.

NOTES AND REFERENCES

1 *Procedure for the Selection of the Leader of the Conservative Party*. Generally, and for the party leadership rules of each of the three main political parties, see: Rodney Brazier, *Constitutional Texts* (1990), Ch. 1.
2 Otherwise known as the Conservative Private Members' Committee. It is an organization which comprises all backbench Conservative Members of the House of Commons.
3 For a recent detailed version of events, see: A. Watkins, *A Conservative Coup* (1991).
4 Generally see: S. A. de Smith and R. Brazier, *Constitutional and Administrative Law* (6th edn, 1989), Ch. 9; and E. C. S. Wade and A. W. Bradley, *Constitutional and Administrative Law* (10th edn, 1985), Ch. 14.
5 See: G. Marshall, *Constitutional Conventions* (1984), pp. 55–56.
6 *Erskine May's Treatise on the Law, Privileges, Proceedings and Usage of Parliament* (21st edn, 1989, by C. J. Boulton); Wade and Bradley, *Constitutional and Administrative Law*; and see Marshall, *Constitutional Conventions*.
7 Quoted in *The Times*, 19 November 1990.
8 From a television interview in the USSR, quoted in *The Independent*, 29 May 1991.
9 Quoted in *The Times*, 9 February 1991.
10 One such critic was the SDP leader, David Owen.

11 Rules 6 and 8.
12 Interview on Channel 4 News, 20 November 1990.
13 *The Times*, 19 November 1990.
14 Communication with author.
15 Interview on Channel 4 News, 20 November 1990.
16 Interview on BBC 1 News, 18 November 1990.
17 Interview on BBC Panorama, 19 November 1990.
18 House of Commons Debates, 22 November 1990.
19 *The Constitution of the United Kingdom* (1991), especially Article 41, pp. 37/8, and Commentary pp. 29–30.
20 *Ibid.*, Ch. 8 and Schedule 3.
21 This was the main function of the Commons, according to Walter Bagehot; see: *The English Constitution* (1867, Fontana edn 1963), pp. 150/1.
22 See: R. H. S. Crossman, 'Introduction' to Walter Bagehot, *ibid.* and *Inside View: Three Lectures on Prime Ministerial Government* (1973); J. P. Mackintosh, *The Government and Politics of Britain* (6th edn, 1984); and for commentary, G. W. Jones, 'Cabinet Government since Bagehot', Ch. 2 of this book.
23 R. H. S. Crossman, 'Introduction' to Walter Bagehot, *The English Constitution* (1987, Fontana edn 1963), p. 51.

4

The Nationalization Legislation of the 1940s and the Privatization Legislation of the 1980s: A Constitutional Perspective

JOHN McELDOWNEY

SUMMARY

This chapter compares and contrasts the nationalization legislation in the 1940s with privatization in the 1980s. The major concern for constitutional lawyers is how accountability and efficiency may be combined in the running of industries which are vital to the nation's well-being. The relevant industries include the major utilities such as electricity and gas as well as transport, water and the steel industry. The theme of the chapter throughout is that privatization can simply replace state ownership with extensive regulation and private monopoly.

Privatization of British telecommunications, water and gas are examined. The recently privatized electricity industry is given particular attention, the Electricity Act 1989 being explained from a constitutional perspective. It is concluded that the Secretary of State has greater legal powers under the 1989 Act than under the nationalization legislation with implications for political power and control over the industry.

The chapter concludes with an evaluation of the Conservative government's privatization strategies. It is argued that the lessons from the experience of nationalization have not been applied in the privatization policies of the government. In common with nationalization in the 1940s, privatization is driven more by ideological beliefs than the demands of accountability and efficiency. New institutions may be required to meet the needs of protecting the consumer, the industry and the government. Possibly the role of the courts may be expanded or there may be set up a new regulatory framework to provide inter-regulatory co-ordination.

INTRODUCTION

Thirty years ago, William Robson defined the meaning of nationalized industry in Britain as:

> State intervention of a positive kind in the ownership, operation or regulation of industries and services in a vast movement of world wide dimension.[1]

Robson listed the public undertakings which fell within his definition. These included the major utilities such as water, gas, electricity and transport, including rail, bus and air. It also covered the British Steel Corporation, the Post Office and the United Kingdom Atomic Energy Authority.

Robson also acknowledged that the movement in favour of nationalization was vast, of bewildering diversity with unquestionable political, economic and social significance. Constitutional lawyers have recognized that nationalization has posed questions about the role of law and constitutional questions on the effectiveness of ministerial accountability for the industries.[2]

This chapter first seeks to explain how the nationalization process in the 1940s gave rise to a regulatory structure which was weak and which eventually led to demands for greater efficiency and accountability within the nationalized industries. Such demands led successive governments to devise techniques to influence the nationalized industries, often based on short-term political expediency. Secondly, the chapter examines the privatization process in the 1980s and the setting up of new regulatory frameworks. In particular it examines the recent example of the privatization of electricity under the Electricity Act 1989. It also examines the earlier examples of telecommunications, gas and water privatizations and considers how accountability and efficiency are to be achieved post-privatization. In fact, paradoxically in the case of electricity, the new powers given to the Secretary of State for Energy under the Electricity Act 1989 are greater than the power available under the nationalization legislation in 1947. Thus the potential for ministerial control or intervention is increased. Has the increase in legal powers been accompanied by an increase in the techniques of accountability?

NATIONALIZATION IN THE 1940s

Forty years ago the establishment of the main nationalized industries was achieved through the creation of public corporations. The characteristics of the public corporation included a wide range of statutory powers granted by Parliament to allow the particular activities to flourish. Statutory powers usually included the grant of a monopoly over the supply to the sectors that the utilities served and a framework which effectively separated the day-to-day working of the corporation from government intervention. A wide range of statutory formulations existed to achieve these characteristics. Sometimes the government took a major shareholding in an existing company; in other cases regulatory mechanisms were placed through the structure of the corporation itself, such as the Central Electricity Generating Board in the case of electricity.[3] Here state ownership of the electricity supply industry provided an entire structure for the generation, supply and distribution of electricity through one uniform system. This replaced a system of electricity generation which in the nineteenth century had resulted in many failed corporate enterprises. Local government areas had been regarded by entrepreneurs as a convenient size for electricity generation and distribution. In the two years from 1880 the number of local authority electricity companies had risen from 14 (1880) to 102 (1882).[3] Most of the companies attracted share speculators but the financial returns proved disappointing. The quick profit sought by shareholders was rarely achieved. As a result many of the companies ended in disaster with bankruptcy, and the shares subsequently became worthless.

The parliamentary supervision of such enterprises was strengthened by the Electric Lighting Act 1882. This Act insisted on a licence period before a local authority could be given the right to purchase any undertaking. Instead of a collection of private bills, containing enabling powers for local authorities to run electricity companies, the 1882 Act substituted a system of provisional orders allowing companies to be set up with the necessary statutory powers. In effect this was an arrangement based on a bargain, whereby Parliament granted statutory powers in return for closer supervision of the activities of the companies. It also reflected on the lack of adequate Company Act provisions to meet the needs of national monopolies. At the end of 1883, 69 provisional orders were issued with the result that 55 electric companies were set up. However, this attempt to reconcile municipal enterprise with the monopolistic tendencies of Company Act companies did not result in a satisfactory electricity supply industry. Companies and their municipalities found their franchised supply areas were too small. Inefficiencies and replication of working practices were common features to such enterprises. This was to lead to major changes in the techniques of regulation of the electricity supply industry.

The use of different forms of regulatory bodies is noticeable. In 1919 the Electricity (Supply) Act established the Electricity Commission to promote, regulate and supervise the supply of electricity on a national basis. In 1926 the Central Electricity Board was founded to construct and operate a national system of generating status interconnected and organized on a national basis.

The interwar years saw an increase in public ownership in the electricity industry. Prior to nationalization in 1947 there were over 560 separate electricity suppliers and only one-third were privately owned. Nationalization in this context followed the established pattern of a movement away from private to public ownership.

In common with most industries which were nationalized, the electricity industry had revealed defects in its organization and structure. Inefficiency and a lack of co-ordination were obvious problems. But such shortcomings were not the only basis for nationalization. Ideological reasons for public ownership were if anything more important than the desire to remedy defects.

Labour Party thinking emphasized the belief that certain activities were essential to the well-being of the nation and should be run by the State. Industries with a natural monopoly were an obvious target for nationalization. Accompanying the desire to run the natural monopolies was the idea that excessive profits should not be accumulated by exploiting a monopoly. Added to this there was a strong belief that industry should be working to the benefit of the nation and provide services rather than rely on the market as a regulator.

The model adopted for most nationalized industries followed the Morrisonian model[4] named after Herbert Morrison, whose ideas were the most influential. Thus the public corporation was the chosen form, with statutory powers to provide services for the newly nationalized industries. Such arrangements were heavily influenced by ideology:

> The public corporation must not be a capitalist business . . .
> it must have a different atmosphere at its board-table from
> that of a shareholders' meeting; the board and its officers
> must regard themselves as high custodians of the public
> interest.[5]

A number of influences could be exercised by government upon the nationalized industry. Such influences included the power of appointment to the boards of nationalized industries, the issuing of general directions as to policy, and specific ministerial approval over financial planning. Also included were ideas about encouraging the buying of British goods, an emphasis on the direction of returns on profits which could be ploughed back into the industry, and overall policy objectives on employment conditions such as wage bargaining. The theory of ministerial supervision could in practice allow ministers to 'run the industry'. Critics of the nationalized industries and the structure of control feared that such intervention might interfere with the efficiency of the industry itself.

Nationalization, however, did not come about as a coherent and well-considered plan. It is a fact that initially corporations were given little guidance on the policies they were to follow. There was general uncertainty as to the precise role such industries should play in the economy and confusion over the extent to which government influence should dictate managerial decisions. In general it was considered sufficient to appoint prudent managers to allow the industries to run themselves. The major issue was whether the nationalized industries required more direct intervention. The answer to this question was slow in coming.

GOVERNMENT POLICY ON THE NATIONALIZED INDUSTRIES

The early nationalization[6] policy from 1945 to 1950 was built on the expectation that profit in the industry would be directed to the public interest. The means to achieve or even define this aim became more crucial as the government of the day defined the running of the nationalized industries as an important part of the general economy.

Three government White Papers, in 1961, 1967 and 1978, set out policy considerations which were influential. The 1961 White Paper set out financial targets[7] to be achieved, specified as a rate of return on assets set by ministers. The formula used was crudely expressed; each nationalized industry was required to manage its affairs with the requirement of 'taking one year with notice to be sufficient to meet all items chargeable to revenue account'. Thus 'targets' were set for the industry to pay its way. Within this framework the industries were remarkably free to develop their own management strategies.

The 1967 White Paper[8] marked a more significant development in providing detailed guidelines as to how the nationalized industries were to perform. Specific financial targets were set with a requirement on capital investment projects of a certain minimum rate of return fixed for all the industries by the government. Further requirements included:

1 The separation of non-commercial responsibilities in accounts with investment based on a social cost–benefit evaluation.
2 Prices were to be set on the basis of long-run marginal costs. This meant that cross-subsidization between markets was to be avoided.
3 Investment was to be based on a value of the expected future return on projects.

NATIONALIZATION AND PRIVATIZATION

The means to monitor the operation of the 1967 White Paper was the Prices and Incomes Board. A weakness in the arrangements was the emphasis on financial instruments and a lack of attention devoted to productive efficiency. A major concern was the potential power of ministers to intervene, thus causing confusion over the exact boundaries of decision-taking between ministers and the nationalized industries. Thompson and Molyneux concluded:

> In particular, the institutional framework provided for ministerial intervention in decision-making in ways which blurred ultimate responsibility for particular actions. The specification of objectives and accountability of performance against them both emphasised in the business management literature were thus absent.[6]

A further deficiency was that in the early 1970s government policy to counter inflation required public corporations to hold down prices at a level which made productivity uneconomic. Compensation for this policy appeared in the form of subsidies, paid to the industry in order to mitigate the economic consequences of loss-making activities. Critics regarded the government's short-term limited objectives based on political choices to be inconsistent with the need to develop efficient industries.

The 1978 White Paper[9] went further than the two previous White Papers and set the following targets for the nationalized industries in an attempt to provide for the weaknesses in government policy. In effect the targets set were intended to make the nationalized industries more efficient and avoid the problem of recurring losses.

1. It strengthened financial controls by the government over public corporations through external financial limits (EFLs) adopted for each industry.
2. Financial targets became the prime instrument of government policy, requiring each industry to publish performance indicators to assess the efficiency of each industry through the relevant government departments.
3. The level of pricing was set to meet the financial targets.
4. Investment was to be examined on the overall performance of the corporations' investment programmes rather than individual projects.

Although the 1978 White Paper was broadly unclear as to how the level of financial targets was to be estimated, there was ample opportunity for ministers to intervene on the basis of determining 'each industry's target in the light of general policy objective, including consideration of social, sectoral and counter-inflation policy'.

The 1978 White Paper[10] had resulted in a major shift towards auditing the efficiency of the nationalized industries. The 1980 Competition Act allowed the Monopolies and Mergers Commission to undertake efficiency audits at the request of ministers. Productive efficiency became the basis of the overall financial controls set on each industry. The 'non-commercial objectives' of the nationalized industries characterized by the Labour Party[11] in its early nationalization policies were set to one side in favour of greater financial scrutiny through efficiency audit. As Paul Craig has observed, 'The tension between the exercise of commercial freedom and the utilisation of public corporations as part of a broader governmental strategy is apparent once again.'[12]

It is important to recognize the major 'constitutional actors' evident in the process of control over the nationalized industries. The main ones which deserve mention are as follows.[13]

Ministers

The 1978 White Paper left the broad policy framework of the government's financial control over the nationalized industries in the hands of ministers, and, in theory, the day-to-day decision-making in the industry on specific projects in the hands of managers. In practice, ministers have exercised specific financial approval over specific projects, especially when large sums of money have been involved. The purchase of VC 10 aircraft in the 1960s, the investment in Concorde and the purchase of British goods by specific nationalized industries are examples of such influence.

Parliament

Although the governing bodies of nationalized industries were not directly accountable to Parliament, in theory ministers were responsible through the relevant department. The main opportunity for discussion arose from legislation affecting the industries, the reports of committees such as the Select Committee on Nationalized Industries. It has been argued that a major weakness of such control was the absence of direct control through information becoming available to committees rather than to industry. The Select Committee on Nationalized Industries was set up in 1956 but in 1979, with reforms of the select committee system, it was abolished. It was replaced by provision for *ad hoc* subcommittees of two or more of the relevant departmental select committee to look at matters affecting nationalized industries. Elliott[14] believes that, if implemented properly, departmental committees could be more effective than the old Select

Committee on Nationalized Industries could ever be. Since then reports have been prepared on aspects of the nationalized industries. Regret was expressed that in 1983 in the reforms introduced in the setting up of the National Audit Office no provision was made for the nationalized industries, which remain outside the ambit of the Comptroller and Auditor General. Efforts to have the nationalized industries included was defeated by government intervention in adopting the private bill originally introduced by Norman St John-Stevas.

Thus parliamentary control appears to depend very much on ministerial accountability, which is seen as a weakness of the existing arrangements.

Treasury

Here the major influence over the nationalized industries is the use of financial targets. The 1978 White Paper introduced the concept of external financing limits (EFLs) on each industry. These represent the total of public financial support for each corporation and are included in the public expenditure White Paper. They are subject to cash limits and in theory would seem to represent a positive statement of the sum that government may make over to the industry. In fact, as Elliott has pointed out, they were used in the financial year 1983-1984 to produce a price increase in the gas and electricity industries because they bound the industries to meet their EFLs through their own financial resources rather than additional government grant.

The Monopolies and Mergers Commission (MMC)

Since 1980 the MMC has offered a ministerial influence over the nationalized industries through reviews of efficiency. In fact this power has been increasingly used since 1982 as a means of increasing the efficiency of commercial objectives of the industry, thereby decreasing the amount of public funds available.

In 1983 reports by the MMC into the National Coal Board (Cmnd. 8920) and the Serpell Committee of Inquiry into Railway Finances, together with a memorandum from the Comptroller and Auditor General to the Public Accounts Committee on the monitoring and control activities of three departments sponsoring nationalized industries, complained of the way in which huge public subsidies were being used inefficiently or for purposes other than those originally intended. The main point of such criticisms was directed to the failure by departments to devise and operate an effective system of control. Although the objects of the MMC inquiry may be determined by ministers, concern that the MMC itself may not exercise a sufficiently independent function in its reports seem to be unfounded. Collins and Wharton concluded in their 1984 study that the MMC reports demonstrated an independent remit. However, they admitted that there was no consensus on what basis the reports were made. Thus the follow-up to reports is unclear and the procedures for improvement left a lot to be desired.

The process of nationalization in the 1940s left unanswered the question of how accountability and efficiency in the nationalized industries might be achieved. There was also a remarkable failure to give a clear meaning to the terms employed to judge the performance of the nationalized industries. Accountability means in this context an obligation to explain or justify actions. Here it is important to recognize that obligations may be achieved through a managerial form of accountability as well as accountability to the legal duties of the industry and ultimate political accountability. In each there must be some quantitative measurement of how resources and objectives have been properly managed. Similarly, the expenditure of money raises issues of efficiency. A prolonged economic debate has taken place over the question of whether the public sector's use of public expenditure is efficient. An underlying assumption in that debate is that the market is an efficient system of self-regulation. This assumption has not been adequately researched or tested. In reality efficiency is a complex term which embraces economic considerations as to the best method by which resources are allocated between competing uses and the best use made of them. By the 1980s, as the Conservative government began to embark on its privatization programme, both questions remained unsatisfactorily answered. This point was succinctly explained by Maurice Garner when he wrote:

> The object of all accountability is to increase efficiency. The object of autonomy for the management of nationalised industries is efficiency. In Britain autonomy and accountability have come to be seen as antithetical.

Garner questions[15] the effectiveness of ministerial accountability when government policy is unable to interfere with day-to-day management. The latter seemed isolated from the demands of efficiency. The 1978 White Paper had gone a long way to improve overall efficiency by providing a realistic pricing structure for the nationalized industries.[16] Both Molyneux and Thompson in their study of the performance of the nationalized industries called for more reforms in the direction indicated by the 1978 White Paper, particularly in respect of increased competition. Such encouragement and optimism was short-lived, as after 1979 the Conservative government's ideological policies sought to reverse the nationalization process through privatization. This policy was implemented in a number of stages which are considered below.

PRIVATIZATION AND THE GOVERNMENT'S IDEOLOGICAL BELIEFS

Nationalization and privatization when compared share at least one common underlying principle. They are both based more strongly on government ideology than on any coherent and systematic plan designed to implement a number of clearly worked-out objectives based on a non-ideological diagnosis of existing problems. Craig has identified a number of reasons for privatization and his list included many of the objections to the nationalization programme of the 1940s:

> The reasons for privatisation are, like those for nationalisation, eclectic. They include the following: improving efficiency, reducing government involvement in decision-making of industry, ordinary share ownership, encouraging share ownership by employees, alleviating problems of public sector pay determination, reducing the public sector borrowing requirement and the enhancement of economic freedom.[17]

The claims made for privatization exceed the reality of the results actually achieved. Government ideology has sought to label nationalized industry as inefficient, while in reality this claim is open to challenge and fails to take account of the developments arrived at from the experience of the 1978 White Paper. Indeed, the striking feature of privatization is that the critical elements in its success depend largely on competition and efficiency within the privatized industry as well as the use of regulatory powers to oversee consumer protection and quality control. Paradoxically, questions of accountability and efficiency arise in privatization strategies to the same extent as they had done in the nationalized industries.

Privatization may be examined according to its historical development. It is necessary to make a crucial distinction between smaller privatized companies and larger activities. For example, smaller companies such as Amersham International, Jaguar, Sealink and British Aerospace operate within a competitive framework[18] and are of little concern to the constitutional lawyer as to how their activities may be regulated.[19] The government's initial forays (Table 1) into implementing its privatization policy were based on identifying these smaller activities, which were privatized as the first phase of the

Table 1

Company	Date of privatization	Net proceeds to HMG (£ million)
British Petroleum (residue sale)	1979	276
	1981	8
	1983	543
	1987	5322
British Aerospace	1981	43
	1985	347
Cable and Wireless	1981	181
	1983	263
	1985	580
Amersham International	1982	60
National Freight Consortium	1982	53
Britoil	1982	626
	1985	426
Associated British Ports	1983	46
	1984	51
Enterprise Oil	1984	382
Sealink (trade sale)	1984	66* to British Rail
Jaguar	1984	297* to British Leyland
British Telecom	1984	3681
British Shipbuilders Warship Yards (trade sale)	1984–1985	54* to British Shipbuilders
British Gas	1986	7731 includes £2500 debentures repayable to consolidated fund
British Airways	1987	850
Royal Ordnance (trade sale)	1987	185
Rolls-Royce	1987	1028
BAA	1987	1183
Rover (trade sale)	1988	150
British Steel	1988	2437
10 water companies	1989	3480 includes £75m repayable in repayments to consolidated fund
Anglian	1989	
Northumbrian Water	1989	
North West Water	1989	
Severn–Trent	1989	
Southern Water	1989	

Table 1 (continued)

Company	Date of privatization	Net proceeds to HMG (£ million)
South West Water	1989	
Thames Water	1989	
Welsh Water	1989	
Wessex Water	1989	
Yorkshire Water	1989	

*Proceeds to nationalized industries.
This table is in abbreviated form from a table taken from material provided in a written answer: *Hansard*, 27 April 1990, Written answers cols 357–360, which is reproduced in Beauchamp, *Public Money and Management*, (Summer, 1990).

government's policy. Stage 1, as it may be referred to, made privatization acceptable and attractive to the public and an electoral asset.

In contrast, the larger privatizations, such as British Telecom[20] in 1984 and British Gas[21] in 1985, required a regulatory framework which attempts to deal with the larger market to which the newly privatized industry belongs.[22] These larger privatizations were the second stage of the government's privatization[23] policy and were notable for the weak regulatory structure used to secure the effective provision of services from the industry.

The privatization of British Telecom (BT) in 1984 is our starting point. The Telecommunications Act 1984 was the first major reform of an industry which had been from 1912 until 1981 a state-owned monopoly. In 1981 the first stage prior to privatization took place, when legislation, the British Telecommunications Act 1981, separated telecommunications from postal services, thereby establishing BT as a public corporation. The 1981 stage relaxed the restrictions on supply of customers' equipment and allowed licensing of other telecommunications systems. The 1984 Telecommunications Act created a Director General of Telecommunications (DGT) with regulatory powers based on guidelines as to how the DGT is expected to perform his duties. The hallmark of this particular privatization was the need to find a suitable competitor for BT. The government effectively promoted the creation of a competitive rival, Mercury, which is the only competitor licensed to date to compete with BT. The experience of nationalization may be seen in the power under the 1984 Act to refer, for example, BT to the MMC if the matter is one which operates against the public interest.

Another characteristic is the requirement to build a pricing structure into the regulatory arrangements. Currently BT cannot increase prices by more than the retail price index minus 3 per cent. The success of the pricing mechanism is to be gauged on how efficient and cost-effective the industry may be, and this remains to be seen.

The creation of the DGT as a means to secure effective competition, economy, efficiency and growth and development of the telecommunications business in the UK, both national and international, depends on how effective the regulatory system might be. Criticism of the 1984 Act focuses on three matters. First, the legislation fails to provide any requirement that adequate information is available to the DGT. Second, there is concern that the resources of the DGT may not be adequate to maintain supervision of the organization. Third, the DGT and Office of Telecommunications (OFTEL) may be perceived as being too closely linked with the industry. Thus their independence and impartiality might be questioned if their perceived role became too protective of the industry.

In fact few referrals have been made by the DGT to the MMC and there is an added difficulty. Legal powers do not exist to prevent BT becoming an owner or participating in industries outside the telecommunications area. The desire to do so may conform with the interests of BT but not necessarily the interests of a competitive telecommunications industry in Britain. In this respect the 1984 Act is defective.[22]

The 1984 regulatory structure was perceived to be weak, overcomplicated and bureaucratic. Privatization had thus encountered similar difficulties in efficiency and competitiveness as had the nationalization legislation of the 1940s. Paradoxically the government in the recent Duopoly Review (1990) accepted that the duopoly policy of fostering competition between BT and Mercury will end. The government will consider on their merits applications for a licence to offer telecommunications services over fixed links within the UK. This will encourage greater competition. There is also to be a requirement of 'no cross-subsidy from the utility's main business'. This marks a considerable shift in the government's policy, and a recognition that the policy behind the 1984 Act was misplaced. However, there are no 'current plans to amend the 1984 Act' and the question is one which will be kept under scrutiny.

Similar issues concerning effective competition arose with the privatization of the gas industry. In 1985 the government decided to privatize British Gas and the question of how competition and efficiency might be achieved was given serious consideration but with disappointing results.

NATIONALIZATION AND PRIVATIZATION

The nationalization of the British gas industry[24] in 1948 and its centralization in 1962 had created a single industry centralized under a public corporation responsible for the activities of 12 area boards who had autonomy over the manufacture and supply of gas. Sole rights to purchase gas from producers had been granted to the corporation in 1982 and pricing had been characteristically low, with a resultant lack of investment. This lack of investment has been attributed to poor policy direction by the government of the day.

Privatization was undertaken by the Gas Act 1986, which followed the model set by telecommunications in 1984. A regulatory structure was set up under a Director General of Gas Supply (OFGAS) and an OFGAS office. The newly created company, British Gas, did not have any competition and, unlike the case of BT and Mercury, none was created by the 1986 Act for the gas industry. No attempt was made to restructure the industry in the 1986 Act. The 12 regional boards could have become gas companies with a separate company to control the transmission system. The strong ideological belief that the timetable of the government's privatization strategy should not be altered or slowed down meant that restructuring of the gas industry was avoided. As Craig noted:

> The decision not to reorganise the industry had been termed a response to interest group pressure from management and consumers, in which short term electoral considerations assumed precedence over longer term considerations of economic efficiency.[25]

It is clear that the Gas Act 1986, in practice, insulates British Gas from competition. As no new competitor was created it is difficult not to see the monopoly of British Gas as virtually impregnable.

Finally, the 1986 Act provided a complex formula for pricing supervised by the Director General of Gas Supply (DGGS) and OFGAS. Legal powers similar to OFTEL were provided to OFGAS to promote efficiency to gas suppliers and users. The DGGS may impose conditions upon the grant of authorization to a public gas supplier and there is a possibility of a referral to the MMC to specify any modification to the authorization. Compliance powers granted to the DGGS and investigative powers over conditions granted in the authorization are all part of the regulatory framework.

Sadly the powers of the regulator are considerably less than the powers possessed by British Gas. For example, it is impossible for the DGGS to alter the legal structure of the gas industry. Some doubts exist as to the powers of the DGGS to be provide transparency of pricing and to open up the transmission system through supplies to third parties. Vickers and Yarrow make a point which has general application to the privatization strategies of the government:

> What has happened is that one of the major deficiencies of the UK control system for nationalised industries – preoccupation with short-term political issues – has been duplicated in the policy framework set for the regulated privately owned gas industry.[26]

In fact the experience gained from the gas and telecommunications privatizations proved to be insufficient to meet the challenge posed by electricity privatization. The government's proposals to privatize the electricity supply industry faced a sterner test because the electricity industry was the largest of the UK's nationalized industries in terms of turnover and capital employed. For example, in 1985 revenue was £11 on a capital stock of £40 billion. In the run-up to electricity privatization the government went ahead with water privatization.

Similarly, the privatization of water proved to be a greater problem than gas or telecommunications. Water privatization[27] had to address one of the most complex legal arrangements for water services. There were ten existing public authorities and major health and environmental factors to be taken into consideration during privatization. The result under the Water Act 1989 is the creation of a new public body, the National Rivers Authority (NRA), with the rights and liabilities of the existing water authorities divided between the NRA and successor companies. The 29 statutory water companies are retained as water undertakers for their areas. The successor companies inherit the responsibilities of sewerage and water subject to the terms of the instruments of appointment. There is a Water Services office with a Director General of Water Services.

The NRA has responsibilities for the control of river and coastal water pollution, water resource management, land drainage, fisheries, navigation and flood defence. A major feature of the legislation is a complex pricing formula, detailed environmental protection arrangements, and a new regulatory body under the Director General of Water Services. The latter is required to balance the protection of the consumer from monopoly exploitation and the efficient running of the utility. There is protection from voluntary winding up by the successor companies and the MMC exercise a review of competition. Concern is expressed by critics of the legislation that competition will be ineffective and the costs required to provide environmental protection will be expensive to the consumer.

Clearly the water privatization plans present yet more examples of problems concerning efficiency and accountability. The present

NATIONALIZATION AND PRIVATIZATION

statutory formulation would seem to do little to achieve competition between the different parts of the industry.

It is electricity which poses the greatest test to date for the government's privatization policies. Electricity privatization[28] also poses some of the most complex legal problems. It is a natural monopoly, involves the use of fuels as diverse as solar power and nuclear energy, and is a heavy polluter of the environment. Under nationalization the generation, supply and transmission of electricity were integrated by the 1957 Electricity Act. The Central Electricity Generating Board (CEGB) was put in charge of both generation and transmission. A national grid was created with 12 area boards for distribution purposes. These purposes were left to the autonomy of the boards, particularly in respect of financial matters. Consumers' interests in England and Wales are represented by 13 district organizations. There are 12 area electricity consultative councils, one for each area board, and an Electricity Consumers' Council set up in 1977 at the national level.

The electricity supply industry provides for the virtual separation between the generation and transmission of electricity undertaken by the CEGB. Distribution and retailing were undertaken by the area boards. Overall direction and the electricity requirements set up by the 1957 Act are required to be met by the CEGB, such as supplying British Rail with electricity.

The privatization strategy adopted by the government was contained in a 1988 White Paper[29] which set out six objectives to be followed, namely: the needs of customers should be considered an important part of the industry; competition is an essential guarantee of customers' interests; regulation was required to promote competition, oversee prices and protect customers' interests; security and safety should be maintained; customers should be given new rights; share ownership should include those who work for the company.

The government's ideological preference was to privatize the entire electricity supply industry, including nuclear power. To those ends a complicated organizational structure was created. Competition in generation is to be provided by the division of the CEGB into two companies, National Power, with 70 per cent of capacity, including nuclear, and PowerGen, with the remaining 30 per cent. The CEGB will be disbanded.

The national grid is to be placed under a separate grid company (the National Grid Company) jointly owned by the 12 distribution companies (DISCOS) replacing the existing 12 area boards.

Despite objections to such proposals and the belated recognition that the nuclear power side of generation was too much of a high risk in terms of economic cost (partly due to decommissioning costs), the government pushed ahead with the existing proposals. In October 1989 and after the Electricity Act 1989 had been passed for the privatization of the industry, the government reluctantly removed the nuclear side of the industry from privatization and it will remain under government control. It will form a separate company under government ownership. More recently the government announced that it favoured selling PowerGen as a private sale rather than as a public flotation. All this is further evidence of the difficulties posed by privatization.

The separation of the grid from the generation side is intended to provide a competitive element in the industry. The government has also set up an Office of Electricity Regulation with a Director General of Electricity Supply (DGES).

The 1989 Electricity Act provides further evidence of the difficulty that privatization faces in providing an adequate structure which combines efficiency for the industry with accountability for policy. The most important elements in electricity privatization are the pricing, competition and regulatory supervision by the DGES.

The 1989 Act provides a complex electricity pricing mechanism based on the retail price index. Regulatory supervision is provided by both the Secretary of State for Energy and the DGES. For many of the duties contained in the Act, such as competition in the generation and supply of electricity and the requirement that all reasonable demands for electricity are served, many of the regulatory functions are *shared* with the Secretary of State and the Director.

It is this feature which is distinctive about the electricity privatization structure contained in the 1989 Act. For the first time the Secretary of State for Energy can intervene directly in the running of the electricity supply industry to an extent which would never have been politically or legally[30] possible under the nationalization legislation.

The Secretary of State's powers include the power to grant licences to generate, transmit or supply electricity. This power may be exercised in consultation with the DGES, who is appointed by the Secretary of State for Energy. It is also possible under section 6 of the 1989 Act to delegate the licensing power to the DGES. Even here the Secretary of State may direct the DGES not to make modifications to a licence.

The 1989 Act follows the pattern in the privatization of British Gas which allows the DGES a discretion to make a referral to the MMC. But the Secretary of State for Energy can direct the MMC not to proceed with the referral. Once a report is prepared the Secretary of State may prohibit publication of 'any matter' if it appears to him that it would be against the public or commercial interest of 'any person'.

The Secretary of State possesses wide powers to keep a register of information on licences, modifications and the like. Effectively placing the Secretary of State as the electricity supply industry's licensing authority of the 1989 Act allows intervention in the work of the DGES as a regulator that challenges any sense of independence or freedom from political influence which the DGES may want to develop. While the DGES has a duty to review the 'carrying on' of electricity generation, transmission and supply, the Secretary of State may give the DGES directions as to the priorities or matters which form the DGES's remit.

The Secretary of State's powers extend to the day-to-day operations of the electricity supply industry. The constitution of generating stations and the consents required may be supervised by the Secretary of State under section 36 of the Act. The use of fuel stocks, and the requirement that electricity is available from non-fossil fuel sources, are all part of the wide powers possessed by the Secretary of State.

The management functions of the person operating the general station could be directed by the Secretary of State as well as the 'specified objectives' which may be given to the National Grid Company to operate the transmission system. It is clear that the legal powers contained in the 1989 Act provide the Secretary of State with the means to take over the operational management of the industry.

Finally, wide emergency powers are included in Part III of the 1989 Act which provide the Secretary of State with extensive powers to give directions to the industry. The term 'civil emergency' is widely defined in subjective terms in section 96 of the 1989 Act. It includes any national disaster or other emergency which, in the opinion of the Secretary of State, is against the interests of national security or commercial interests. The power to give directions does not contain any requirement of laying the direction before Parliament. The 1989 Act provides the Secretary of State with unparalleled powers in the history of the electricity supply industry to intervene in the day-to-day running of the industry. The successful regulation of the electricity supply industry depends on the competition which the 1989 Act is intended to initiate. Determinations made by the Director General have had to arbitrate between competing claims of power companies in their supply of electricity. To a large extent many large consumers feel that the complexity of the regulatory framework and the use of contracts for the supply of electricity have left the major influence in the hands of the major players in the generation, supply and production of electricity. This in effect gives National Power and PowerGen a duopoly influence which has been relieved of the burden of nuclear power, which remains in public ownership.

CONCLUSIONS

The question of accountability[31] and efficiency raised by the nationalized industries in their relationship with the government of the day led to a wide range of techniques introduced to allow competitive industries to become consistent with political ideology. As Prosser pointed out:

> Thus the nationalisation process was seen as almost exclusively a matter of transferring property rights whilst issues of control and accountability were treated as determined by ownership and so of little interest in their own right.[32]

The steps taken since 1978 to provide a framework for a coherent nationalized industry policy seem, on an economic analysis, to be working. Molyneux and Thompson found:

> The upturn in performance since 1978 points to the success of the various institutional reforms that have been implemented . . . We suggest that the type of reform indicated by our analysis is one that would place emphasis on increased competition, a proposal substantially at variance with current initiatives involving the privatisation of the State Monopolies.[6]

The experience to date of privatization has indicated that the difficulties experienced in nationalization of providing a satisfactory basis for both the industry and government to operate under remain. In the case of telecommunications and gas a weak regulatory framework has little impact on the essential requirement of competition. Constitutional lawyers can sense that the regulatory bodies constructed under both major privatizations lack clearly defined objectives and the means to achieve them. The privatization of electricity has provided in the Electricity Act 1989 a stronger framework for direct political intervention in the industry than under nationalization.

This raises the question in constitutional terms of accountability. Constitutional lawyers may seek to find the answer in a number of institutions: first, the various regulators (including the MMC) who should be seen to have adequate powers to oversee the industry; second, the courts and the power of judicial review; and third, the Secretary of State in terms of ministerial responsibility to Parliament. All three forms of accountability exist but seem unlikely to be able to provide a coherent set of objectives for the industry to act efficiently and at the same time to satisfy consumer demands for a good-quality service. The courts are expensive, unduly technical and pragmatic in operation and historically ministerial responsibility has proved ineffective in providing an objective standard to check policy decision-taking. Under its guise ministers remain remarkably free to act within the overall policy objectives often set by the political demands of the day. Despite assumptions to the contrary, electricity privatization has permitted the granting of additional ministerial powers which allow direct intervention in the industry. This presents the government of the day with political opportunities to interfere in the day-to-day functioning of the industry. Privatization has produced what government policy on nationalization was heavily critical of, that is potential for powerful intervention in the market.

Constitutional lawyers may perceive the obvious difficulties which privatization poses. Sir Gordon Borrie has pointed to the prospect of increased use of judicial review. His observations are that the complex pattern of regulation over the private sector through privatization may not be sufficient. Perhaps the courts have a role to perform? In summary he suggests that litigation can play a useful regulatory role.

There are increasing signs that the powerful facility of judicial review proceedings may now be available against bodies other than public bodies and that the courts are willing to encourage such a development.

Cases such as the *Panel on Take-overs and Mergers ex parte Datafin plc* [1987] QB 815 suggest that Borrie's analysis is grounded in judicial decisions. The Court of Appeal reviewed the powers of the city take-overs and mergers panel, expressing a clear preference to have jurisdiction over such a body. Such jurisdiction might not extend to a purely contractual matter such as a private arbitration where the arbitrator is not subject to judicial review.[33] However, such reliance on the courts' ability to develop techniques of judicial intervention seem optimistic. Judicial review is, as Professor de Smith has reminded us, 'sporadic and peripheral'. Privatization is extremely diverse in its policy implementation. Indeed, privatization represents a particular specialism with its own internal arrangements set to balance consumer protection, market strategies and efficiency. The mechanism for its control, as with its efficient regulation, fits uneasily with the present development of judicial review, where clear principles have not been a hallmark of its developments. Economic analysis and market strategies seem ill-suited to the winner-takes-all culture of court cases.

Future development of judicial review will depend on whether new agencies can be created to overcome the burdens of expense and uncertainty which limit the availability of judicial remedies to ordinary members of the public. For example, the proposal of a Director of Civil Proceedings made by Sir Harry Woolf in his Harry

Street lecture is one change which may overcome some of the disadvantages mentioned above.

Changes are possible in the role of regulatory bodies and in the development of inter-regulation agencies in the style of the United States Federal Administrative Procedure Act. Setting up such procedures might provide a more satisfactory solution to the problems posed above, allowing data, analysis and rules to be correlated. The past lessons of nationalization point to the difficulty of government setting targets and setting strategies and financial planning for the nationalized industries. The experience of privatization has shown that the lessons of the nationalized industries have not been learnt. The questions of accountability and efficiency remain largely unresolved for the newly privatized industries in the same way as they had been unresolved for the nationalized industries.

Constitutional lawyers have to meet the challenges set by privatization. The legal requirements of licences and regulatory controls apply techniques from private law to public law. New techniques of analysis and new regulatory bodies are required. The change of ownership which privatization has secured has barely affected the fundamental relationship between the industries and the consumer. Future government policy and shifts in ideology in the life cycle of party politics need to be addressed in the requirement of efficiency and accountability which the privatized industry must meet.[34]

NOTES AND REFERENCES

1 W. Robson, *Nationalised Industry and Public Ownership* (1960, 2nd edn, 1962), p. 17. Also see: L. Gordon, *The Public Corporation in Great Britain* (London, 1938); E. Goodwin, *Forms of Public Control and Ownership* (London, 1951). Generally see: D.J. Gayle and J. Goodrich, *Privatization and Deregulation in Global Perspective* (London: Pinter, 1990).

2 T. Prosser, *Nationalised Industries and Public Control* (Oxford: Blackwell, 1986). Also see: T. Prosser and M.E. Dimcook, *British Public Utilities and National Development* (Chester, 1983).

3 L. Hannah, *Electricity before Nationalisation* (Electricity Council, 1929). Also see: H.H. Ballin, *The Organisation of Electricity Supply in Great Britain* (1946).

4 H. Morrison, *Socialisation of Transport* (1933).

5 *Ibid.* For a background study of nationalization as part of the public economy see: J. Tomlinson, *Public Policy and the Economy since 1900* (Oxford University Press, 1990).

6 R. Molyneux and D. Thompson, 'Nationalised Industry Performance: Still Third Rate?', *Fiscal Studies*, **18** (1987), 48–82.
7 *Financial and Economic Obligations of the Nationalised Industries*, Cmnd. 1337 (1961).
8 *Nationalised Industries: A Review of Economic and Financial Objectives*, Cmnd. 3437 (1967).
9 *The Nationalised Industries*, Cmnd. 7131 (1978).
10 C. Graham and T. Prosser, 'Privatising Nationalised Industries: Constitutional Issues and New Legal Techniques', *MLR*, **50** (1987), 16.
11 T. Prosser, *The Privatisation of Public Enterprises in France and Great Britain: The State, Constitution and Public Policy*, EUR Working Paper No. 88/364 (1988), p. 37.
12 P.P. Craig, *Administrative Law* (London: Sweet and Maxwell, 1989, 2nd edn), pp. 84–87.
13 Prosser, *Nationalised Industries*. But see: J.F. McEldowney, 'The National Audit Office and Privatisation', *MLR*, **54** (1991), 933–955. The role of the National Audit Office is analysed in its examination of the departmental supervision of privatisation.
14 M.J. Elliot, 'The Control of Public Expenditure', in J. Jowell and D. Oliver (eds), *The Changing Constitution* (Oxford University Press, 1985), pp. 149–173.
15 M. Garner, 'Auditing the Efficiency of Nationalised Industries: Enter the Monopolies and Mergers Commission', *Public Administration*, **60** (1982), 426.
16 B. Collins and B. Wharton, 'Investigating Public Industries: How Has the Monopolies and Mergers Commission Performed?', *Public Money* (September 1984), 15–23.
17 Craig, *Administrative Law*. The MMC powers refer to (Section 11, Competition Act 1980) public corporations and certain other statutory bodies. In practice such companies are thereby excluded from review. See: C. Veljanovski, 'Privatization: Progress, Issues and Problems', in D.J. Gayle and J. Goodrich (eds), *Privatization and Deregulation in Global Perspective*, pp. 63–79.
18 C. Veljanovski, *Selling the State: Privatisation in Britain* (London: Weidenfeld and Nicolson, 1987).
19 L. Hancher and M. Moran, *Capitalism, Culture and Economic Regulation* (Oxford University Press, 1989).
20 M.E. Beesley, *Liberalisation of the Use of the British Telecommunications Network* (London: HMSO, 1981).
21 Deloitte, Haskins and Sells, *British Gas Efficiency Study* (1983).
22 J. Vickers and G. Yarrow, *Privatisation: An Economic Analysis* (London: MIT Press, 1988), p. 248.
23 Heald and Steel, 'Privatising Public Enterprise: An Analysis of the Government's Case', in J. Kay *et al.* (eds), *Privatisation and Regulation - The UK Experience* (Oxford University Press, 1986). See: Blanche Sas, 'Regulation and the Privatised Electricity Supply Industry', *MLR*, **53** (1990), 485.
24 See: Mayer and Meadowcroft, 'Selling Public Assets: Techniques and Financial Implications', in Kay *et al.* (eds), *Privatisation and Regulation*.
25 Craig, *Administrative Law*, pp. 164–169.
26 Vickers and Yarrow, *Privatisation*, p. 263.

27 See: R. MacRory, *The Water Act 1989 Current Legal Statutes* (London: Sweet and Maxwell, 1989).
28 McAuslan and McEldowney, *The Electricity Act 1989 Current Legal Statutes* (1989). See: James Capel, *Reshaping the Electricity Supply Industry in England and Wales* (London: James Capel, 1990).
29 *Privatising Electricity*, Cm. 322 (1988).
30 Generally see: G. Borrie, 'The Regulation of Public and Private Power', *Public Law* (1990), 552. See also: D. Helm and G. Yarrow, 'The Regulation of Public Utilities', *Oxford Review of Economic Policy*, 14 (1988), No. 2.
31 For a general discussion of the Monopolies and Mergers Commission see: B. Collins and B. Wharton, 'Nationalised Industries: Responses to the Monopolies & Mergers Commission', *Public Money*, 4, (1984–85), 30–32; M. Garner, 'The White Papers on the Nationalised Industries', *Public Administration*, 57, (1979).
32 Prosser, *The Privatisation of Public Enterprises*, p. 272. See also: C. Graham and T. Prosser, *Privatising Public Enterprises* (Oxford University Press, 1991).
33 See: *R. v. National Joint Council for the Draft of Dental Technicians (Disputes Committee), ex parte; Neate* [1953] 1 QB 7040.
34 Prosser, *The Privatisation of Public Enterprises*. See also: D. Heald, *Public Expenditure* (Oxford: Blackwell, 1987). The need for an inter-regulatory agency becomes apparent as more of the privatized industries engage in activities outside their original remit. An example would be if British Gas owned shares in BT or in electricity companies.

5

Administrative Law: Is the System Now in Place?

ANTHONY BRADLEY

Administrative law in this country [the UK] is not really a system at all, but is simply an exercise of arbitrary power in relation to certain matters which are specified or indicated by statute, not on any definite principle, but haphazard, on the theory, presumably, that such matters are better kept outside the control of the Courts, and left to the uncontrolled discretion of the Executive and its servants.

To members of a university law school, this quotation may sound like one of those fictitious quotations made up by the examiners, and followed by the word 'Discuss', in an attempt to put at least one question into an examination paper that will inspire the best students to display a brilliant level of analytical insight while enabling the weakest students to write something vaguely relevant.

The quotation in fact comes from Lord Hewart's *The New Despotism*, published in 1929.[1] As that judicial figure warmed to his subject, he preferred to call it not administrative law but 'administrative lawlessness'. Doubtless many administrative lawyers today would deride the Hewart view out of hand, as being old-fashioned, biased and idiosyncratic even in its time. So too might they dismiss with scorn the Committee on Ministers' Powers in 1932, who advised 'without hesitation' against the adoption of a system of administrative law, which (in the committee's view) would be inconsistent with the sovereignty of Parliament and the supremacy of the law.[2] Be that as it may, we could hardly contend, given such contemporary evidence, that a system of administrative law was in place in the 1920s or 1930s.

In the 1990s, we live in a more enlightened age and we can point to such notable developments in public law since 1945 as: the Crown Proceedings Act 1947; the Franks Report on administrative tribunals and inquiries, the Tribunals and Inquiries Act 1958 (now 1971), and the work of the Council on Tribunals; the rapid growth of ombudsmen in the public sector since the Parliamentary Commissioner Act 1967, providing remedies for maladministration that has caused injustice to individuals; and the success of the procedure of the application for judicial review created by Order 53 of the Rules of the Supreme Court in 1977.[3]

We would also wish to point to judicial recognition of administrative law and argue that the judges now see it as an important branch of the UK's constitutional arrangements. Undoubtedly this owes much to academic writing on the subject.[4] Important progress towards recognition can be found in Lord Reid's dictum in 1963:

> We do not have a developed system of administrative
> law – perhaps because until fairly recently we did not need it.[5]

And in 1981, in opposing reliance by a government department on technical restrictions on the applicant's *locus standi*, Lord Diplock said that to accept such restrictions would be

> to reverse that progress towards a comprehensive system of
> administrative law that I regard as having been the greatest
> achievement of the English courts in my judicial lifetime.[6]

This judicial recognition is evidenced in a different way by the burgeoning volume of administrative law cases now being reported.[7] We could also point to the official recognition of administrative law that was given in the civil service leaflet, *The Judge over Your Shoulder*,[8] and a related memorandum from the cabinet to all departments in 1987 entitled *Reducing the Risk of Legal Challenges*.[9] More recently still, according to Sir Robert Andrew's report, *Review of the Government Legal Service*: 'administrative law now rates with resource control as a major element in civil service top management courses . . .'[10] In other words, the importance of this branch of law is well recognized within the heart of the executive machine.

Should we assume from this that the system of administrative law is now in place and can best be allowed to keep itself in motion? In fact the expert commentators are not unanimous on these matters. Three examples may be given. First, the Justice/All Souls Committee on Administrative Law, whose chairman was Sir Patrick Neill, published its report, *Administrative Justice: Some Necessary Reforms*, in 1988. This committee did not recommend anything as radical as the creation of an Administrative Division of the High Court, still less the introduction of an institution on the lines of the French Conseil d'État.[11] But it had a wealth of criticisms to make of the present situation, and many proposals for reform.

Secondly, Lord Justice Woolf, one of the leading exponents of administrative law on the English bench, in 1990 published his Hamlyn Lectures, *Protection of the Public - A New Challenge*. He too had extensive criticisms to make.

Thirdly, Lord Scarman, who had been chairman of the English Law Commission when it first proposed a royal commission to examine the whole of administrative law, commented that

> administrative law has to be a developing legal science, which it is the duty of judges aided by practitioners and scholars to keep abreast with the pace of change in the public administration.

Lord Scarman continued:

> The judges are doing their best: but will Parliament really permit the growth of a body of coherent and comprehensive administrative law? . . . Today's administrative law is made up of bits and pieces . . . It is still no more than an ad hoc bunch of restraints, controls and procedures wrung from government and encapsulated in statutes and statutory instruments of limited operation.[12]

Passing over the striking similarity that this bears to the quotation from Lord Hewart at the start of this chapter, how can it be that Lord Scarman and the other experts are so critical? The question becomes even more urgent in the light of the buoyant statistics concerning the present volume of administrative law litigation.[13]

In 1989, no fewer than 1580 applications for leave to apply for judicial review were received by the Crown Office, 256 of which concerned criminal matters, and 419 immigration matters, leaving 905 others over the whole field of public administration.[14]

In the three years 1987–1989, the average annual total of applications was 1446. If this figure is compared with the average of 823 applications in the years 1982–1984, we see that an increase of 76 per cent has occurred in only five years.

During 1989, leave was granted in 905 applications, and 187 applications for judicial review were allowed either by a single judge or by the Divisional Court. In addition to cases under RSC Order 53, 436 other appeals and applications were received in the Crown Office under statutes dealing with town planning, compulsory purchase and the like.

Indeed, the Judicial Statistics since 1977 show that the detailed figures for 1989 are for the most part the highest on record, except that in several recent years (1979, 1985, 1987) rather more applications were successful than in 1989. Possibly this exception indicates a falling off in the success rate as the total number of applications has grown. It is difficult to suppose that the figures for the 1990s will show any reverse in these trends.

Given this busy hum of forensic activity, some may wish to apply the old saying, 'If it ain't broke, don't fix it'. They would also point out that administrative law in general, and the law relating to judicial review in particular, is in an exciting period of development – as the ambit of judicial review is tested in new situations, as judges are called on to solve difficult questions as to the limits of 'public law',[15] and as new powers of government are created by legislation along with the problems of interpretation and decision-making that accompany such laws.

The situation of vigorous activity in the courts is likely to continue. For the full picture of relevant processes, we would also need to look at statistics of public inquiries and administrative tribunals, and also of the various ombudsmen's investigations. Nonetheless, it is worth trying to stand back from this intense activity and to consider whether the present working machinery is as effective and as efficient as an important branch of the modern legal system should be. Is the centre in danger of being swamped, as Lord Lane LCJ considered to be the case in 1990?[16]

THE PURPOSES OF ADMINISTRATIVE LAW

In administrative law there is no lack of problems of law and judicial discretion to which solutions may in time emerge as the courts have opportunities to resolve them. But some features of the system fall outside the kinds of question that the judges may answer. To give but two examples, the office of ombudsman and the procedure of application for judicial review could not have been created by judicial decision.

The need to consider institutional questions is bound to bring into play one's views about the definition and purposes of administrative law. Is its main function to keep the acts and policies of public authorities under close scrutiny and restraint (as though Gulliver in the island of Lilliput can be tied down only by the effect of innumerable strings) or to enable a democratically elected and responsible government to achieve its policies for the public good?[17] Or can one adopt the intermediate position of seeking to ensure that government policies, whatever these may be, are adopted by lawful means and administered fairly and even-handedly?

Our attitudes to government and current policies of government necessarily affect our attitudes to the work and decisions of the High Court. Thus some consider that too many applications for judicial review are made (or at least too many that have no chance of success) or even that the procedure is being abused – as Sir William Wade did in 1989 when the Greenwich council took the unremarkable but resourceful step of testing the legality of the government's poll tax leaflet.[18]

But others may consider that public authorities get away with it too often, that the government's dominance over legislation means that too few applications for judicial review succeed in the face of Parliament's plain intent.

Some again may be concerned at problems of access, whether these arise from the unequal distribution of resources in society or from the structure of the judicial system. (Why should a homeless person in the north-east of England or a dismissed public employee in Cardiff be unable to get relief without recourse to London?) Some obstacles to access are raised by the courts themselves, as in the *Rose Theatre* case.[19] Can we be sure that the deserving cases always reach the Divisional Court? And in any event should the Divisional Court be regarded as the primary point of entry into the court system?

Nevertheless, no-one can doubt that a system of administrative law must include a residual procedure for enabling a court to review the legality of governmental decisions. Nor may it be doubted that the present procedure is serving important public purposes. The government certainly has no such doubts, both from the way in which it defends proceedings and itself institutes them against recalcitrant local councils. The 1990s will surely see an intensification of present trends, with increasing significance being attached to procedures for protecting individual and minority rights. The impact of European public law will be felt in demands for an ever more sophisticated scheme of legal protection, so there can be no doubt that, at least to serve as a residual remedy against public authorities, Order 53 is here to stay as machinery for enabling aggrieved individuals to take officialdom into court where no better solution is available.

As I have already suggested, the purposes that judicial review serves cannot be looked at in isolation from the demands of public policy generally or from other channels for the redress of grievances. As is shown by many cases brought by homeless persons, would-be immigrants and prisoners, the need to go to the Divisional Court to seek judicial review often reflects the lack of a custom-built, impartial and trusted remedy for the grievances of vulnerable people.

Where large numbers of decisions that directly affect individuals are regularly made by officials, the High Court should provide not the front line of review but the secondary line of supervision, reviewing the work of tribunals rather than reviewing at first hand the decisions of the administrators. In this respect, a backward step was taken with the abolition of the right of appeal to a tribunal when the Social Fund was created.[20] Legislation creating a right of appeal against local decisions affecting homeless persons, or providing wider rights of appeal in immigration matters, would not only have an effect on the workload of the Divisional Court: it might also serve the needs of the individual and the ends of administrative justice rather better than reliance on Order 53 alone.

Again, many lawyers might be less concerned over the proper scope of *Wednesbury* unreasonableness (i.e. the extent to which the merits of official decisions can be scrutinized on judicial review) if government were now to accept the recommendation of the Whyatt committee made as long ago as 1961[21] that there should in principle be a right of appeal to an impartial tribunal on the merits against discretionary decisions taken by public authorities (as the report of the Council on Tribunals for 1989–90 was urging).[22] And if a desire to avoid a proliferation of specialized tribunals seems to bar the adoption of this principle, a working model of a general purpose tribunal may now be found in the Administrative Appeal Tribunal in Australia.[23]

ASPECTS OF ADMINISTRATIVE LAW NEEDING TO BE REFORMED

What then are the main changes that might help towards the introduction of a comprehensive system of public law, bearing in mind the needs both of government and the governed?

The duty to give reasons

First, it is a matter for regret that public authorities are under no general duty to give reasons for their decisions that directly affect individuals. In the most cogently argued chapter in the Justice/All Souls report, this issue is fully explored and the position in English law and other jurisdictions is reviewed. Under the Tribunals and Inquiries Act 1971, there is already a qualified duty to give reasons for decisions made by tribunals or where a public inquiry has been held.[24] But this does not apply to many separate decisions made by public authorities in the regular course of their functions. Where an authority is acting in a responsible manner, reasons for its decisions there must be. Yet in *R.* v. *Lancashire County Council, ex parte Huddleston*,[25] the Court of Appeal achieved the feat of laying down admirable principles of disclosure for bodies whose decisions are subject to judicial review, while causing the unsuccessful applicant for a discretionary student grant to leave the court without knowing why her request for a grant had been rejected.[26]

Of this matter, Lord Justice Woolf has written:

> If I were to be asked to identify the most beneficial improvement which could be made to English administrative law I would unhesitatingly reply that it would be the introduction of a general requirement that reasons should normally be available, at least on request, for all administrative actions.[27]

In the 1989 Lonrho litigation the House of Lords was unwilling to take further the dicta in *Padfield* v. *Minister of Agriculture*[28] about the giving of reasons; and it was not contended in the House by Lonrho either that there was a general duty to give reasons, or that the Fair Trading Act 1973 imposed a duty on the Secretary of State to give reasons for refusing to refer the Harrods take-over to the Monopolies and Mergers Commission.[29]

The absence of a general duty to give reasons does not, however, exclude the court deciding in a particular situation that it (the court) is entitled to reasons, even if the individual directly affected was not originally so entitled.[30]

If a general duty to give reasons for decisions were enacted, the duty itself would be a skeleton to which some flesh would have to be added. Thus in Australia, the legislation requires the decision-maker to state the findings made as to material facts and to refer to the evidence on which those findings were based.[31] But the judges would also have an important role in developing the duty, through deciding what amounted to an adequate statement of reasons in a given case.[32]

Closely related to reasons is the broader question of the right to have information about the authority's case when judicial review is sought. In some European public law jurisdictions, the process of review is inquisitorial rather than adversarial. Lord Justice Woolf, commenting that the co-operation of government departments with the judicial review process had contributed to its success, gave the example that

> when there is a challenge to some departmental decision, it is the practice for the department to set out frankly in an affidavit the matters which were taken into account in reaching a decision. The decision-making process is fully disclosed.[33]

If that were indeed the universal practice of public authorities, then many procedural benefits would be felt. But I am not so confident as Lord Justice Woolf that the Order 53 procedure has yet struck the balance between the interests of applicant and respondent in this respect that is appropriate in a public law jurisdiction. If indeed the campaign for a Freedom of Information Act were to succeed, this would be likely to have significant implications for future litigation.[34]

Compensation

The present limited scope of financial remedies on judicial review should be widened. While Order 53 allowed the remedy of damages to be sought together with the prerogative orders, it did not alter the substantive law:

> the result is that the citizen's ability to obtain compensation for wrongful and arbitrary administrative action is extremely limited.[35]

In the light of such Judicial Committee decisions as *Dunlop* v. *Woollahra Council* and *Rowling* v. *Takaro Properties Ltd*,[36] no movement towards widening the scope of governmental liability is likely to come from judicial decision. While I do not believe it to be necessary or desirable to rewrite the law of torts wherever a public authority is the defendant, I do favour extending the power of the court on an application for judicial review so that the court may

> grant compensation to those cases where the alternative remedies provided by judicial review are insufficient to secure substantial justice in the case and material hardship would be caused to an applicant if compensation were not awarded in lieu of or in addition to other relief.[37]

It is indeed already an accepted public policy that compensation should, through the ombudsman system, be available to individuals who are shown to have suffered injustice as a result of maladministration. How then can compensation not be payable on at least some occasions in which an individual suffers loss because of unlawful official action?[37]

Aspects of Order 53 procedure

Some aspects of Order 53 procedure deserve to be mentioned in view of their importance for the working of judicial control.

So far as the *time limit* for seeking judicial review is concerned, the three-month limit for all applications (capable of being extended at the discretion of the court) was introduced only in 1980, but an awkward discrepancy exists between Order 53 itself and section 31 of the Supreme Court Act 1981. The awkwardness has not been satisfactorily resolved by the decision of the House of Lords in *R.* v. *Dairy Produce Tribunal, ex p. Caswell*.[38] Some would argue that an application for review that succeeds on its merits should never be rejected on the issue of time alone. Indeed, there is no express limit in the Scottish procedure of judicial review that was introduced in 1985[39] and the Justice/All Souls report was against the three-month rule.[40] In my view, it is not the three-month rule as such that needs reform so much as the conflicting criteria that come into play between the stage of leave and that of relief. Compared with time-limits in other European systems of administrative law, the three-month rule is not unduly restrictive.

As for the vexed question of *interim relief against government departments*, it may be that the recent flurry of litigation concerning the power of the High Court to grant temporary relief against decisions by ministers and other officers of the Crown has achieved a stable state.[41] However, the majority decision of the Court of Appeal in *R. v. Secretary of State for Education, ex p. Avon CC*,[42] which upheld the power of the court under Order 53, rule 3(10)(a) to order a stay of proceedings in respect of a minister's decision, seems vulnerable until it has been confirmed by the House of Lords.[43] To quote Lord Justice Woolf again,

> it is not right that the protection of the individual should be entirely dependent upon the willingness of the Crown to hold its hand as a matter of grace.[44]

In an up-to-date system of public law, there is no place for executive privileges that are justified solely in terms of the historic position of the Crown.

The controversy over *O'Reilly v. Mackman*[45] has already been well aired. I consider that the principle which the House of Lords was seeking to establish, namely that the Order 53 procedure should be utilized in very many situations in which the legality of official action is questioned, has had beneficial effects. At a more principled level, the decision has caused there to be searching consideration of the public law/private law distinction. This does not mean that I agree with all the applications of *O'Reilly v. Mackman*, especially so far as scope for what has been called collateral review is concerned.[46] Thus the recent decision of the Court of Appeal in *Foster v. Chief Adjudication Officer*[47] is plainly wrong in holding that the Social Security Commissioners have no jurisdiction to rule on the validity of delegated legislation when this question has to be decided for the Commissioners to determine a disputed claim for benefit.

As for the requirement for preliminary leave to be obtained under Order 53 before an application for judicial review can proceed, I believe the requirement to be beneficial, despite the opposition to it expressed by the Justice/All Souls Report.[48]

Other aspects of judicial review which may be mentioned briefly are as follows. First, there is the enactment of a 'code' of judicial review.[49] This could well be on the lines of recent Australian legislation, declaring the general grounds on which review may be sought and the scope of this form of control. Such a 'code' would need to be framed loosely at the edges, so that scope for judicial development of the law would remain.

Secondly, there is a continuing danger that a supreme Parliament will use its legal authority to exclude or restrict judicial review in a potentially oppressive way. Two recent examples are found in the Interception of Communications Act 1985, and in the Security Service Act 1989.[50] Again, the Local Government Finance Act 1988 specifies that judicial review and no other remedy is available in respect of certain decisions; and what the court shall do if an application for review succeeds.[51] If the legislature takes the view that judicial review is something to be conferred in such precise terms, then this is but a brief step away from legislation purporting to restrict review, or to take it away altogether. Such legislation would add a further dimension to the situation which the Master of the Rolls mentioned in the poll-tax capping case, namely that the judiciary's task is more complicated than that of a World Cup referee, since Parliament 'tends to lay down different rules for different situations' and the judges 'are therefore continually being faced with the need to study, interpret and apply new versions of the rules'.[52]

The availability of judicial review is surely a constitutional fundamental. As the *Factortame* decision of the European Court of Justice indicated,[53] limits upon its scope imposed by national law are not always going to survive scrutiny at the European level.[54]

Institutional changes

Many developments in the law are certain to come about from the future decisions of the courts. But what case law cannot achieve is any assessment of the institutional structure within which public authorities operate and their decisions are brought under scrutiny. I will mention three matters.

First, there is at present an informal dualism between the work of the courts and the work of the ombudsmen for central and local government and the National Health Service. This dualism comes about through an overlap of functions between judicial review and the tasks of the ombudsman in investigating the actions of public authorities and recommending suitable remedies for injustice caused by maladministration. Both the courts and the ombudsman inhabit the land of administration and the principles applied in the two systems need to be broadly in harmony with each other.[55] Ways of accomplishing this are discussed in the Justice/All Souls Report, but the report sees no real need for the two systems of redress to be brought closer together.[56] In general the report is much too complacent about the present effectiveness of the ombudsman.[57]

Secondly, I strongly support the same report in its recommendation for creation of an Administrative Review Commission that would, like the similarly named council in Australia, have continuing responsibility for oversight of the principles and methods of public administration and the operation of remedies for the individual, including judicial review. The commission would seek to do on a broader canvas what is at present done in respect of tribunals and inquiries by the Council on Tribunals.[58] In due time, the Council on Tribunals should be subsumed within the overall structure of the Administrative Review Council.[59]

Finally, several eminent lawyers have recommended the appointment of a Director of Civil Proceedings, whose functions would be closely involved with judicial review proceedings and whose mission would be to act in the public interest.[60] The role of this new personage would include initiating and conducting review proceedings and acting as an *amicus curiae* when necessary. For me this remains a somewhat shadowy figure, even as his or her role is described by Lord Justice Woolf. While it seems wrong that relator proceedings can be brought only with the consent of the Attorney-General, the function of giving such consent could well be entrusted to the court.[61] And I am uncertain how one could draw up a sensible budget for such a Director's activities, given the vagueness of his remit. The most significant procedural task that needs to be fulfilled is for the power of the High Court to be more readily available to an applicant in securing discovery of relevant information from public authorities; such a power could be well exercised directly by the Crown Office or a designated judge.

CONCLUSION

The purpose that underlies these proposals is to demonstrate that a good many parts of the system that the United Kingdom has are in need of attention. The argument is not that such reform is essential to the continued health and vigour of administrative law regarded as a forensic activity, but that significant improvements in the effectiveness of the present system are both desirable and attainable. Lord Scarman again:

> The sad truth is that we in Britain will not achieve a principled and coherent body of administrative law unless Parliament enacts it. And this is unlikely.[62]

I would share Lord Scarman's pessimism if I shared his views that progress can be made only by a once and for all exercise of legislative authority. There is certainly much that could be achieved by such legislation, but this is not the only way in which worthwhile advances could be made.

NOTES AND REFERENCES

A shorter version of this chapter appeared in the *New Law Journal* for 22 March 1991.

1 p. 46.
2 Cmd. 4060 (1932), p. 110.
3 The procedure was revised in 1980 (S.I. 1980 No. 2000) and given a seal of approval by the Supreme Court Act 1981, s. 31.
4 S. A. de Smith's *Judicial Review of Administrative Action* was first published in 1959. *Principles of Administrative Law*, by J. A. G. Griffith and H. Street (1952) was first in the post-1945 field. The leading treatise is now Sir William Wade, *Administrative Law* (1988, 6th edn). Of more recent textbooks, P. P. Craig, *Administrative Law* (1989, 2nd edn) is of particular value.
5 *Ridge* v. *Baldwin* [1964] AC 40.
6 *R.* v. *I.R.C., ex p. National Federation of Self-Employed and Small Businesses* [1982] AC 617, 641.
7 The *Crown Office Digest* was first published in 1988, and was soon followed by the *Administrative Law Reports*.
8 See: [1987] PL 485.
9 See: [1988] PL 1.
10 Cabinet Office (1989), p. 72, cited at [1989] PL 374, 379.
11 *Administrative Justice: Some Necessary Reforms* (1988), pp. 168–170.
12 'The Development of Administrative Law: Obstacles and Opportunities' [1990] PL 490, 491–492.
13 See: M. Sunkin, 'What Is Happening to Applications for Judicial Review?' *MLR*, **50** (1987), 432; and 'The Judicial Review Caseload, 1987–1989' [1991] PL 490.
14 See the Judicial Statistics 1989. In 1990, over 2000 applications for judicial review were filed.
15 See, for example, the case law on non-statutory agencies with regulatory powers following *R.* v. *Panel on Take-overs and Mergers, ex p. Datafin plc* [1987] QB 815.
16 See his speech at the Lord Mayor's Dinner, 19 June 1990.
17 Cf. C. Harlow and R. Rawlings, *Law and Administration* (1984), Ch. 1 and 2.
18 *The Times*, 18 May 1989; and see [1989] PL 487.
19 *R.* v. *Secretary of State for Environment, ex p. Rose Theatre Trust* [1990] 1 QB 504, criticized by P. Cane at [1990] PL 307.
20 See: Council on Tribunals, *Social Security: Abolition of independent appeals under the Proposed Social Fund*, Cmnd. 9722 (1986); and R. Drabble and T. Lynes, 'The Social Fund: Discretion or Control?' [1989] PL 297.

21 *The Citizen and the Administration: The Redress of Grievances* (Justice, 1961), part II.
22 *Annual Report of the Council on Tribunals 1989-90* (HC 64, 1990-91), p. 5.
23 See: *Administrative Justice*, pp. 253-256.
24 1971 Act, s. 12.
25 [1986] 2 All ER 941, discussed at [1986] PL 508.
26 In *R. v. Civil Service Appeal Board, ex p. Cunningham* [1991] 4 All ER 310, the Court of Appeal held that the board was required by natural justice to give reasons when deciding whether the dismissal of a prison officer was fair and when assessing compensation due to him. Lord Donaldson MR said: 'The applicant may still not be entitled to reasons, but the court is' (p. 316) – once, that is, the court concludes that it is arguable that the board's decision was unlawful.
27 H. Woolf, *Protection of the Public – A New Challenge* (1990), p. 92.
28 [1968] AC 997.
29 *R. v. Secretary of State for Trade and Industry, ex p. Lonrho plc* [1989] 1 WLR 525.
30 See: *R. v. Civil Service Appeal Board* (n. 26 above).
31 The Administrative Decisions (Judicial Review) Act 1977 (Australia) as amended, s. 13.
32 In *R. v. Secretary of State for the Home Department, ex p. Swati* [1986] 1 WLR 477, the standard for performing a statutory duty to give reasons was set at such a low level that the mere recital of statutory grounds proved to be sufficient.
33 H. Woolf, *Protection of the Public*, p. 16.
34 As it has in Australia. See P. Villanti, 'Freedom of Information as an Instrument of Discovery', in M. Harris and V. Waye, *Administrative Law* (1991, Sydney), pp. 68-79.
35 H. Woolf, *Protection of the Public*, p. 56.
36 Respectively [1982] AC 158 and [1988] AC 473.
37 H. Woolf, *Protection of the Public*, p. 59. See also: *Administrative Justice*, Ch. 11; and A.W. Bradley, 'Administrative Law and the Law of Torts' *The Law Teacher*, **23** (1989), 109.
38 See, for example, *R. v. Dairy Produce Tribunal, ex p. Caswell* [1990] 2 AC 738, where a farmer's milk production licences were unlawfully withheld, but no compensation was payable.
39 See: [1987] PL 313.
40 *Administrative Justice*, pp. 155-157.
41 The questions raised by *R. v. Home Secretary, ex p. Herbage (No. 2)* [1987] QB 1077 and *R. v. Licensing Authority, ex p. Smith, Kline and French Laboratories (No. 2)* [1990] 1 QB 574 have now been settled by *R. v. Secretary of State for Transport, ex p. Factortame Ltd* [1990] 2 AC 85.
42 [1991] 1 All ER 282.
43 The Judicial Committee have held to the contrary in *Minister of Foreign Affairs v. Vehicles and Supplies Ltd* [1991] 4 All ER 65, where *ex p. Avon CC* was not cited.
44 H. Woolf, *Protection of the Public*, p. 64. And cf. *M. v. Home Office* [1992] 2 WLR 73.
45 [1983] 2 AC 237.
46 See: [1988] PL 169, and also *Doyle v. Northumbria Probation Committee* [1991] 4 All ER 294.
47 [1991] 3 All ER 846, criticized at [1992] PL 185.

48 *Administrative Justice*, pp. 152–155. And see A. Le Sueur and M. Sunkin [1992] PL 102.
49 *Administrative Justice*, pp. 157–158 and apps 8 and 9.
50 1985 Act, s. 7(8); 1989 Act, s. 5(4).
51 Ss. 138 and 142.
52 *R.* v. *Secretary of State for the Environment, ex p. Hammersmith LBC* [1990] 3 All ER 589, 614.
53 [1991] 1 All ER 70.
54 And see *Johnstone* v. *Chief Constable, RUC* [1987] QB 129.
55 A.W. Bradley, 'The Role of the Ombudsman in Relation to the Protection of Citizens' Rights' [1980] CLJ 304.
56 *Administrative Justice*, Ch. 5.
57 See: G. Drewry and R. Gregory, 'Barlow Clowes and the Ombudsman' [1991] PL 192, 408.
58 See: *Administrative Justice*, Ch. 4.
59 See: [1991] PL 6.
60 In particular, J.A.G. Griffith [1985] PL 564, 582 and H. Woolf, *Protection of the Public*, pp. 109–113.
61 See: *Administrative Justice*, pp. 186–189. The importance of relator proceedings has been much diminished by the capacity of councils to sue under the Local Government Act 1972, s. 222 (discussed by B. Hough [1992] PL 130).
62 [1990] PL 490, 493.

6

Political Parties: Conservative Political and Constitutional Ideology

JOHN RAMSDEN

British Conservatives have usually eschewed ideological imperatives, seeing their policies as being motivated more by pragmatic and material considerations than by the theoretical. Disraeli advised his contemporaries to confine their reading habits to novels and biographies, and post-war surveys of the reading habits of Conservative MPs show that biography and political history figure far more prominently than do works of theory or ideology (it is very different for Labour MPs). Serious attempts to present a party philosophy, for example in Hugh Cecil's *Conservatism* or Quintin Hogg's *The Case for Conservatism*,[1] have almost always been written in periods of opposition, times when it was impossible to show what the party stood for by its actions and when it was therefore necessary to say something. These serious works trace Conservative philosophy back to Richard Hooker, Lord Falkland, John Locke, Edmund Burke and W.H. Mallock, a consistently conservative tradition in British political thought, and therefore useful ammunition for a party that was (in opposition both in 1913 and in 1947) trying to resist changes that were being pushed through from the left.

But it is difficult to find the slightest evidence that any major Conservative politicians have actually been influenced by such a tradition when they were themselves in office; more characteristic perhaps was Baldwin's confession, when asked which political thinker had most influenced him, that he had been much impressed as an undergraduate by the writings of the constitutional lawyer Sir Henry Maine, but could no longer remember what Maine's ideas were.[2] Equally characteristic was the remark of Lord Salisbury, that Iain Macleod was 'too clever by half',[3] an epithet that stuck to him for life and served as a warning to others. In practice, then, the party's very real tradition of distrusting intellectuals may have led to the deliberate suppression of ideological argument, except in such desperate circumstances as 1947. Historians and political scientists, working on the assumption that everyone has an ideological position even if he or she is not conscious of it, itself something of an unconscious ideology, have not been slow to fill the interpretative gap left by the party's lack of ideological self-assignation.

This whole area of explanation is a minefield. It is after all usually the case that 'ideology' can be assumed to be working on the conscious as well as the unconscious mind, that it is an active and not merely a passive state. It is in practice even more difficult than this suggests, because to analyse unconscious ideology, it is necessary to find that underlying ideology in actual policy, and the Conservative Party does not have any very clear definition of what constitutes official party policy anyway. This is largely a consequence of the party's not having a constitution: there are, of course, sets of rules for constituency parties, for the National Union, standing orders for the 1922 Committee and so on, but no single co-ordinating document that links these separate units into one constitutional entity. (By comparison, all segments of the Labour Party can be assigned defined roles within the 'constitution' of the party as adopted in 1918 and much amended since, there being in that constitution rules about its own amendment.) The problem is particularly acute when it comes to policy, because the rules of the various Conservative bodies do not have much to say on the subject, and those bodies that seem to exist to deal with policy, the Party Conference and the Advisory Committee on Policy, have very well-defined memberships but equally ill-defined powers.[4] It has usually been assumed that when in office the actions and speeches of Conservative ministers are the definition of party policy: Central Office (which is, after all, a party, not a government, agency) certainly works on this assumption, supporting the work of ministers and the prime minister, and limiting and even denigrating on occasions the work of other Conservatives who have different views. In practice, then, the 'policy' of the party may just be what Conservative governments do (as Herbert Morrison cynically, but in constitutional terms quite incorrectly, observed about Labour: party policy for Labour and the Liberal Democrats is defined by specific constitutional provisions and may or may not be the same as what their leaders do in office). The search for ideology in party policy therefore runs the risk of identifying as underlying ideological changes policy choices that really are no more than the consequences of fashion, of tactics and of new leaders who use a different vocabulary and practise a different style. All the same, ideology has to be defined widely, because it is otherwise impossible to study it at all for a party that has strenuously resisted ideological categorization.

For this chapter, 'present' is being taken to include the quarter-century since 1965 when the party seemed to shift decisively away from the stance of the previous two generations. In the summer of 1965 Conservative MPs for the first time actually elected their leader (though, confusingly, the word 'election' had often been used in the past to describe the formal enthronement of a single candidate that followed the 'customary processes'). The new leader, Edward Heath, appeared to mark a real change of mood, generation and social character from the 'grouse-moor' style of the Eden–Macmillan–Home years – a coming into their inheritance of the middle classes, after their permeation of the party for over a century.[5] The first policy document of the new regime, *Putting Britain Right Ahead*, formally committed the party to European integration, to rolling back the State, to lowering taxation, and to curbing the powers of the trades unions. The very title of the document was significant; the final word, *Ahead*, was added at the last moment only when it was pointed out that *Putting Britain Right* would encourage the question 'who had put Britain wrong?' and this would be an inconvenient question for the party that had ruled for the previous 13 years. Adding *Ahead* accorded with the desire to seem modernizing and thrusting, and so compete with Harold Wilson's promises of white-hot technological innovation, but the addition of the word was in part misleading – it accorded with Heath's bluff, no-nonsense introductory statement, but less so with the catalogue of detailed, radical proposals in the document itself.[6]

In effect, the Conservatives did decide in 1965 that they needed to put Britain right and that they were as responsible as anyone for its having gone wrong by 1964 (though most Tories were not yet ready to say quite that). Enoch Powell, the storm petrel of the coming revolution in thinking, was already saying it, for example in his early speeches on the need for a change of monetary policy, speeches collected as early as 1965 in *A Nation Not Afraid*. Sir Keith Joseph, Margaret Thatcher's acknowledged mentor, has now himself acknowledged that Powell led the way for 'Thatcherism' and that it was characteristic of Powell's clearsightedness that he reached the intellectual conclusion many years ahead of the field.[7] In effect, the Conservative Party set its course for 'Thatcherism' in 1965, even if Margaret Thatcher, like most other MPs, was entirely unaware of the fact. The tactical shifts of the 1970s and the change of leadership style in 1975 served only to conceal continuity over the 25 years of the Heath–Thatcher era.[8] It seems reasonable to assess this 'present' phase of British Conservatism against the longer context of the historic Conservative tradition.

It is possible to find in the Conservative history of the previous century some principles and practices that were pursued consistently or continuously enough to be free of the danger that they represented only fashion or tactics.[9] The first principle would be that the best should be preserved, since it is both easier and quicker to destroy things than to build them, and that there should therefore be a presumption for continuity and against change: Lord Falkland argued that 'if it is not necessary to change, then it is necessary not to change', and Sir Rhodes Boyson more recently translated this as 'if it ain't bust, don't fix it'.[10] The second principle would be that the present generation is the inheritor of the past and the trustee of the future, a Burkeian concept that is also a powerful argument for continuity and caution. Thirdly, Conservatives have been highly pessimistic about human nature, sometimes rooting their views, as Hogg did, in a theological concept of original sin, and they have been dubious about the possibilities of human improvement; in practical politics this often surfaced in fears for the survival of civilization if change were allowed and controls relaxed, all related to arguments about 'slippery slopes' and the 'thin end of the wedge'. Baldwin was haunted by the way in which democracy had arrived 'at the gallop' in Britain (it took five Reform Acts spread over a whole century, one of the slowest transitions to democracy in Europe!) and spoke of the thin crust of civilization covering the seething masses below. Lord Salisbury when prime minister was even more gloomy about the future of 'the race' itself. Fourthly, it was claimed as the Conservatives' special role in British politics to resist fashionable extremes, and Conservative history was raided somewhat selectively to provide evidence for this: so it was argued that in the 1830s and 1840s Conservatives sought to protect the weak and underprivileged against unscrupulous industrial capitalists; in the 1870s and 1880s Conservatives stressed the Tory principle of church and state against the exaggerated Liberal claims for individual liberty; in the inter-war years, the Conservatives championed liberty against socialism.[11] This is in fact an explicitly anti-ideological principle. Fifthly, and crucially (since it is on this principle that the party claims its name), the Conservatives have been unreactionary; from the time that Peel assumed the leadership in 1834 and promised not to repeal the 1832 Reform Act, it was clear that the party would not turn the clock back, that resistance to change would not necessarily involve pledges to reverse the changes that opponents made. The few exceptions rather prove this rule: Bonar Law's promise to repeal the 1913 Trades Union Act caused endless trouble to him and his successor for the next 20 years; Churchill's promise to denationalize the steel industry was no more than a symbolic act, and his rather rash pledge to re-create university constituencies when they were abolished in 1948 was simply ignored when it came to the drafting of the next manifesto. It was generally accepted that a Conservative government took up where its opponents left off, not that it started from where the previous Conservative administration had got to. This was often cited, as for example by Macleod in the 1950s, as the Conservatives' greatest political gift – the ability to learn from their opponents, to recognize that the electorate was always right – and hence claimed as the secret of long-term party survival and success.[12]

Alongside these clear principles may be cited some continuous practices which amount almost to principle. Firstly, Conservatives have regularly played the role of English nationalists within UK politics, and, when the occasion justified it, argued the case for Britain's power and prestige internationally; they have not generally been squeamish about the military consequences of such attitudes, or even about the financial consequences. From at least the time of Disraeli, Conservatives have fought for the Irish Union (and, when necessary, for the Welsh and Scottish Unions too), have pursued policies in support of British expansionism and imperialism, and even of adventurism, as with Disraeli's Sudanese expedition of 1868.[13] More negatively, they have not been squeamish either when it came to questioning the patriotic credentials of opponents, Liberals who 'allowed' the death of General Gordon in the 1880s, pro-Boers in 1900, pacifists in 1914–1918, and Labour for questioning the Suez expedition in 1956.

Secondly, the party has supported the preservation of privileges and argued explicitly in favour of equality of opportunity but against egalitarianism; Baldwin once quoted Rousseau's tag about all babies being born equal and challenged all the mothers in the audience to agree with him that this was nonsense.[14] The actual privileges to be supported differed over time, often the consequence of having to give supporters what they most wanted; at different times, landowners, the drink trade, the Church of England, the owners of inherited wealth, and the grammar schools were beneficiaries of this defence of privilege. There is considerable overlap here with my first and second principles outlined above.

The third principle deriving from practice is leadership as such, in the party and in the country at large. Within the party, Conservative leaders have been accorded an astonishing freedom of action in setting the agenda of politics, choosing their ministers and shadow ministers, running the party machine and deciding policy at manifesto time. All hinges, of course, on the ability to win, and those leaders who delivered parliamentary majorities had great freedom of manoeuvre. Churchill summed this up epigrammatically in 1922 when he said of the Conservative leader that 'if he trips he must be sustained, if he sleeps he must not be disturbed, if he makes mistakes they must be covered, but if he is no good he must be pole-axed'.[15] There is some obvious logic in this, for the mere winning of an election denies office to the left and prevents them from legislating, and is therefore in itself a major success in the promotion of Conservative objectives. It is no doubt easier for a Conservative grouping to unite around this self-consciously opportunist strategy, for they already have (in the status quo) most of what they want to achieve; on the radical and fissiparous left, it is necessary (and *far* more difficult) to get agreement on the promotion of something that has never yet existed. As a result of this practical principle, Conservative leaders have almost never been overthrown solely for policy reasons – Neville Chamberlain in 1940 being the clearest exception – but leaders who have lost or seemed likely to lose elections have had a difficult time. Joseph Chamberlain's disruptive campaign for tariff reform was opposed by Conservative free traders partly because they did not like the policy itself, but more because they did not expect to win with it, and so (by losing to the Liberals) they saw the Empire, the House of Lords, the Irish Union and the Welsh Church all being put needlessly at risk. But it was only Balfour's third successive election defeat that brought him down.[16] In the next generation, Baldwin was disliked and distrusted by many of his supporters between 1924 and 1929, but was in no danger until he lost the 1929 general election, and in no further danger after the 1931 election produced another Conservative majority.[17] The *Fuehrerprinzip* is carried beyond the party, too; in both of the World Wars, Conservatives overwhelmingly backed prime ministers that they had previously hated and distrusted, because the national cause seemed to require it. In May 1918 they kept Lloyd George in office while most of them believed him to be a liar and a cheat, simply because they saw him as the best war leader. At the end of that year, they kept him in office for a further term because he seemed more likely than a pure Conservative government to stave off revolution. Outside the party as well as inside, practical principles and tactics overlapped.

The final practical principle lies in simply being in office; not only has the occupation of government denied opponents the chance to legislate changes, it has also left to Conservative ministers the opportunity to administer the country for two-thirds of the last century. Institutions are shaped not only by the Act that creates them but also by what follows: British Coal as an organization owes far more to the (mainly Conservative) administrations since 1951 than to the Attlee government that nationalized it. Occupying office gives opportunities to make countless appointments in the public sector, as well as the wider patronage opportunities of the Church of England and the honours system. More generally, the occupation of office shapes public perceptions of what office-holding should look like and forces opponents to match it if they want to live up to the apparent needs of the job. In 1924, when Ramsay MacDonald's Labour colleagues donned knee breeches and top hats to visit the Palace, they were anxious to show their fitness to govern (interpreting that idea largely by what they had seen from their predecessors).[18]

These five principles of theory and four practical principles having been deduced from Conservative history prior to 1965, the 'present' may be matched against them to see how closely it fits.

It is on the face of it difficult to see how recent Conservatism has practised the first of my theoretical principles. In opposition between 1964 and 1970, almost every area of British policy was subjected to a searching scrutiny, and proposals for change were made in almost every case. The 1966 election manifesto contained 131 specific pledges, and on returning to power in 1970 the party had made unprecedentedly detailed preparations – ministers were ready briefed, bills were drafted, and the first year's parliamentary timetable had been planned.[19] This was not exactly a government proceeding to legislate with caution, but rather one that seemed to think that it had limited time in which to carry out a revolution, albeit one that it described optimistically as a 'quiet revolution'. In opposition again after 1974 the pattern was far more complex; on the one hand the party's desire to make major changes (for example, in trade union law) was even more determined after the failure of the Heath government's initiatives and the humiliations of its end in 1974, but on the other hand it was widely thought that over-preparation before 1970 had been one of the causes of Heath's difficulties in office. The new leader, Margaret Thatcher, had difficulty in establishing her authority in a shadow cabinet most of whose members had not wanted her to be their leader in the first place. For these reasons, the policy strategy adopted between 1975 and 1979 was to 'let a hundred flowers bloom', to let everyone and anyone make policy suggestions but to get committed to none of them before the election;[20] the Maoist language was to turn out to be far more appropriate than anyone foresaw, as Thatcher herself turned into a permanent revolutionary when once in office. Meanwhile, Sir Geoffrey Howe assured a Party Conference that the next Conservative government would introduce a moratorium on legislation, that it would not make changes unless the case for doing so was overwhelming, a commitment for which he was warmly applauded. How wrong he was. In office, Thatcher's team embarked on a torrent of legislative and administrative reform: local government, and especially local government finance, was changed almost every year, there was almost an annual education reform bill, and the National Health Service underwent several structural reorganizations (in all these fields the Heath government had already introduced major changes ten years earlier). It was a far cry from the earlier period in which major education reforms were introduced only cautiously and about once in each generation. Even the vocabulary of Conservatism as the resistance to change was largely dropped, and the prime minister and such close associates as Norman Tebbit cheerfully appropriated the word 'radical' to describe themselves. It was argued from the platform at Party Conferences that Conservatives were now the force for change,[21] a concept that appears not even to have attracted attention to its sheer illogicality.

In this context, it is not surprising that my second principle has also taken something of a battering. Rhetorically, the idea of the present generation as the bridge between past and present has remained important. The Heath insistence on the historic importance of his European policies and the Thatcher appeal to British history for support for her scepticism about Europe indicate the limited connection between rhetoric and reality here. Thatcher's championing of 'Victorian values' may seem a more valid appeal to history, but her raid on the history books to find ideological ancestors was in fact a highly selective one. There were certainly Victorians who supported the sort of philosophies that Thatcher was articulating on their behalf, but they were not for the most part Conservatives in their own time (they were more likely to have been radical utilitarians) and they were certainly not associated specifically with the Peel/Disraeli Conservative Party. Most of Thatcher's Victorian heroes would have detested all that Victorian Conservatism seemed to them to stand for. Moving on from rhetoric to personnel, the Heath–Thatcher period did see the turning of a social corner by the party, if not as decisively as some observers suggested. By 1990, the Conservative back-benches were far less the preserve of a socially narrow elite than in 1960, and the retirement from the Commons of Jasper More, whose predecessors had sat there more or less continuously since the Long Parliament, and usually for the same Shropshire seat, seemed a milestone on this road. The election of John Major as leader (only the party's second since Bonar Law who had not been to a university) seemed to suggest that this social movement would continue. But the changes were slow and limited; by 1990, there were far fewer Etonians and Harrovians on the backbenches, but still most Conservative MPs and candidates had been to minor public schools and to Oxbridge.[22]

The third principle, the pessimistic view of humanity and the inevitability of things getting worse, had always been one used mainly to resist change when on the opposition benches and it was much in evidence for these reasons in 1964–1970 (when, for example, it was used to deride the National Plan of 1966 or the 'solemn and binding agreement' with the TUC in 1969) and in 1974–1979 (as, for example, over Michael Foot's Employment Protection Act). In the latter period, the party toyed even with ideas for the limitation of parliamentary sovereignty, with several Conservatives putting the case for proportional representation and with Lord Hailsham arguing for a Bill of Rights, but these were little more than products of the party's frustration with a Labour government which had full parliamentary power derived from a historically low share of the vote. As Conservative confidence returned in and after 1979, these ideas withered on the vine, which was just as well when it is remembered that election victories in the 1980s were also won by Conservative governments with rather small shares of the national vote. By 1990, with some considerable irony, it was Labour that was considering both a Bill of Rights and PR. The one constitutional development that can be traced to Conservatives in these years was one that needed no legislation, the refinement of the principle of the mandate. In the past, Conservatives had been reluctant to get committed to policies very closely in periods of opposition: Churchill after 1945 positively refused to bind the hands of the next prime minister (himself) by promising too much before the 1951 election.[23] As we have seen, this was again the view in 1979. But in 1966, 1970, and especially in the 1980s, Conservative manifestos were very explicit and subsequent Conservative governments justified their prosecution of radical reform programmes on the argument of a contract with the voters. Given the lack of consultation *within* the party over the content of manifestos, as for example in the abolition of the GLC in 1983 or the introduction of the poll tax in 1987, this new approach became a powerful engine of change in the hands of a prime minister. The engine was usually intended to be turned on cabinet colleagues and Conservative MPs rather than the other parties, but in doing so Thatcher created a formidable weapon that could be used by any party in the future, as Tony Benn pointed out. How would Conservatives resist radical change that had derived from a future Labour government's winning manifesto?

My fourth principle was triumphantly vindicated by recent Conservatism. Both Heath and Thatcher represented themselves as correcting a discredited consensus in British politics – reducing taxation that was too high, reducing the power of the State (though necessarily using the State's power to an unprecedented extent in enforcing change everywhere else, as in local government), and reversing the balance in industrial relations. They both saw themselves as abandoning or at least redefining a failed consensus from the previous generation.[24] Both saw Britain as a nation in decline, socially, morally, economically and internationally, and saw it as their particular duty to reverse that decline. This principle of correcting the balance has been largely used to justify the profoundly *un*conservative policies they pursued and which are analysed above.

On the other hand, the fifth principle, being *un*reactionary, seems hard to apply to the most recent past. Even in vocabulary, such words as 'dismantle', when applied to the public sector, or 'return power to the members', when applied to trade unions, explicitly endorse the idea of reversion rather than progression. Indeed, a key concept in the emergence of Thatcherism was Joseph's enunciation of the 'ratchet effect' whereby (he said) each Labour government had moved Britain towards socialism, and each Conservative administration merely consolidated these changes by braking the wheel, but never changing the direction; in a seminal essay he argued for 'Reversing the Trend' so that Conservatives would henceforth set the direction and their opponents would merely be able to apply the brake.[25] It was precisely this principle, as applied in a step-by-step reform of trade union law, that moved the fulcrum of political debate so far during the 1980s; by 1990 all the parties accepted as axiomatic in the trade union field ideas that had seemed wildly improbable in the 1970s. As Michael Heseltine said in an election broadcast in 1979, 'Forward or back? Because we cannot go on as we are'.[26]

My four practical principles are easier to evaluate, relying as they do more on practice than on ideas. There is little need to make the case for Conservatives continuing their nationalist stance. The defeat in 1979 of devolution proposals for Scotland and Wales owed a great deal to the Conservatives' opposition (they were the only party in either country that campaigned unitedly for a 'No' vote in the referenda). The abolition of Stormont and the Anglo-Irish Agreement upset Ulster Unionist allies but the Conservatives have not indicated any weakness on the basic principle of the Union; there have been no 'troops out' supporters on the Tory benches. Likewise, the Falklands War of 1982 provided a chance both to show off Britain's remaining military potential in a mainly post-colonial world, and for the party again to play the patriotic card in domestic politics. With Arthur Scargill substituting for General Galtieri and the South Yorkshire Police for the armed forces, the Orgreave battles of 1984 reinforced the message of Goose Green in 1982.

The question of inequality is a more complex one. In education, there was certainly an attempt to preserve elite institutions and reinforce them through new foundations.[27] The statistics about economic inequality will bear more than one interpretation, but it seems likely that the gaps between rich and poor have increased. In the 1980s, in the rhetoric of the 'enterprise culture', this was an explicitly open reinforcement of success, but such phrases as 'lame duck industries' and 'standing on your own two feet' entered regular political currency in the Heath period. Thatcher's emphasis on wealth creation (as in arguing that the Good Samaritan would have been no use to anyone if he had been bankrupt) and Heath's stressing of the responsibilities that accrued with wealth (as in his attack on 'the unacceptable face of capitalism') conceal a great area of common ground. Any emphasis on removing class barriers has been on removing the barriers as such, not on reducing the distances between social groups, and there is little in this that conflicts with Conservative tradition.

Leadership has certainly been a prominent feature under Thatcher, freely compared during her time as leader to Winston Churchill – for Conservatives the epitome of leadership ever since 1940 – and especially so after the Falklands War. She also pushed the practical powers of the party leader well beyond all precedents, as in the way that she developed personal policy initiatives, sought at times to undermine fellow ministers,[28] and on occasion made policy off the cuff (as, for example, over immigration policy in 1978). Both she and Heath before her were actually strengthened by their having been democratically elected; he, after all, survived the humiliations of early 1974 and was overthrown only when defeated in three elections out of four, and she not only survived the making of an unprecedentedly large number of enemies among MPs but survived to become the longest-serving prime minister of modern times – and fell in the end only because the chances of her winning for the party a fourth election seemed to be fading.

The final practical principle, that of office-holding in itself, may not at first seem strictly relevant since the most recent period has anyway been one of continuous Conservative government. The shifts and changes of policy while in office, like the changes of leader in 1975 and in 1990, owed at least something to the party's desire to win again. The 'U-turn' on economic policy in 1972 certainly owed much to ministers' genuine conviction that both unemployment and social division were reaching unacceptable levels, but they were influenced too by the more mundane indicators – opinion polls, by-elections and the loss of control in town halls. After the indecisive February 1974 election, Heath sought desperately to make a deal with the Liberals that would enable him to stay in office even as a minority prime minister, so anxious was he to deny office to Labour.[29] (Callaghan was to return the compliment by actually making a Lib–Lab pact to keep Thatcher out in 1977.) History did not repeat itself when in 1981 unemployment and social tensions again reached high levels; one reason was the prime minister's strong nerve and her inflexible determination, but it may nevertheless be the case that a stronger opposition than Labour was in these years would have enforced a change of policy, or that electoral calculations would have enforced one anyway but for the fortuitous 'Falklands factor' of 1982. The redefinition and relaxation of 'monetarism' in the middle years of the Thatcher period certainly owed much to the electoral perspectives.

There is no doubt either that Thatcher understood well, as Heath perhaps did not or did not care to, the value of patronage and of the government machine to the office-holding party. The honours system was plied more systematically in the 1980s than for decades past, and applied to categories of people like working newspaper editors who might have seemed inappropriate recipients of honours to a previous generation. Similarly, the political role of a few key civil servants – Charles Powell or Robert Armstrong – went well beyond most precedents and may demonstrate the considerable strengths that can accrue to a party if it occupies office for a lengthy period and hence appoints over a decade all its own senior professional advisers.[30] It was difficult to see how another party would have worked easily with such a team of advisers had it come to power. There were certainly Conservative precedents for playing the office-holding game in this way, though few that had done it so unashamedly since Disraeli. This was one example of Victorian values.

The tally can now be made. From my list of theoretical principles, the present matches the past on at most two counts out of five and is highly contradictory to at least two of the others. On the practical principles, there is a better score, for on all four counts there is a positive answer, even though on a couple of these the 1980s in particular witness a different way or a different extent of putting the principles into practice. Six out of nine indicates considerable continuity of ideology even if the emphases have sometimes bcome rather different. (It should be noted that in no previous period of Conservative history would there have been a perfect fit with this deduced tradition.)

The final lesson then is to reinforce the leadership point: with so much depending on who is the leader at a particular time, and with the leader chosen and retained by MPs largely with their own electability in mind, there is bound to be some considerable shift to match the public's changing perceptions, and there is bound to be a shift, too, to reflect the leader's own predilections. Back in 1922 Bonar Law argued that 'this is a question in regard to which our system . . . has hitherto gone on this principle: that the party elects a leader, and that the leader chooses the policy, and if the party does not like it, they get themselves another leader'.[31] As for policy, so for ideology?

NOTES AND REFERENCES

1 H. Cecil, *Conservatism* (1912); Q. Hogg, *The Case for Conservatism* (1947).
2 Lord Longford, *Born to Believe* (1953), pp. 71–72.
3 N. Fisher, *Iain Macleod* (1973), p. 21.

4 J. Ramsden, *The Making of Conservative Policy: The Conservative Research Department since 1929*, (1980), pp. 3–5.
5 J. Ramsden, 'Churchill to Heath', in Lord Butler (ed.), *The Conservatives* (1977), pp. 427–428.
6 Ramsden, *The Making of Conservative Policy*, p. 249.
7 *Contemporary Record*, Vol. 3, no. 3, p. 38.
8 J. Ramsden, 'The Conservative Party since 1945', in A. Seldon (ed.), *UK Political Parties since 1945* (1989), p. 33.
9 This approach was also taken by R. Hornby, *Political Quarterly* (1961), 229.
10 *Sunday Times*, 17 December 1989.
11 Hogg, *The Case for Conservatism*, p. 15; C. Patten, *The Tory Case* (1983), p. 7.
12 Ramsden, 'Churchill to Heath', p. 425.
13 F. Harcourt, 'Disraeli's Imperialism: A Matter of Timing', *Historical Journal*, 23 (1980), 87–109.
14 J. Ramsden, *The Age of Balfour and Baldwin, 1902–1940* (1978), p. 210.
15 Quoted in P. Norton and A. Aughey, *Conservatives and Conservatism* (1981), p. 241.
16 Ramsden, *The Age of Balfour*, pp. 37–42.
17 S. Ball, *Baldwin and the Conservative Party: The Crisis of 1929–1931* (1988).
18 R. W. Lyman, *The First Labour Government* (1957), pp. 106–107.
19 Ramsden, *The Making of Conservative Policy*, pp. 280–281.
20 C. Patten, 'Policy-Making in Opposition', in Z. Layton-Henry (ed.), *Conservative Party Politics* (1980), pp. 18–19.
21 D. Kavanagh, *Thatcherism and British Politics* (1987), p. 281; N. Tebbit, *Upwardly Mobile*, paperback edition 1989, pp. 344–345.
22 Ramsden, 'The Conservative Party since 1945', p. 24.
23 Lord Butler of Saffron Walden, *The Art of the Possible* (1971), pp. 132–133.
24 E. Heath, *The Great Divide in British Politics*, CPC pamphlet 355, 1966.
25 K. Joseph, *Reversing the Trend* (1975).
26 R. Worcester and M. Harrop (eds), *Political Communications: The General Election Campaign of 1979* (1982), p. 15.
27 C. Knight, *The Making of Tory Education Policy in Post-war Britain, 1945–1986* (1990).
28 R. Harris, *Good and Faithful Servant: The Unauthorised Biography of Bernard Ingham* (1990).
29 D. Hurd, *An End to Promises: A Sketch of a Government, 1970–74* (1979), pp. 134–135.
30 H. Young, *One of Us* (1988), pp. 336–338.
31 G. H. Le May (ed.), *British Government, 1914–1963: Selected Documents* (2nd edn, 1964), pp. 367–368.

7

Political Parties: The Constitution of the Social and Liberal Democrats

CHARLES RADCLIFFE BEALE

PREFACE

A competitive party system is at the heart of a healthy political democracy. Parties articulate and reconcile different views about how a nation should be governed, and they generate ideas, and mobilize consent, for reform. But above all, parties represent people. To do so effectively, they must do so proportionately. At the 1987 election, we saw the Labour Party, with 8 million votes, win a handsome 36 per cent share of the seats in Parliament, while the Alliance, with 7 million votes, was almost completely eliminated, scraping home with just 3.5 per cent of the seats. The 7 million victims were Liberals and Social Democrats. In the wake of their 1987 defeat, they voted in favour of negotiations aimed at securing a merger between their two parties. This chapter is about those negotiations, and the party which they produced. It is unashamedly written from a centrist viewpoint.

Uniting two proud political movements was never going to be easy. Parties are not simply mechanical devices designed by engineers to gather votes and execute decisions. They are bodies of women and men held together by a common conviction and an indestructible passion of belief which can withstand the strains of electoral battle. As Robert Maclennan, a leading actor in the events which dominate this chapter, said, 'Convictions, not constitutions, are what breathe animation into political parties.' Within the SDP, those convictions boiled over during the summer of 1987 when the debate over whether or not to open merger negotiations with the Liberals escalated into an emotionally charged fight for the party's soul. Many Social Democrats were reluctant to give up their position of parity with Liberals, which the existing Alliance arrangements afforded them, and exchange it for the prospect of a merged party in which they risked being swamped by Liberals, unable to exert anything like their former influence on policy-making. A brief account of the civil war which plagued the SDP from June to September of that year is included on pp. 94–96 as a backdrop to the tense negotiations which followed. The division which the row created had conflicting effects on the bargaining position of the SDP negotiators. On the one hand, they could demand extra concessions from their Liberal counterparts, on the ground that a significant part of the party had shown itself, in the summer membership ballot, to be as yet unconvinced by the arguments for merger. On the other hand, however, isolated from their anti-merger colleagues, the SDP negotiators had effectively closed off their options and had nowhere else to go, other than into a merged party.

The new party's constitution dominated negotiations throughout the autumn of 1987. On pp. 96–105, the central plank of this chapter, a contrast is drawn between the constitutions of the two old Alliance parties. The constitution which emerged from the discussions is analysed, with special attention given to key aspects of it: the policy-making process; the federal structure; the membership system; women in the party; and the name and constitutional preamble. An account of how and why certain decisions were reached by the negotiators is also included, drawn principally from first-hand accounts and press reports. Pages 105–112 are devoted to a separate episode in the merger story. It was the SDP side which insisted that a clear and unequivocal statement of policy must be anchored into the unity package, to reassure SDP waverers. But the publication of such a statement, in January 1988, caused uproar in the Liberal Party and brought the whole process of merger and the future of the Alliance suddenly into a chaotic state of collapse. The policy 'fiasco' dramatically exposed the gulf which had opened up between the Alliance leadership and its membership, ironically strengthening the will of the majority and creating the necessary wave of support which finally swept the two parties across the threshold of union a few weeks later.

Finally, pp. 112–115 take a look at the new party in practice. Trailing badly in the polls and almost annihilated at the 1989 Euro-elections, the Liberal Democrats look, to many, like a spent force. Two-party politics has bounced back into fashion among Fleet Street pundits and the next election promises to centre on a straight fight between Labour and the Conservatives. Time alone can tell whether the merger paved the way for long-term success, or whether its promise was false. The chapter concludes by looking at the prospects for the centre at the next election and asks, 'Was merger worth it?'

The information presented in this chapter has been gathered from a diversity of sources, including material written by members of the merger negotiating teams, press reports from the period, David Steel's autobiography and other published accounts of proceedings. I am indebted to the former SDP leader, Robert Maclennan, for sharing so many of his records and reminiscences with me, during the 18 months I spent working as his research assistant. What follows is therefore a compilation of information – official and unofficial – together with some personal impressions and, inevitably, a few prejudices too.

INTRODUCTION

The SDP/Liberal Alliance came away from the polls in 1987 with 23 per cent of the popular vote but just 22 MPs (out of a total of 650). Dreams of a breakthrough had been destroyed by the realities of a crippling electoral system, a lacklustre campaign and disabling internal party problems. David Steel's decision to force the question of a merger on to the agenda within 36 hours of the polls closing, and the manner in which he did it, has been the subject of much criticism. In his autobiography, *Against Goliath*, he enlists the authority of Macbeth in his defence on the grounds that 'If it were done when 'tis done, then 'twere well it were done quickly'.[1] Whatever view one takes about the rights or wrongs of the Liberal leader's action at the time, it is clear that the furore which followed could hardly have been more disastrous for Alliance morale and credibility.

It was on Saturday 13 June 1987 that David Steel lit the fire which was to rage all summer long. He composed a memorandum, addressed to his own party but shared with the press, in which he set out what, in his view, were the options open to the Alliance parties in the aftermath of electoral defeat. There could be no standing still, he warned – the choice was between 'democratic fusion' and separation:

> I would prefer the formation of a single Liberal Democratic Alliance. We should learn the lessons of the more logical and coherent constitution of the SDP and blend that with the more powerful, decentralised grass-roots organisation of the Liberal Party.[2]

In a passage curiously headed 'My Own Position', the Liberal leader announced:

> I see it as my immediate task to see this period of discussion through. I will thereafter discuss my own position and decide my possible role.

At the time, few doubted what David Steel intended that role to be.

The long and bitter merger debate opened up a chasm within the SDP and dominated the front pages of the national press throughout the months of July and August 1987. Its various arguments and counter-arguments are well documented and perhaps still too painfully fresh in the minds of many to warrant extensive coverage here. In any case, the available space precludes it. Suffice it to quote the leader in *The Daily Telegraph* on 25 August:

> A political party must either be in charge of a national crisis or
> be suffering from a catastrophe of its own if it is to remain in
> the news throughout an Englishman's August.

There was no question about it. The SDP was in the throes of the most serious catastrophe of its short but eventful life. With a view to bringing the conflict swiftly and decisively to a head, the SDP's 58,904 members were balloted on the question of whether or not merger negotiations with the Liberals should take place. On 6 August the results of the ballot were declared. The party had ignored the advice of its leader and the majority on its National Committee and voted by a margin of just under three to two in favour of negotiations taking place. It was a victory for the 'Yes to Unity' campaign led by Shirley Williams, Roy Jenkins, Bill Rodgers and William Goodhart. David Owen, 'sad and distressed' at his party's decision, announced his resignation. The result of the ballot, far from settling matters, precipitated a second, even more traumatic, bout of civil war within the party. David Owen promised to carry on the fight from within, warning that, if the merger did take place, he would resurrect a 'continuing' Social Democratic Party on the centre ground of British politics.

By now the SDP was drifting, rudderless, deeper into chaos and danger by the day. It was Robert Maclennan – a Scottish MP and, until now, a key supporter of David Owen – who arrested this drift with his sudden and unexpected decision to step into the leadership vacuum and carry out the instructions of the majority of the party's members by negotiating terms for a merger with the Liberals. Writing in *The Independent* a month earlier, Maclennan had suggested that a merger between the two parties would 'clap our members into the closed room of a single party, like Sartre's Hell, from which there is no exit.'[3] But his mind had been changed by the outcome of the ballot of members and Owen's reaction to it. He was concerned that the will of the majority would be frustrated and the interests of the party seriously undermined unless a new leader stepped into the breach and opened up negotiations with the Liberals. Realizing that if talks were going to take place they had better take place with someone in charge who was determined to drive a hard deal, he decided that the task must fall to him. After consulting Shirley Williams in New England, Maclennan put out a statement to the press, in which he said that the membership had expressed its view that a new party organization with the Liberals was needed to advance social democratic objectives and that 'the SDP must therefore enter in good faith into constructive discussions to try to give effect to that purpose'.[4] At the end of August, Maclennan was elected, unopposed, as party leader.

Within days of the twist which had installed Maclennan at the helm of the SDP, the party assembled for its annual conference at Portsmouth. It was an occasion marred by acrimony and division. At moments, the party appeared to be on the verge of disintegrating on the spot. But a skilful speech from the new leader succeeded in stabilizing the situation: Maclennan urged fellow Social Democrats to adopt a 'wait and see' attitude towards the negotiations for merger and not to prejudge them one way or the other until the final package was on the table. He laid down tough requirements which, he warned, must be met before he personally could find any merger acceptable. In particular, the new party could not fudge crucial policy issues – it must accept the case for the British independent nuclear deterrent, the social market economy, and the expansion of civil nuclear power. He also made it clear that the SDP's constitution (of which he was the author back in 1981–1982) must form the bedrock of any new united Alliance organization.[5] In effect, Maclennan was taking a double-edged gamble. In setting such high standards he ran the risk not only of preventing the merger altogether, but also of pushing himself into a position in which most of his party and most of his negotiators could accept a merger deal, but he, in the light of his tough demands, could not. During the negotiations he was repeatedly to put his own position in jeopardy by threatening to call the merger off, thereby, in effect, offering to throw his party back into a state of leaderless confusion and commit personal political suicide in the process. Thus having raised the stakes for merger Maclennan succeeded in quelling the fears of sceptics and cooling the war of words and warnings which had torn the party apart since the general election in June. The SDP was as split as ever, but it had been pulled back from the brink.

Two weeks later, the Liberal Party Assembly, meeting in Harrogate, voted by a staggering margin of 44 : 1 in favour of merger negotiations. The path was now clear for the talking to begin.

THE CONSTITUTIONAL NEGOTIATIONS

The Liberal Party and SDP constitutions compared

The Liberal and Social Democratic Parties had always operated in very different ways. The difference was largely traceable to the contrast in the historic origins of the two parties. Below is an outline of the Liberal and SDP constitutions. We shall be returning to some aspects of them in more detail later as part of the discussion about the new merged party's constitution, and the negotiations which produced it.

The Liberal Party constitution
The Liberals were the proud inheritors of a political tradition rooted in the great social reform movements of the nineteenth century. But history had bestowed a certain sanctity on the party's archaic institutions, a sanctity which made change both slow and difficult. Liberals' suspicion of headstrong leadership made it even harder for those seeking to improve or modernize the party's internal infrastructure. The result was a party in which power was widely dispersed among local activists who united only for the annual assembly where, their numbers and views unknown, they could effectively assert control over the leadership in key policy votes. As a safeguard against dictatorship by eccentric activists, the leader was empowered with a veto over the final content of the party's general election manifesto. The principal criticisms of the Liberal constitution were that it was shambolic and inefficient. It prevented the party's leaders from leading; it muddled the party's national image and message; it increased the risk of damaging splits on policy issues and of confrontations between the party and its leadership; and it put too much power into the hands of activists who, by the very fact of their active commitment, were likely to be more extreme in their views than the broader membership.

The SDP constitution
The constitution of the SDP was shaped by very different factors. Unlike the Liberal Party, whose constitution sought to enshrine the rights of activists, the SDP was born out of growing alarm at the rise of militant activism in the Labour Party. Those who broke away from Labour in 1981 committed themselves to building a model party democracy in which all members had a say in the party's affairs, through elections to the party's main policy-making body, the Council for Social Democracy (CSD), and through the use of postal ballots; policy-making was careful and consensual; and leadership was purposive and effective. Other pioneering features of the SDP's constitution included positive discrimination in favour of women and a centralized system of membership.

Uniting two such different organizations took an unimaginable force of effort and understanding. Although David Steel readily acknowledged, early on, the advantages of the SDP constitution as a model for the new party, there were many in his party, particularly those whose agreement was essential for a merger to take place, who were deeply suspicious of what they saw as SDP centralism and who were protective of the tradition of local autonomy which ran thick through the Liberal Party's veins. Below, the draft constitution, which emerged from over 200 exhausting hours of negotiation, is analysed. As will be seen, on the SDP side, carefully pre-planned negotiating tactics, combined with a degree of brinkmanship, ensured that on most major issues it was the Liberals who were forced to give the most ground. The end product, therefore, owes much to its Social Democratic parentage. As *The Independent* reported on the day of its publication:

> The SDP has won almost everything it wanted – in particular, membership ballots and a tight policy-making machinery which is ultimately accountable to individual party members.[6]

The negotiated constitutional package

Five aspects of the negotiated package warrant special attention here: (a) the policy-making process; (b) the federal structure; (c) the membership system; (d) women in the party; and (e) the name and the preamble.

The policy-making process[7]
Policy in the Liberal Party was generated at the annual Joint Liberal Assembly (JLA). Voting rules at the assembly were, to say the least, loose. It was sometimes cruelly said of Liberal Assemblies that anyone who turned up would be given a vote. While this is technically incorrect, it is not so very far from the truth. The JLA was large – up to 10,000 people could potentially take part, although usually the number actually doing so was nearer 2000. It was dominated by activists and party pressure groups, which gave it a slightly chaotic and unpredictable atmosphere. No one quite knew who was there and how they would vote. In the past this had occasionally resulted in poor decision-making, for example the famous anti-nuclear vote on defence at Eastbourne in 1986, which contradicted both the view of the leadership and the mood of the wider party membership. Similar assemblies took place in Scotland and Wales – they were expected, although not obliged, to toe the JLA line in the event of any disagreement. Apart from the leader's veto over the manifesto (which had never been exercised), the JLA was regarded as sovereign and no policy committee or parliamentary meeting could block its decisions. The Liberal Policy Committee's role was to stimulate debate at the JLA and produce detailed policy papers via its various policy panels. In addition it was responsible for drawing up the party's general election manifesto, in consultation with the MPs, the Candidates' Association and the policy panels. Its members were partly elected by the activist-dominated Party

Council (see below), and partly *ex officio*. In addition to the JLA, the Scottish and Welsh Assemblies and the Policy Committee, there was the Liberal Council. The Council was a small hard core of activists who met four times a year and made decisions which the leadership was expected to 'bear in mind'. The leadership, in fact, had very little time at all for the Council. In his book, *Against Goliath*, David Steel refers to the 'somewhat unrepresentative Party Council'. He recalls one 'cramped and squalid' meeting he attended: 'The TV cameras recorded elder statesmen such as Baroness Seear and Lord Bonham-Carter picking their way through the previous night's beer barrels to get to the meeting. It didn't even look business-like.'[8]

The SDP's structured approach to policy-making could hardly have been more business-like, which is just why many die-hard Liberals resented it. SDP policy was determined by two bodies – the Council for Social Democracy (CSD) and the Policy Committee. The CSD was composed of around 500 representatives elected by area parties. It met four times a year to debate, and vote on, both matters of general policy and specific policy papers commissioned by the Policy Committee. The Policy Committee had an inbuilt majority of MPs (irrelevant once the number of MPs dwindled in 1983), and was chaired by the leader of the party. To be adopted as official party policy, any motion or paper had to be endorsed by both the CSD and the Policy Committee. In the event of deadlock between the Committee and the CSD, either body could call for a ballot of the membership, although in practice this was never needed (usually the Committee got its own way). The general election programme was drawn up by the Committee.

The merged party's policy-making process was debated by the negotiating teams on 20 October and 17/18 November 1987. Immediately, negotiators split into two camps: those who wanted to see an efficient, tightly controlled policy-making process accountable, ultimately, to the membership of the party, and those who wanted a less regulated process in which power over policy ultimately lay with those who were the most active in their support for the party, i.e. local activists, through a sovereign conference and a wider consultative network of party councils.

The SDP side accepted that the Conference should be sovereign, except in one case. The Policy Committee, they argued, should have the power to defer any Conference decision with which it disagreed for one meeting and/or order a ballot of all members if it wanted to pursue the disagreement further. They were strongly opposed to the idea of a Party Council, along the lines of that which met in the Liberal Party four times a year, and argued instead for Conference to meet twice a year. The Liberals were prepared to accept the Policy

Committee's right to delay Conference decisions (effectively by six months), but were split over the question of ballots and the abolition of the Party Council. Eventually David Steel, himself anxious to bury the troublesome Council once and for all, pressed for a straw vote to be taken in which the SDP side and Liberal minority joined together to swing the vote in favour of the SDP demand for two Conferences a year and no Party Council.[9] In the face of SDP pressure, the Liberal negotiators also caved in on the issue of ballots, which they had initially opposed on the grounds that they took the final say away from activists and gave it to less committed party members. But as Shirley Williams argued, 'In the last analysis we have to trust our members.'[10] The teams agreed that membership ballots, which were to be regarded as consultative rather than binding, could be called for by the Executive Committee, either on its own initiative or at the request of the Policy Committee or the Conference. It was unanimously agreed that one-member, one-vote ballots (where appropriate using STV) should also be used for the election of the leader and president of the federal party, and for prospective parliamentary candidate (PPC) selection.[11]

So, the new party was to have a 2000-strong Federal Conference, meeting twice a year, composed of representatives sent by local parties in proportion to their membership. The Conference would be empowered to approve, amend or reject interim policy proposals (Green Papers) and definitive policy statements (White Papers) introduced by the Policy Committee, but would be subject to the check that its decisions could be delayed by the Policy Committee or even overturned by a ballot of the whole membership. Preparation of the party's general election manifesto was to be the responsibility of the Policy Committee, in consultation with the parliamentary party.[7] It was agreed that the party leader should not have a right of veto over the Conference since the delaying powers of the Policy Committee and the balloting powers of the Executive together provided an adequate check on Conference power.[12]

Divisions soon opened up between the Social Democrats – who argued that parliamentarians and councillors should enjoy an in-built majority, and that women should have guaranteed places, on the Committee – and the Liberals – who wanted as many members as possible to be freely elected by the Conference with no in-built majority for parliamentarians and councillors and no guaranteed places for women. The SDP position on guaranteed places for parliamentarians, especially MPs, was summarized by Robert Maclennan, who said:

> The MPs are those who have to face the electorate. They must have an input as of right, though the sovereignty of the Party lies with the membership at large.[13]

A compromise was reached. The Federal Policy Committee was to comprise 27 members, including the leader and 4 other MPs elected by the parliamentary party in the Commons, the president, one peer, elected by the parliamentary party in the Lords, and three councillors, elected by the Councillors' Association. This gave parliamentarians and councillors a third of the places (a little short of the original SDP demand). The Committee was also to contain two representatives from the Scottish party, two representatives from the Welsh party and 13 members directly elected by the Conference. The SDP principle of positive discrimination in favour of women, in the form of guaranteed places on committees and shortlists, was later accepted for everything, including for the Federal Policy Committee, which had to contain at least four women and four men.

The federal structure[14]

A federal structure is one which is divided into local units, each with the power to take decisions on local issues, subject to the will of an over-arching federal organization where issues of national importance are involved. Its principal advantage is that decisions are likely to be better informed – since they are taken as close to those affected as possible – and more participatory. On the other hand, the dual system of local and national decision-making inevitably involves both duplicity and, occasionally, division. Thus it is a question of balancing quality and democracy against efficiency and unity.

Federalism was a Liberal precondition of merger – although the idea of devolving day-to-day decision-making, on issues which are of exclusive interest to a particular region or locality, was one which Social Democrats found easy to embrace. There was never going to be any bitter dispute about the principle of federalism. However, finding a mechanism which would be both democratic *and* efficient, in practice, proved much more difficult than expected. It was not clear whether the party should be split into three straight state parties – the English, Scottish and Welsh parties – or whether England itself should be subdivided into regional state parties, e.g. Greater London, the South, the Midlands and the North.

Eventually, agreement emerged along the following lines. First, it was decided that there should be three state parties, one each for Scotland, Wales and England, and a federal organization. Second, on policy matters it was agreed that the federal party (through its Conference and Policy Committee) should be responsible for the preparation of UK-wide policy, including through the submission of Green and White Papers at the bi-annual Federal Conference and the production of the general election manifesto. Each state party should have the power to adopt its own policies on issues relating specifically to the state concerned. Third, on non-policy matters, each state party (through its State Executive Committee) should be largely responsible for its own affairs, e.g. collecting and renewing party memberships and PPC selection. Within England there should be a regional structure, and an English conference drawn from the English members of the Federal Conference, a co-ordinating committee for England, and a Council of the Regions of England. Finally, in Scotland, the main organs of the party should be a Conference, an Executive Committee and a Policy Committee. In Wales, the main organs of the party should be a Council, an Executive Committee and a Policy Sub-committee.

The membership system[15]

It was agreed that, as in the old SDP, membership was to be recorded centrally by each state party. There was to be no constituency affiliation to the party, as used to happen in the old Liberal Party. Every member of the party would automatically be registered as a member of the federal party, the relevant state party and the relevant local (i.e. constituency) party.

Women in the party

In-built discrimination in favour of women was a pioneering feature of the SDP's constitution and a principle to which Social Democrats were strongly committed. Yet it was also a principle which many in the Liberal Party found deeply offensive. But on this issue, as on many others throughout the negotiations (e.g. ballots, party council, committee composition, name and preamble), the Liberal negotiating position crumbled as parts of the team split off to join the SDP, producing a decision which was very close to the original SDP demand.

The provision for women finally agreed at the negotiating sessions of 1/2 December was as follows:

- at least four women and at least four men should be elected to the Federal Executive and Federal Policy Committees;[16]
- each parliamentary shortlist between two and four should include at least one woman and one man, and shortlists of five or over at least two women and two men;[17]
- local parties which, by virtue of their size, should be entitled to elect three or more representatives to the Federal Conference must include at least one woman and one man.[18]

The Liberals agreed to positive discrimination for women in return for a concession from the SDP on youth and student representation at the Conference. The SDP negotiators, laying aside nightmare memories of Young Liberals at past Assemblies rebelling against the leadership, agreed that the new party's youth and student organizations should each be entitled to send a (deliberately small) number of representatives to the Federal Conference.

The name and the preamble to the constitution
The issues of the new party's name and the wording of the preamble to its constitution were the two most troublesome and damaging constitutional issues discussed by the negotiators. Perhaps for that reason they were left until towards the very end of the negotiating process, when other contentious issues had been dealt with and a tight timetable demanded speedy solutions. The choice of the new party's name did not, of course, lend itself to a speedy solution. The pride and passion attached to political labels should not be underestimated. To the outside world, protracted wrangling over the question of what the new party should call itself seemed illogical and frivolous. Yet the reason why the question of the name caused the new party so much trouble is exactly because it is not a logical or rational question – it is wrapped up in emotion and tangled in the ties of deep-seated loyalties.

The name was first discussed by the negotiators on 8 December. The two sides put forward their respective proposals: from the Liberals, 'the Liberal and Social Democratic Party', with no short title; from the SDP, 'the New Social and Liberal Democratic Party', or 'the Democrats' for short.[19] Both sides accepted that a long title should incorporate the names of both of the parent parties, although they disagreed in what order the incorporation should appear, but were at odds over suggestions for a short title. The Liberals refused to accept anything which did not contain the word 'Liberal' in it, whilst the SDP argued strongly in favour of the name 'Democrats' on the grounds that it would give the party a genuinely new feel, and would rebut the claims of those who said that the new party would be no more than a Liberal Party Mark II.

When the teams met the next day it became clear that the Liberals were not prepared to compromise on the word 'Liberal', an attitude which caused Robert Maclennan to say

> If we break down on the name that is very unfortunate but
> that is the case and perhaps we can recognise that. We must
> look at the perspectives that are leading us to these differences.
> On the Liberal side you are looking for an enlargement of the
> Liberal Party and not a new party. On the SDP side we are not
> wanting to join an enlarged Liberal Party.[20]

It was a statement which said much about the different approaches of the two sides and gave voice to the fear felt by many Social Democrats about just what the intentions of pro-merger Liberals really were. The argument came to a head with Alan Beith's provocative statement, 'I am a Liberal, I have always been a Liberal and I will continue to be a Liberal until the day I die.' In reaction to this, John Grant, an SDP negotiator, said he was pulling out of the talks altogether. Maclennan then announced that the SDP would have to 'reconsider its position' and walked out, followed by the rest of his team.[21] Some time later, Maclennan let it be known that he was on the brink of calling the merger off, but then returned to the meeting, alone, to warn the Liberals that the SDP team would not be back to the table 'until we hear from you that you have a proposal that meets our requirements'. The Liberal Party leadership prepared for the worst. It was 2.00 p.m. on 9 December. The Liberal minutes recorded:

> In the event of failure of the negotiations, to use the Special Assembly as a Liberal Party relaunch.[22]

The SDP–Liberal merger seemed to have collapsed.

But in fact, the situation was rescued by another Liberal concession. The Liberal negotiators voted ten to three to climb down from their previous refusal to contemplate the exclusion of the word Liberal from the short title and brought an old familiar term back to the table with their proposal: 'The New Liberal and Social Democratic Party, which may be known as the Alliance'. Twenty-four hours later, Maclennan dramatically announced from Brussels airport that the deal was on again. But before the draft constitution, together with the new compromise name, could be finally ratified by the negotiating teams, agreement had to be reached on a text for the preamble to the constitution. The preamble was intended to be a timeless statement of principles. Already two different versions of it had surfaced: a joint draft, composed by two Social Democrats – John Grant and David Marquand – and two Liberals – Michael Meadowcroft and Richard Holme; and a Liberal draft, composed by Tony Greaves in consultation with the rest of the Liberal negotiators. The process of putting together an acceptable text involved blending the styles and contents of the parent parties' respective preambles. The SDP was prepared to accept a more Liberal style in exchange for the inclusion of a reference to NATO (which was a feature of the SDP constitution). The issue became contentious: the Liberals were opposed to including so specific an organization as NATO in the preamble; for the SDP, inclusion of the NATO reference was something of a virility symbol, proving to the world in general that the new party was not 'soft' on defence and to would-be Owenites in particular that there had been no sell-out to the Liberals.

On the morning of 15 December, Shirley Williams and Tony Greaves met to hammer out a third and final version (reproduced in the Appendix), based on the original Liberal draft, but retaining the NATO reference. Later that day their work met with the approval of the re-assembled negotiating teams, who went on to approve the whole constitutional package, into which the Williams–Greaves preamble was inserted under the title of 'The Draft Constitution of the New Liberal and Social Democratic Party, which may be known as the Alliance'. After more than 200 hours of stormy negotiating sessions, often stretching late into the night, the new party had a constitution, a statement of principles and a name. Apart from some minor amendments to the text and the preamble, and a change of name, agreed in mid-January, the constitution stood in its final form and today forms the basis of the merged Social and Liberal Democrats.

The launch of the draft constitution

On 18 December, the document was unveiled at a Westminster press conference by Robert Maclennan, David Steel, Shirley Williams and Adrian Slade. Shirley Williams told reporters that the new constitution was 'decentralized, democratic, deliberative and discriminating in favour of those groups in our society who have been effectively left out of the political process'.[23] David Steel proclaimed the document as the foundation stone of 'the most democratic and decent party in the country', adding that he had 'absolutely no doubt that this package will be overwhelmingly endorsed'.[24] A noticeably less enthusiastic Robert Maclennan would only say that it was far too early to predict whether there would be a merged party because they had yet to agree a declaration of policy 'which will be critical in determining the attitude of many SDP members to the proposed union'. Writing in *The Guardian* on the same day, Maclennan had warned that: 'Until the policy declaration is agreed we shall not have a complete package, and until we have a complete package I cannot call on Social Democrats to endorse the merger.' Meanwhile, die-hard Liberals Tony Greaves and Rachael Pitchford took the opportunity of the launch to voice their criticisms of the draft for being 'too centralized, too inward-looking and too elitist',[25] comments which no doubt cheered on-looking Social Democrats considerably.

THE POLICY FIASCO

Negotiations on the new party's constitution came to an end on 15 December 1987. The negotiating teams returned home to re-establish normal living, working and sleeping patterns as the press turned its attention to more festive matters. But for the SDP leadership, the most testing business of the merger was about to begin. Tucked away in meetings and libraries, installed in front of word processors, Robert Maclennan and his staff settled down to work on the new party's policy declaration.

The now notorious policy declaration, launched early in the new year, came within a whisker of wrecking the merger and blasting apart the Alliance. Its heralded publication was followed within minutes by a furious rebellion amongst Liberal MPs and a hasty and humiliating retraction by the two party leaders. The embarrassment was deepened by the fact that the whole extraordinary crisis unfolded under the full glare of mass media attention. As Matthew Parris put it, speaking on LWT's 'Weekend World' shortly afterwards:

> The row was undeniably one of the most highly coloured events of recent politics. It had, for neutral observers, perhaps the ambiguous fascination of a traffic accident – gruesome but riveting.[26]

Meanwhile, the wrath of the Liberal and Social Democratic Parties fell upon their hapless leaders. The future leadership hopes of both Steel and Maclennan were dramatically and irrevocably dashed in the midst of the policy furore. From the outset, Maclennan had promised his party that union with the Liberals could only take place on the basis of a pre-arranged platform of clear, radical and realistic policy. He said so at the Portsmouth Conference in his debut speech as party leader. Then he warned colleagues that the new party could not fudge crucial issues such as civil nuclear power, Britain's defence policy or a social market approach to economic policy. Speaking to a fringe meeting at the same conference, he restated his point, saying:

> We have got to have that clear policy stand, otherwise we will simply be importing into the new party the problems of the old Alliance. We would perpetuate the lack of clarity which was so damaging to us in the election.[27]

The message was repeated to the Liberals at their Assembly in Harrogate a few weeks later when Maclennan warned:

> I do not favour the blank-cheque approach to this new enterprise.[28]

Having made his point in September, Maclennan continued to repeat it with force throughout the negotiating period. At successive press conferences he reminded observers that any merger was conditional on a tough policy stance being agreed for the new party.

Maclennan had insisted in October that the drafting of the policy declaration be taken out of the hands of the negotiators and left as a matter for the leaders alone. The aim, he told negotiators, was to produce 'a document of its time' which showed 'where we stand on the great issues facing the country at the time of the launch'. He described the declaration as 'unashamedly a leaders' document', although to be authoritative it would need to have the 'imprimatur' of the negotiating teams. He proposed that the declaration should be appended to the constitution and thereby 'given a certain validity during the transitional period'.[29] Soon after securing the reluctant approval of the Liberal negotiators for his plan, the SDP leader commissioned two young journalists to help him write the document – they were Hugo Dixon, 25, and Andrew Gilmour, 23. Meanwhile, he invested time meeting experts and interest groups in various policy fields and consulting with researchers at the Institute of Fiscal Studies. On 22 December, Maclennan and his two protégés arrived at David Steel's home at Ettrick Bridge, in the Borders of Scotland, to discuss the policy declaration. Apart from Steel, also present were Alan Beith MP (deputy Liberal leader) and Alec McGivan (Steel's political adviser). Discussion concentrated on the style, length and scope of the declaration, but also covered the inclusion of some specific policies, among them a firm stance on nuclear defence and a strong commitment to fighting poverty.

Not mentioned at the Ettrick Bridge meeting were Maclennan's radical plans to finance an anti-poverty programme with cash from a broader VAT base and a sliding scale of benefit withdrawal. The plans were developed by the SDP leader in conjunction with the Institute of Fiscal Studies and British and American economists. All over Christmas, Maclennan sent his new thinking flashing across the world by facsimile from Boston, where he was staying with his wife's family, to his young scribes in London, and from there to Steel in the Borders. The principle was simple. In the words of the document:

> Universal child benefit is designed to help the poor but it wastes resources by subsidising the well-off. The same is true of the current exemption of 'necessities' from VAT. We must make sure that tax reliefs and benefits get through to the people who need them. The Party should therefore not be afraid, in its crusade against poverty, to concentrate child benefit on the poor; and extend VAT to food, children's clothing, domestic fuel, newspapers and financial services . . .'[30]

Maclennan had calculated that the VAT and child benefit proposals alone would raise enough money to quite literally abolish poverty and reduce income tax. The document went on to argue for further tax reforms, including the abolition of mortgage tax relief and the married man's allowance, and the phasing out of tax concessions on company cars. The whole package was presented as a means of sweeping away the misplaced subsidies and inefficient flaws of the present system and raising the funds for a carefully targeted onslaught on deprivation and poverty.

Details of the plans were relayed to Steel, who, far from registering alarm, merely made a few complimentary remarks in the margin of his copy before forwarding it to his deputy, Beith. Maclennan's return to Britain coincided with Steel's departure for Kenya and so the two leaders remained continents apart until just days before the launch of the declaration scheduled for lunchtime on 13 January. When the two did meet, it was Monday 11 January. Steel congratulated the SDP leader and his staff on what he described as an 'imaginative and exciting' document. In particular, he highlighted the extension of VAT as an inspired idea which would add credibility to the party's anti-poverty programme.[31] The next day copies of the policy declaration, as yet untitled, were left in the Liberal Party Whips' Office in the House of Commons, for the information of MPs, and laid on the negotiating table at Cowley Street, for the attention of SDP and Liberal negotiators who were reassembling to consider final amendments to the constitution.

The document was discussed at a meeting of the Liberal Party Policy Committee that afternoon. The Committee was aghast at what it considered to be a badly written, sub-Thatcherite, suicide note. David Steel, Alan Beith and Des Wilson were urgently dispatched to Maclennan's office in Cowley Street to demand that publication be abandoned pending further discussions and re-drafting. Maclennan refused point-blank. 'This is, and always has been, a leaders' document', he said, 'there is no question of the Policy Committee, or any other committee for that matter, derailing us over this. I will not change a word of it. If there is any delay, I shall go ahead and publish it alone and the merger will be off.'[32] The most he would agree to was a meeting later that night to consider a few minor textual changes. The launch was still on for lunchtime the next day. That night, negotiators were locked in an ill-tempered argument over demands for a new party name and for changes to be made to the constitutional preamble. Once again, the SDP's negotiating tactics took merger right to the brink, with Maclennan slamming his fist on the table and demanding that the Liberals accept both 'Social and Liberal Democrats' as the new party's name and retention of the reference to NATO in the constitution. He gave them five minutes to climb down or, he said, 'it's all off'. With that, he and his colleagues left.[32]

The Liberals, of course, did climb down, but not without loss. Three Liberal negotiators – Tony Greaves, Rachael Pitchford and Peter Knowlson – walked out of the talks in disgust at what they saw as yet another Liberal cave-in. The others resigned themselves to the

Maclennan terms: 'I'd rather give in to the Social Democrats than to Kinnock or Thatcher', argued Chris Mason, a Liberal negotiator; 'If it's Social and Liberal Democrats or no merger . . .' (Liberal MP Alex Carlile). At just after midnight the SDP negotiators were called back into the meeting and informed of their victory.[33] Having cleared up the issue of the name and approved minor changes to the text of the preamble, the negotiators' attention turned to the policy declaration. By now it was one o'clock in the morning and the weary remnants of the two negotiating teams ploughed through the draft document, agreeing to insignificant amendments and additions. The tone was slightly softened: the opening glowing reference to Margaret Thatcher was made a little less glowing; the controversial commitments on VAT became 'measures to be worked on and costed . . . to be put forward only after widespread consultation'; and a few adjectives were changed here and there. At 4 a.m., the session ended in exhaustion. Steel and Maclennan signed an official final draft to a ripple of applause from the negotiators.

Later that morning, expressions of resistance to the document, now christened *Voices and Choices for All*, poured into Steel's office from across the country. A member of the negotiating team had leaked the document's contents to the press overnight and the news had made the front pages of all the quality newspapers that morning. By mid-morning, Steel realized that the whole Liberal Party was in open revolt against the document. At 11.25, with the press conference to launch the document just 35 minutes away, he called Maclennan over to his office at the Commons. The Liberal leader was emotional. When Maclennan arrived, he cleared the office of staff and colleagues. *The Observer*, in its account of events, reported that 'It is not known what passed between the two men during the next ten minutes. But when the others were re-admitted, they both looked, according to one eye-witness, "as white as corpses" – and the press conference was off.' In fact a distraught David Steel told Maclennan that he could not go through with the deal, he could not deliver his party. In vain Maclennan urged him to 'be tough, be a leader'. Steel's only reply was that he now had no choice but to resign his position as Liberal leader (something which, in the event, he managed to avoid doing).[34]

Meanwhile, as yet unaware of the miserable scene being played out in Steel's office, the press had gathered *en masse* in the Jubilee Room at the Commons, where SDP workers had already distributed copies of the ill-fated document. As noon struck, Steel and Maclennan sent their unfortunate research assistants over to face the reporters. They announced that the press conference had been 'postponed', to allow further time for the leaders to 'consult more fully with their parliamentary colleagues'.[35] Minutes later, the story was the lead item on every news bulletin. 'The SDP/Liberal merger is this afternoon on the rocks', announced the BBC's One O'Clock News. Meanwhile, at Westminster, journalists, sensing impending catastrophe, were congregating around doorways and in corridors, waiting for snippets of information to emerge. An emotional meeting of the MPs and their leaders at 2 p.m. managed to persuade Maclennan against immediately abandoning the merger and he agreed to announce that the process of negotiation was being extended by a few more days. At 5 p.m. the two leaders, flanked by their grim-faced parliamentary colleagues, faced the press. Maclennan said: 'Since we signed and published the document this morning, we have had some predictable reactions, particularly in the Liberal Party, questioning some of these programmes and ideas . . .'[36] However, the SDP leader refused to take back a word of the document: 'We have published this document and we have said that these are our views. Now there is no question of us unsaying them. We have no intention of unsaying them.' Steel admitted that he did not 'see a way forward at the moment, but give people a few days, give them some sleep, and some hope that there might be a way'. The next morning brought an outpouring of fierce criticism from the press. The headlines were eloquent: 'Suicide: Loopy Steel Finished Amid Merger Chaos', declared *Today*; 'Kamikaze Steel Crisis: Mac the Knife Carves Up Liberal Leader', *The Daily Express*; 'The Greatest Farce on Earth', *The Sun*; and 'Alliance Merger in Disarray', *The Independent*. Talking to senior Alliance politicians, commented *The Observer* a few days later, 'is like talking to the survivors of a major accident. They are still in shock.'[37]

But out of the jaws of defeat, the Alliance was salvaged. For the rest of the week, and over the following weekend, a burst of frenzied activity within the two parties produced a compromise, consensual, policy document which found a form of words to cover most contentious issues and succeeded in offending no-one in the process. The paper, written by six 'wise men' appointed for the task by the leaders, was endorsed by the negotiating teams, the Liberal Policy Committee and the parliamentary parties on Monday 18 January. As *The Guardian* newspaper commented in an editorial on 20 January:

> The single-minded determination with which Liberals and
> Social Democrats rewrote their policy declaration over the
> weekend was undeniably impressive in its way.

Maclennan pronounced himself satisfied. The document, called *A Democracy of Conscience*, was an updated version of the Alliance manifesto at the previous election, which they had all been proud to fight for just seven months earlier. Moreover, the SDP leader argued, on the crucial question of nuclear defence, the new document went further than the old manifesto, which had committed the Alliance to cancelling Trident. Instead, the new document recognized that the SDP's principle of a modernized nuclear deterrent would have to be 'reconciled' with the reality that Trident will have been 'substantially paid for and probably already deployed' by the time of the next election. In fact, the SDP leader's swallowed pride and change of heart owed less to the merits of the worthy but bland *Democracy of Conscience* than to the sudden urgency with which the frustrated majority in the SDP were pressing for unity. As news of the collapse was beamed into the homes of party members up and down the country, switchboard operators at Cowley Street were deluged with calls pressing for merger to take place at once, lest the agony of the break-up be prolonged. As party leader, Maclennan was honour-bound to put their wishes before his own face-saving concerns.

The process of hauling the merger back on to the rails ended with a bizarre eleventh-hour twist – involving a late-night taxi dash by Maclennan to the Limehouse home of his predecessor, David Owen. Minutes after endorsing the new policy statement at a meeting of the two negotiating teams, Maclennan appeared on the steps of the SDP's Cowley Street headquarters to announce live to millions of TV viewers of the BBC's Nine O'Clock News that he was off to visit David Owen – to seek to change his mind about merger and to commend the 'magnificent new package' to him. Maclennan was then whisked across London, a gaggle of journalists and cameramen in hot pursuit, only to be met, in Limehouse, by a furious Owen, who accused him of setting up a cheap publicity stunt. Just 15 minutes later, Maclennan re-emerged, looking drained and upset. Pushing his way past the waiting crowd of astonished journalists, the SDP leader paused only to say: 'I came here to visit an old friend – I held out an olive branch and it was rejected.' He has since described Owen, that evening, as being 'on a pinnacle of pique'.[38] The whole extraordinary episode ended in another blaze of melodramatic front-page newspaper headlines: 'Owen Snubs Peace Plea: Maclennan Humbled in Most Humiliating Climbdown in British Political History!', revelled *The Daily Mail*.

A few days later, on 23 January, Liberals meeting at a Special Assembly in Blackpool voted by a margin of six to one in favour of merger. On 31 January, the Council for Social Democracy followed suit, although with slightly less enthusiasm. Ballots of the membership of each party, a month later, endorsed the merger package by similar margins – 7:1 in the Liberal Party and 2:1 in the SDP. The day after the results of the membership ballots were declared from the steps of Cowley Street, and almost nine months after David Steel had initiated the merger debate after the election, the Liberal Party and the Social Democratic Party, in its original form, ceased to exist. (David Owen became leader of a minority, 'continuing' SDP.) The Social and Liberal Democrats were in business.

CONCLUSIONS

The state of the centre in the wake of the merger

The immediate consequence of the SDP–Liberal merger was the division it created in the centre ground of British politics. Far from welding together that vast body of sensible and compassionate opinion which lies at the heart of the electorate, the acrimonious process of merging scattered it to the winds and thereby threw away years of painstaking effort and achievement. The general impression in the minds of most voters is still that the events of 1987–1988 paved the way not for a happy marriage, but for a messy divorce.

The bitter and prolonged wrangling which the merger debate produced set back the Liberal and Social Democratic cause immeasurably. Understandably, most voters found it quite incredible that two men, David Steel and David Owen, who had spent the previous four years appearing happily together in soft-focus photographs and talking about their parties' mutual love affair should, within days of the general election result being declared, suddenly turn on each other with such extraordinary ferocity. The electorate was made to feel foolish and deceived, as if it had been taken in by this shallow display of amity, shielded from the animosity and disagreement which, it later turned out, were all the time beneath the surface. The Alliance stood for partnership, for working together in pursuit of the common good. As an ideal, it embodied the new politics of consensus and coalition which its members wanted to replace Britain's battle-weary political system. The row which preceded the merger seemed to expose Social Democrats and Liberals as just 'ordinary' politicians, rather than the new brand of co-operative people they had claimed to be. In comparison, the *Voices and Choices for All* fiasco was much less damaging. In fact, the crisis actually brought members of both parties closer together, in the same way that survivors of a shipwreck, awaiting rescue, might desperately cling to one another for comfort. The price of what was first and foremost a public relations folly was ultimately paid by the two leaders, Steel and Maclennan, both of whom later stood down to make way for a fresh face to take over the leadership.

So was merger worth it? An initial reaction is negative. The week after their launch, the Liberal Democrats (as they are now retitled) limped into the opinion polls registering around 7 per cent support, vying for third place with David Owen's reconstituted SDP. In 1989 there was the rise of the Greens, humiliation at the Euro-elections, and a series of cash crises. Membership languished stubbornly at around the 90,000 mark, and thousands of activists, many of them brought into politics for the first time with the triumphant launch of the SDP in 1981, became increasingly detached. Meanwhile the turmoil in the centre, coupled with Labour's sudden half-conversion to social democracy, ensured that the long-awaited flood of support away from the Tories by-passed the new party and went direct to Labour. But there are crumbs of comfort for Liberal Democrats. As a constitutional structure, a campaigning organization and a policy-making body the new party is working far more efficiently and effectively than its predecessor, the Alliance.

The party's constitution, built on the twin pillars of democracy and decentralization, seems superior to the old-fashioned systems of party management which stifle debate and participation within the two main parties. The union block vote continues to diminish Labour's local and conference democracy, while the Conservatives manage everything from the centre, excluding the wider membership and allowing the leadership to assume dictatorial status. Both might learn from the Liberal Democrats' constitution. At local elections and by-elections, Liberal Democrat candidates continue to poll, on average, well over a quarter of the vote, a considerably higher share than predicted by national opinion polls and a firm foundation from which to launch a wider recovery. The policy-making process has operated smoothly, producing coherent and realistic decisions on matters such as the nuclear deterrent, economic policy, radical tax and benefit reform, and now new thinking on the reform of welfare services.

Challenges from the Greens and David Owen's SDP have been seen off. Under Paddy Ashdown, the party has found a clearer philosophical vision, one which concentrates on new ways of expanding social choice, through an enabling State, and wider access to a competitive market economy. Central to the new party's approach to politics is the decentralization, the dispersal, and the sharing, of power – within the economy, industry, the political system, and the European Community. Indeed, taken separately, Liberal Democrat policies on proportional representation, a Bill of Rights and a united Europe represent three valuable pieces of political real estate to which no other party has yet laid claim.

The implications for Britain's party system

So, we now see a third party which has regained some sense of purpose and direction, and which looks strong across the country in local politics, but whose chances of national power appear, at first glance, more remote than ever. Many leading Labour and Conservative figures have spent much time appearing on Britain's television screens to reassure the nation that it can breathe a sigh of relief: two-party politics is back. Their confidence is misguided. The trend away from two-party politics began almost 40 years ago and continues unabated. It is rooted in the long-term break-up of Britain's class structure and the ongoing diversification of interests and influences which today determine political allegiance. The proportion of the electorate voting for either of the two main parties at general elections has declined steadily from 79 per cent in 1951, to 52 per cent in 1987. Virtually half the electorate in 1987 either voted for other parties, or else abstained. Since the 1987 election, the merger, and the fall in the fortunes of the Liberal Democrats, two things have become clear. Firstly, the quarter of the electorate who voted Alliance in 1987 are still refusing to support either of the two older parties. Over the past year or so, between them the Liberal Democrats, the Greens, David Owen's SDP and the nationalist parties have attracted the support of one in every two voters in parliamentary and council by-elections, and of one in four voters in the European elections. As Adam Raphael argued in *The Observer* in September 1989:

> As the icepack of Thatcherism begins to break up, the Liberal Democrats, and the other parties of the centre, far from sliding into irrelevancy, hold the key to the future of British politics. . . . As the Thatcher star fades, at least 25% of the voting electorate continues to be alienated from the two major parties. The splintering of the centre has left many voters footloose.[39]

Secondly, the number of people who are giving up on the process altogether, by not voting, looks set to increase. Some recent opinion polls suggest that 30–37 per cent of the electorate do not intend to vote at all at the 1992 election, compared with the 26 per cent who failed to vote in the 1987 general election.

So there has been no return to two-party politics out in the country, only a redistribution of third-party support and a growing sense of apathy and despair. The choice which Paddy Ashdown has described as 'the dilemma between the devil and deep blue rinse' is no more appealing now than it was a few years ago.

Future prospects

Centre parties traditionally perform well at general elections in which support is slipping away from a Conservative government. In 1964 and 1974, the Liberals, on each occasion, managed to double their share of the vote. It seems probable that a similar pattern will be followed in 1992. If the fight between the Conservative government and the

Labour Party is close in 1992, then the Liberal Democrats will not need a great level of electoral support to hold the balance of power in Parliament. In such a situation, few doubt that Neil Kinnock would submit to pressure, not just from the Liberal Democrats but also from many within his own party, to legislate on PR in return for the keys to Downing Street. It would be a deep irony if the party were to win a place at the cabinet table with only a fraction of the popular support it took to fail at the 1987 election. A decade after the Gang of Four proclaimed it their ambition, the oppressive and divisive (in Liberal Democrat eyes) mould of British politics would finally have been broken.

APPENDIX: EXTRACTS FROM THREE DIFFERENT VERSIONS OF THE PREAMBLE TO THE CONSTITUTION OF THE NEW PARTY

1 Initial SDP–Liberal draft by Marquand, Grant, Meadowcroft and Holme.
2 Williams–Greaves draft attached to the constitution unveiled at December press conference.
3 Final version produced in mid-January 1988.

Opening statement

(1) The New Liberal and Social Democratic Party exists to create and defend an open, classless and more equal society in which every citizen shall possess liberty, property and security and none shall be enslaved by poverty, ignorance or conformity.

(2) The New Liberal and Social Democratic Party, which may be known as the Alliance, exists to build and safeguard a fair, free and more equal society shaped by the values of liberty, justice and community in which no-one shall be enslaved by poverty, ignorance or conformity.

(3) The Social and Liberal Democrats exist to safeguard a fair, free and open society in which we seek to balance the fundamental values of liberty, equality and community and in which no-one shall be enslaved by poverty, ignorance or conformity . . . We aim to disperse power, to foster diversity and to nurture creativity.

Comment: Style becomes more Liberal, removal of SDP word 'classless' and demotion of SDP word 'equal/equality'.

On the economy

(1) We seek to build a competitive, sustainable and prosperous economy, free from doctrinaire interference in private, public and co-operative sectors. We stand for enterprise and high employment promoted through market freedom where possible and the positive use of government power where necessary . . . We encourage workers, management and government to recognise their mutual dependence and to co-operate to achieve common interests: we will foster workplace democracy and industrial partnership.

(2) We will foster a strong and sustainable economy in which there is a just distribution of the rewards of success, working to the benefit of all and using and developing the skills of the people. We encourage democracy and participation in industry and commerce within a competitive enviroment in which the state allows the market to operate freely where possible but intervenes where necessary.

(3) We will foster a strong and sustainable economy which encourages the necessary wealth-creating process, develops and uses the skills of the people and works to the benefit of all, with a just distribution of the rewards of success. We want to see democracy, participation and the co-operative principle in industry and commerce within a competitive environment in which the state allows the market to operate freely where possible but intervenes where necessary.

Comment: Different ways of describing the social market. Final version better balanced with its reference to encouraging the 'necessary wealth-creating process'.

On property

(1) We recognise the personal ownership of property is a safeguard of independence, seek to spread capital, income and property and to ensure a fair participation in the fruits of success and the appreciation in land values.

(2) We recognise that the independence of individuals is safeguarded by the personal ownership of property. We also recognise that the market alone does not distribute wealth or income fairly. We support the widest possible distribution of wealth and promote the rights of all citizens to social provision and cultural activity.

(3) We recognise that the independence of individuals is safeguarded by their personal ownership of property, but that the market alone does not distribute wealth or income fairly. We support the widest possible distribution of wealth and promote the rights of all citizens to social provision and cultural activity.

Comment: Curious Liberal-style reference to rising land values taken out; strengthened SDP-style commitment to redistribution of wealth.

On the European Community

(1) We work for an integrated and united European Community, and the ending of the barriers which divide our continent.

(2) We will work together with other countries towards an equitable and peaceful international order and a durable system of common security . . . by playing a full and constructive role within the framework of the European Community.

(3) Setting aside national sovereignty when necessary, we will work with other countries towards an equitable and peaceful international order and a durable system of common security. Within the European Community we affirm the values of federalism and integration and work for unity based on these principles.

Comment: A much stronger endorsement of European integration is added to final version. Reference to 'Setting aside national sovereignty where necessary' is particularly significant. Specific commitment to European federalism.

On the Third World

(1) We are shamed by the continuation of vast imbalances within the world and commit ourselves to fight and dispel ignorance, poverty and hunger.

(2) We will contribute to . . . the elimination of world poverty.

(3) Our responsibility for justice and liberty cannot be confined by national boundaries; we are committed to fight poverty, oppression, hunger, ignorance, disease and aggression wherever they occur.

Comment: Very strong commitment to Third World aid watered down in second draft but partially revived in final version. End result is something much less passionate but wider in scope.

NOTES AND REFERENCES

1 D. Steel, *Against Goliath* (1989), p. 282.
2 Memorandum from David Steel Addressed to Officers of the Liberal Party, 13 June 1987. Source: private papers.
3 R. Maclennan, in *The Independent*, 29 June 1987, 'Passion as the Better Part of Politics'.
4 Press release from Robert Maclennan. Release date: noon, 15 August 1987. Source: private papers.
5 Speech by Robert Maclennan to the SDP Conference in Portsmouth, 1 September 1987. Source: private papers.
6 *The Independent*, 19 December 1987.
7 See Constitution, Article 7.
8 Steel, *Against Goliath*, p. 288.
9 R. Pitchford and T. Greaves, *Merger* (1989), p. 33.
10 *Ibid.*, p. 58.
11 See Constitution, Articles 10 (leader), 12 (President) and 11 (PPCs).
12 *The Times*, 19 November 1987.
13 Pitchford and Greaves, *Merger*, p. 32.
14 See Constitution, Article 2.
15 See Constitution, Article 3.
16 See Constitution, Articles 7 and 8.
17 See Constitution, Article 11.
18 See Constitution, Article 6.
19 Pitchford and Greaves, *Merger*, p. 88.
20 *Ibid.*, p. 90.
21 In conversation with Robert Maclennan.
22 Pitchford and Greaves, *Merger*, p. 98.
23 Press release from Robert Maclennan. Release date: noon, 18 December 1989. Source: private papers.
24 *Financial Times*, 19 December 1987.
25 *The Guardian*, 19 December 1987.
26 LWT transcript of 'Weekend World', 'The Alliance in Crisis: Can It Be Saved?', Sunday 17 January 1988.
27 *Daily Telegraph*, 2 September 1987.
28 Speech by Robert Maclennan to Liberal Assembly in Harrogate, 16 September 1987.
29 Pitchford and Greaves, *Merger*, p. 37.
30 *Voices and Choices for All* (1988) pp. 8–9.
31 In conversation with Robert Maclennan.

32 In conversation with Robert Maclennan.
33 *The Guardian*, 14 January 1988.
34 In conversation with Robert Maclennan.
35 Joint statement to the press from Robert Maclennan and David Steel, noon, 13 January 1988.
36 *The Guardian*, 14 January 1988.
37 *The Observer*, 17 January 1988.
38 In conversation with Robert Maclennan.
39 *The Observer*, 10 September 1989.

8

Fairness and Political Finance: The Case of Election Campaigns

DAWN OLIVER

The financing of the activities of the political parties in the UK is a broad subject. This chapter will focus on the aspects of the subject that are raised by election campaigns. The purpose will be to use this as a test of what is often said to be a defect in the present system, namely that it is unfair as between the parties.

The financing of parliamentary election campaigns[1] in the UK differs from systems in other Western democracies in a number of ways. The amounts spent are relatively modest; there is no provision of public funds to the parties for the purpose; there are strict controls on local expenditure and no controls at all on national expenditure; and considerable assistance in kind is given to candidates and to national party organizations for their campaigns. This chapter will consider to what extent the present arrangements are satisfactory and will briefly discuss some of the reforms that have been suggested to meet shortcomings in the system. We shall start by considering the controls on expenditure by candidates in their constituencies.

CONSTITUENCY EXPENDITURE

Expenditure at constituency level is strictly controlled under the Representation of the People Act 1983. The limits are updated from time to time, although there is no statutory provision for automatic index-linking. Inflation has meant that this has resulted in a reduction in real terms of the amount that may be spent for periods before the limits are increased. The limits are relatively low. In the 1987 election they worked out as a limit of £5000–6000 in most constituencies. The limits were raised in 1991 to £4144 plus 3.5p per registered elector in borough constituencies and 4.7p per registered elector in county constituencies.[2] The Representation of the People Act 1989 quadrupled the permitted maximum in by-elections.

To prevent the circumvention of the controls on candidates' expenditure there are strict legal prohibitions against other people or organizations incurring expenses with a view to promoting or procuring the election of a particular candidate under section 75 of the Representation of the People Act 1983. But these controls leave open the possibility of persons or organizations other than the candidate incurring expenditure in order to promote a party or a set of ideas associated with a party rather than a candidate.[3]

Of the relatively modest sums that may be spent in the constituency campaigns the Conservative Party raises a large proportion through fund-raising events. Labour raises money from sponsoring trade unions and from fund-raising activities. The Liberal Democrats and other small parties tend to rely substantially on subscriptions and fund-raising activities.

There seems to be general satisfaction with the controls on the incurring of expenditure on election campaigns at local level. As far as the attitude of the general public is concerned, the MORI poll in March 1991[4] found that 80 per cent of respondents thought that there should be (as there is) a set limit to the amount of money that political parties can spend on local campaigns during general elections. The parties too seem generally satisfied and in their responses to the Hansard Society's request for evidence none of the three main parties sought to challenge the general principle of limiting local expenditure.[5] The parties' principal complaint is that there is no legal requirement that the amounts that may be spent should rise in line with inflation.

There are, I suggest, positive advantages in a system which differentiates between expenditure in the constituencies and at national level and imposes particular controls of the sort that exist under the present system on the former. Even if there were to be controls on national campaign expenditure they could not be the same controls as those that operate at local level, and their rationales would not be the same. The controls at local level mean that there is no question of wealthier people 'buying' their candidatures by offering to meet substantial campaign expenses which the party organizations themselves would not be able to meet. They mean that at local level candidates can compete on equal terms. And they encourage a highly personal style of local campaigning by candidates and their supporters which in my view strengthens the relationship between MPs, their local party organizations and their constituents. If anything, it is suggested, the law should be changed to encourage even more the local side of election campaigning: at present elections tend to be fought on national rather than local issues and to focus on national rather than local figures in the party. Good constituency members or candidates get less credit than they could do for their efforts in their constituency. (By way of an aside, this position is exacerbated by section 93 of the Representation of the People Act, which makes it an offence for candidates to take part in a broadcast about themselves or the constituency without the consent of the other candidates. This effectively gives candidates a veto over broadcasts of local election coverage, and encourages the concentration on national personalities and issues. The provision may well be a breach of Article 10 of the European Convention on Human Rights, which protects the right to receive information. It is unpopular with the media, but popular with politicians. It ought to be repealed.)

There are, however, difficulties in the present system of control of local expenditure, for example in determining what is and what is not election expenditure, and this causes problems for agents and candidates: if the party leader visits one or even three or four constituencies on a day in the course of an election campaign, to what extent is the expense of such a visit to be regarded as that of the local campaign, or of the national campaign? There are also problems in determining when an election campaign begins so that the taxi meter starts ticking: the parties each issue to their agents guidance on this matter. Given the anxiety felt by candidates and agents about the possibility of a challenge to their election expenditure there is a strong case for clarifying the rules in this area. The Home Office is preparing guidance on these matters for candidates and their agents, but these of course will have no legal force. It remains for consideration whether legislation is required to deal with the uncertainties, or whether provision should be made for the issue of guidelines which would have statutory relevance if not statutory force, just as the Highway Code is relevant in court proceedings.

An aspect of the financing of election campaigns in the constituencies that does attract criticism is the requirement that candidates find a deposit of £500, which is forfeit if the candidate fails to win one-twentieth of the votes cast. The objective of this when it was introduced was to provide a 'safeguard against candidacies which added to the cost and complexity of the election whilst having no serious prospect of polling a sufficient number of votes to influence the result'.[6] The main justification, then, was administrative convenience.

While £500 may not seem a large sum for an individual candidate to raise, the reality is that candidates usually stand for parties and the parties may have to provide the deposit. The requirement presents an obstacle to parties such as the Greens which would wish to campaign nationally. With 650 seats in the House of Commons the party would have to raise £325,000 in order to contest every seat, a very substantial sum, much of which would be at risk.

There is no reason to believe that a means test is the best way of discouraging candidates with little support. If that is what is required, then a test of public support should be imposed, for example by increasing the number of signatures to a nomination to, say, two hundred as opposed to the present ten. It is suggested that the latter would be a better approach to avoiding the administrative problems caused by a proliferation of candidates. Rawlings is of the view that such a system would be unworkable because of the difficulties in checking so many signatures,[7] but this is a system that operates elsewhere, and difficulties as to the validity of nominations could be avoided by the candidates if they obtained more than the required number of signatures, so allowing the nomination to stand even if some of the signatures were found not to meet the strict statutory requirements.

THE NATIONAL ELECTION CAMPAIGN

By contrast with the position in the constituencies, as indicated above there are no legal limits on the amount that the parties – or other bodies – may spend on national election campaigns. In practice these are the most important and influential aspects of campaigns, especially in general elections.

As is well known the present position is that the money for national campaigns is provided from private sources and there is no public cash subsidy. The source of the money raised by the parties is largely institutional for the Conservatives and Labour, donations from companies and trade unions respectively. There is a view that donations from companies are unlawful as being *ultra vires* the company[8] but the point has not been decided. The Liberal Democrats rely very heavily on members' subscriptions, individual donations and fund-raising activities.

Trade unions may make donations to political parties only out of a political fund, and there has to be a ballot of trade union members every ten years on the question whether the union should have such a fund.[9] When this legislation was passed, the Conservative government expected the vote to go against political funds in some unions, but in practice these votes have been overwhelmingly in favour of political funds. There is an argument that, in order for the law to be even-handed between the parties, companies should be under a similar obligation to ballot their shareholders about using funds for political purposes.[10] We shall return to this approach to the regulation of campaign expenditure shortly.

There has been public concern about these sources of finance and their effect on the policies of the parties. It is suggested from time to time that the Labour and Conservative Parties are beholden to their financiers in such a way that they may feel under pressure to pursue policies favourable to them. This was the basis of the Conservative poster campaign 'Who runs Labour?' in the autumn of 1991. And the Conservatives laid themselves open to a great deal of criticism in late 1991 when there were reports of large donations to party funds from foreign businessmen and various suspect sources. The present system certainly does not look good from this point of view.

Respondents in the MORI State of the Nation poll were asked whether they thought there should be prohibitions on contributions from trade unions and companies to political parties. Forty-six per cent thought contributions from trade unions should be banned, 44 per cent contributions from companies. Forty-three per cent and 45 per cent respectively thought they should not be banned. Although opinion on the subject is fairly evenly divided, these figures do indicate considerable public unease about the system.

As indicated earlier, overall the amount of money spent by the parties on election campaigns in the UK is modest, and there is as yet no trend towards increasing the amount spent in real terms in national campaigns. In 1991 the Conservatives were reported to be trying to raise £20 million for the forthcoming campaign, but with an accumulated deficit of £12 million they were experiencing difficulty in doing so. One difficulty in looking at the amounts spent is that the parties' accounts are not uniform in their presentation and do not make it easy to identify election campaign expenditure with great accuracy or to compare like with like. But according to figures obtained by Pinto-Duschinsky[11] the Conservatives spent more on elections in 1935 and 1964 in real terms than they did in 1987; Labour spent more in 1987 than ever before, but the second largest sum was spent in 1964, the third largest in 1970.

Most criticisms of the present position focus on the substantial disparities between the amounts spent by the Conservatives, Labour and other parties (the Liberals, the SDP, now the Liberal Democrats, and the Greens, and SNP and Plaid Cymru). Again it is difficult to obtain accurate information, especially since the exercise of separating campaign from other expenditure is artificial: in practice the election campaign is fought for many months before the election is announced. But subject to these important reservations, we can get some indication of the scale of party expenditure and the disparity between the parties in the 1987 general election from Pinto-Duschinsky's figures: on these the Conservatives spent some £9 million on the national campaign, Labour £4 million, and the Alliance in the region of £1.1 million. The ratio between these three parties on these figures was approximately 9 : 4 : 1.

In recent elections the parties have spent large sums on advertising in the press, through leaflets and on posters. In the 1987 election, out of the total spent Pinto-Duschinsky estimates that the Conservatives spent £6.4 million and Labour £2.1 million on these forms of advertising.[12] Butler and Kavanagh estimate that the Conservatives spent £3.6 million on press advertising in the election campaign in 1987, while Labour spent £1.6 million and the Alliance £0.4 million.[13] The ratio was in the region of 7 : 3 : 1.

On the face of it there is, again, a large imbalance between the parties here which may be regarded as 'unfair' to the smaller parties in particular. But it should be pointed out that there is very little firm evidence to suggest that money spent by the parties on posters and newspaper advertisements affects the support for the party; the money spent may in fact be wasted in that respect. Or it may stimulate support for other parties if it strikes voters as unfair or objectionable. This point about the impact of political posters is illustrated by the findings of a MORI poll in 1983: by the day of the election 46 per cent said that they had not seen any political advertisements on hoardings. Only some 35 per cent of respondents had seen any political advertisements on hoardings which they remembered as being Conservative, 34 per cent had seen what they recollected as a Labour advertisement, and 27 per cent an Alliance advertisement.

The MORI poll of 1991 found that 81 per cent of respondents thought that there should be a set limit to the amount of money that political parties can spend on campaigning during general elections. It is not clear whether this response reflected dissatisfaction with the level of expenditure in election campaigns, or with the imbalance between the parties. My guess would be that the response reflects the latter concern. It may also reflect concern about the sources of finance, discussed above.

Is the law's 'hands off' approach to expenditure in national election campaigns appropriate in current conditions? The disadvantage most commonly invoked is that the system is 'unfair' to the smaller parties, and indeed to Labour, which has smaller resources at its disposal than the Conservatives, despite the fact that its support may sometimes be greater, and sometimes not far off that of the Conservatives: in sum this aspect of the objection to the present system is that the level of finances available to the two main parties does not bear much relation to the level of their support and that this is 'unfair'. The implication is either that their expenditure ought to be restricted so that the disparity between them is reduced, or that they should receive a public subsidy, again in order to reduce the disparity.

Restrictions on expenditure on election campaigns would, on balance, have adverse consequences. Even if it does not increase the support for the party, or even if it does increase support, but 'unfairly', campaigning may well have substantial beneficial effects which outweigh any disadvantages in terms of fairness. It may influence turn-out in elections by raising the profile and temperature of the political debate: in this respect the more that is spent the better from the point of view of the general public. It may also sharpen the terms of the debate that takes place between the parties and the electorate at election time, and this in my view is beneficial. In effect it is an opportunity for those who advertise to challenge the other contenders to counter the claims made in the poster or advertisement. And finally, it would be easy for restrictions on expenditure to be circumvented, for example by sympathetic campaigning by outside groups.

ASSISTANCE IN KIND IN ELECTION CAMPAIGNS

So far our discussion has focused on expenditure by the parties in election campaigns. But it is unrealistic to regard this as the sole measure of resources devoted to the system. The scale of the legal provision for the giving of assistance in kind to parties at election time is not widely appreciated. Pinto-Duschinsky has estimated that free postage and the free use of halls for election meetings in the constituencies were worth £0.7 million to each party fielding a candidate in every constituency in the 1987 election. But this contribution pales into relative insignificance against the value of free television time for party election broadcasts. In the 1987 election campaign this was worth some £7 million to each of the three main contestants; taking TV time in the run-up to the election, the value was some £12.5 million to each of these parties.[14] In addition the fact that the broadcasting companies give news coverage to the parties in the same proportion as the allocation of party election broadcasts gives a considerable benefit to the main contenders. Although a price or precise value cannot be put on this it should be regarded as a substantial benefit in kind to the parties and taken into account in estimating the extent of the imbalance between the parties in election campaigns.

The value of assistance in kind puts the amounts of money raised and spent by the parties from private sources into proportion. If we add in the value of benefits in kind of £7.7 million to each of the three main parties the ratio of election expenditure between the three main parties was 17 : 12 : 9 in 1987. Clearly there is a large imbalance between the parties but it is not as acute as is sometimes believed.

The allocation of assistance in kind in the form of free post and the use of halls for election meetings is the same to each candidate. The amount of free television time is not the same for each party. The arrangements for awarding party election broadcasts are purely informal: theoretically the Committee on Political Broadcasting, chaired by the prime minister and including representatives of the major parties and management of the BBC and the IBA, allocates time on the basis of criteria which are agreed but not published. These take account of support for the parties in the previous election and the number of candidates fielded (50 is regarded as the qualifying number nationally). Until 1983, in effect the two main parties carved up the system to their own advantage, and the smaller parties had little influence. But the Committee on Political Broadcasting did not make the decisions in the 1983 and 1987 elections because the parties were unable to agree, and the BBC and IBA made their own allocations. In 1987 they treated Labour, the Conservatives and the Alliance equally and awarded the SNP two election broadcasts in Scotland compared to the five each allowed to the other parties. This formula was reached after informal soundings and consultation between the broadcasters and the whips out of which the equal treatment emerged as commanding general consent. But it is, of course, possible that smaller parties would be excluded by such a 'system'. The consent of the large parties does not necessarily mean that a particular allocation of time is appropriate. There must surely be a case for formalizing this process and publishing the criteria.

'FAIRNESS' IN ELECTION CAMPAIGNS

The point has been made on a number of occasions in the discussion so far that the distribution of resources for election campaigns is alleged to be 'unfair' as between the parties. The fact that the Conservatives have more money to spend in election campaigns than Labour and other parties, the fact that trade unions have to ballot members about political funds whereas companies do not have to ballot shareholders about company donations to political parties, the fact that party election broadcasts do not give 'fair' time or any time at all to smaller parties – all of these points may be cited as instances of 'unfairness' in the system.

But there are major difficulties in deciding exactly what is fair or what guidelines should be applied in making 'fair' allocations, whether of time, money or other resources. This is illustrated by the following questions. Would equality in the allocation of money or TV time between all parties be fair? Or if fair, would the desirability of fairness between the parties be outweighed by other considerations, such as acceptability to public opinion or the need to husband public money? If equality of treatment of all parties is not fair, which parties should be excluded entirely from the quest for fairness, and on what criteria? Should some parties receive less than others? If so, how should allocations be fixed? Should resources be allocated according to support in the previous election, or in recent opinion polls? Would the alternative of matching privately raised funds with public funds be 'fair' given that some parties have access to more in the way of private funds than others? Should subscription income dictate what public funds are awarded? Would it matter that some parties tended to have poorer subscribers than others?

The feeling that the system is unfair has produced a range of proposals for reform, but, as the questions posed above imply, many of them cause more problems than they solve. One way of dealing with the imbalance of resources between the parties would be to limit the amount that the parties are allowed to expend on their national campaigns. This would mean that parties unable to raise large sums of money would be at less of a disadvantage as compared with others than under the present regime. Although this solution had considerable support in the 1991 MORI poll, it presents a number of problems. At present parties are not legally recognized and there is no requirement for them to register or organize themselves in a particular way. So the question would arise, what bodies are to be bound by a limit on the amount that may be spent in national election campaigns? If parties had to register and were then bound by restrictions, these could easily be circumvented by campaigning groups, companies, unions, the press spending money on publicity encouraging people to support a particular *party* or an idea or set of ideas rather than a candidate or candidates, something which is not currently regulated or prohibited. Indeed, almost any attempt simply to restrict expenditure by parties would be open to this sort of circumvention.

A way of avoiding this would be for sympathetic campaigning by other organizations during election campaigns also to be banned. At present this is not covered by the RPA prohibition on the promotion of candidates. In the *Tronoh Mines* case[15] a company inserted an advertisement in a national newspaper criticizing the Labour Party for its proposal to introduce a scheme of dividend restraint and calling for the election of 'a new and strong government' with policies more acceptable to the company. It was held that this was not a breach of what is now section 75 of the RPA since it was not expenditure to promote a particular candidate in a particular constituency. General political propaganda is not covered by the section, even if it incidentally had the effect of assisting a particular candidate among others. To seek to limit the freedom of other bodies to advertise or campaign for a party or a set of ideas would be a substantial inroad into freedom of speech and political activity and would, incidentally, be contrary to the European Convention on Human Rights. There are, in sum, formidable technical and practical problems and major issues of principle in limiting election expenditure by parties at national level.[16]

Another solution to the problem of unfairness as between the parties would be for political donations from companies and trade unions to be banned, thus making all parties dependent on fund-raising events, individual subscriptions and so on and effectively narrowing the gap between the two main parties and the others. As indicated above, public opinion is split on this issue. But such a rule would not produce equality between the parties. Some parties have wealthier members than others and can raise larger subscriptions. And, as with a limitation on party expenditure, a ban of this kind could easily be circumvented by companies and trade unions themselves advertising and rallying support for a party. To ban this would again be a substantial inroad into free speech and freedom of political activity.

Other ways of discouraging reliance on these sources might be worth considering, for example requiring companies to ballot shareholders before making political contributions or spending money on political advertising. Some companies already do this. My own view is that there is much to be said for this sort of requirement, but not in order to make for fairness between the parties so much as to protect the shareholders from having their money spent on causes which they oppose, just as the political fund ballots in unions are to protect members from having their funds spent in a way that they would not wish. In many respects, however, trade union members and shareholders are not in equivalent positions, and the scale of donations to Labour and the Conservatives respectively and the influence of unions and companies in the two parties are very different. The arguments for changing the position of shareholders based on 'fairness' between the parties as opposed to fairness to union members and company shareholders assume more of a parallel than exists in reality.[17]

The obvious result of either restricting expenditure or banning institutional donations would be that less money would be spent on election campaigns overall. They would therefore probably have a much reduced impact and be more low key than at present, and this would have disadvantages in reducing public interest in the campaign, and therefore possibly reducing turnout. It is for these reasons that I would not favour restricting expenditure or banning institutional support as solutions to the 'problem'.

A third solution would be to provide public funds to some or all of the political parties specifically for election campaigns. Proposals for public funding were made by the Houghton Committee in 1976[18] and the Hansard Society in 1981,[19] but these proposals have not found favour with governments since then. At present both Labour and the Liberal Democrats are committed to some form of public funding for parties. The MORI poll found that only 39 per cent of respondents thought that a fixed amount of public money should be given to political parties to finance election campaigns.

There is not the space here to look into the arguments for and against public funding in principle, but if it were to be provided it is clear that difficult questions about fairness would arise. As far as the amount that should be paid to parties from public funds is concerned, it is far from clear what formula could be devised to produce an allocation that was 'fair' to the parties. Amounts could be geared to the votes and/or seats won at the previous general election as is the case with 'Short money' for parliamentary activity. However, the purpose of 'Short money' is not to secure fairness between the parties in Parliament but to enable the opposition parties to perform their functions of opposing the government effectively.

An allocation of public funds for election campaigns on the basis of previous election results would tend to institutionalize the present party balance by offering no help to new entrants in the political race, like the SDP in the 1983 election or the Greens. Is this 'fair'? It would clearly be beneficial to the established parties and for that reason it might command support in Parliament if the matter came to be debated, but the fact that a measure which would benefit them has the support of the two main parties is seldom to be taken to indicate that it is fair to other parties or in any other respect desirable.

An alternative approach would be to make a sum available for each candidate fielded, or to find a formula linking votes won at the previous election, performance in opinion polls and the number of candidates fielded. Smaller parties who could ill afford lost deposits would, however, lose out here again and feel that it was not a fair system.

Yet another approach would be to extend the provision of assistance 'in kind', through, for example, extending rights to radio and television time, advertising in the press, and on hoardings, the free delivery of further election addresses, use of the telephone and so on. Again difficulties could arise over giving what could be valuable assistance in kind to parties with no serious or substantial support. The same difficulties in allocating such benefits 'fairly' would arise as in the options discussed earlier.

These various difficulties raise the issue of whether 'fairness' can be achieved in the financing of election campaigns, and, even if it can, whether 'fairness between the parties' is what the system should be aiming for.

Ewing has urged that 'it is important to ensure that there is a fair distribution of the money that is available'[20] since, as Rawls argues 'a just constitution sets up a form of fair rivalry for political office and authority'.[21] Ewing's view is that this means that if the supply of money into the system does not lead to a situation of fair rivalry, it may be necessary to take steps to do so by law in order to prevent the potential domination of a particular candidate, a particular political party or a particular political ideology. Having considered the differing financial fortunes of the three main parties he suggests that it is wrong that the fortunes of a party or movement such as the Alliance in the 1983 election should be hindered or frustrated simply because it has been unable to attract institutional investors on any substantial scale.[22]

Ewing proposes to secure fairness in elections through, among other things, the publication of party accounts, public funding of parties, extending spending limits to the national campaigns, possible banning of expenditure on election campaigns by other bodies if they exploited the limits on party expenditure, and some kind of mechanism to redress the balance in press coverage, possibly through public funding of the press.

Although I agree about the desirability of preventing a particular candidate, party or political ideology from dominating an election, and about the defects in the system as it operated for the Alliance in 1983, my reasons for doing so are different from those advanced by Ewing. As far as the Alliance is concerned its main problem was the electoral system which denied its voters the opportunity to elect their preferred candidate. Even with many millions of pounds to fight that election it would not have won many more seats.

I do not accept the assumption in Ewing's argument that we should be concerned about fairness to and the fortunes of a party or movement as such; my concern is with the fortunes of the electors and the community, and it seems to me that this is the consideration that should determine our attitude to political finance. As the earlier discussion of possible ways of dealing with the imbalance of resources between the parties indicates, 'fairness' to the parties in election campaigns in any concrete sense is a chimera, a will o' the wisp. In any event, in my view the parties should not be regarded as having interests of their own requiring protection and promotion by the law save to the extent that those interests promote the general public interest in accountable and effective government and a mature citizenry.

WHY DOES THE FINANCING OF ELECTION CAMPAIGNS MATTER?

We have to ask ourselves a fundamental question if we are to reach a conclusion on this issue. What are election campaigns for? Only if we have some notion of the answers (there may be more than one) to this question can we make rational judgements about such matters as their financing.

My answer to that question is that the purpose of election campaigns is to provide information to enable voters to make informed choices about who should represent them in the next Parliament or, in the case of local or European elections, for the next term of those institutions. If we take this as our starting point in the discussion of the financing of election campaigns the rules ought to be geared to enable voters to cast their votes on the basis of full information about the parties and their candidates. Set against this vital role of elections, arguments about 'fairness to parties' seem quite inappropriate. Why should the State have, as Ewing suggests, a role to underwrite more equitable rivalry, except to the extent that it enables voters to make more informed choices? It may be that provisions that enable voters to make informed choices produce some sort of 'fairness' between parties, but to the extent that this is so it seems to me that it can only be regarded as a 'spin-off', desirable from the point of view of the parties, of measures that are justified for quite other reasons.

What aspects of the present system inhibit the making of informed choices about parties, policies and candidates at election time? Of course the absence of public rights of access to official information contributes to the problem, but this is not my main concern in this chapter. Voters need information not only about what each party would do if elected, but about what criticisms the other parties make of those policies, how parties respond to those criticisms, what alternatives are being advocated and what the pros and cons of those are, and how party leaders respond to criticism and pressure and behave in debate. The problems experienced by some, less well-funded parties in putting their views to the electorate and, most importantly, to the other parties in contention, and challenging them to respond, effectively restricts this sort of information.

Another problem is the fact that the public is not aware of where the parties' money comes from and to whom they may be beholden, and this is a strong argument for requiring the parties to publish their accounts in a form that would enable voters to make comparisons between the parties and identify major institutional donors.

These points are part of a larger problem. There is in my view a considerable problem in British politics of unresponsiveness on the part of the two main parties to new ideas and to public opinion and at the same time insufficiently rigorous scrutiny of new ideas. This contributes to the unadaptability of the system at many levels – economic, social, political. The whole system suffers from an inability to adjust not just to new ideas but also to new realities.[23]

The ability of the two main parties to raise far more money than others and to run more high-profile election campaigns as a result produces a singularly two-dimensional, even, at times of political consensus, one-dimensional, view of policy possibilities. The two main parties either agree or disagree with one another. That is all that they can do. What is needed is for other approaches and solutions to be aired – after all, there are likely to be more than two approaches and two possible solutions to any problem. By way of example, in the debate about the alternative to the community charge (poll tax) that took place from December 1990 to the summer of 1991 the two main parties rapidly fixed upon a property tax; although each party had different views on points of detail, there was in effect little difference between them in principle. The Liberal Democrats' proposal for a local income tax was ruled off the agenda by the two other parties, notwithstanding the fact that it is not a self-evidently wrongheaded alternative and indeed has many points in its favour.

If a wider range of approaches and solutions is to be discussed in an election campaign, then other parties (and other organizations) must have access to the public at that time, and that costs money. The introduction of new dimensions to policy issues is what the SDP, the Greens, the Liberal Democrats and the nationalist parties have achieved in the last few years. I think it is clear that these parties have had quite profound influence on public opinion and on the policies and the styles of the two main parties, for example in the areas of environmental policy and constitutional reform – decentralization, proportional representation, reform of the second chamber, citizenship, freedom of information. This raising of issues seems to me to be highly desirable in principle, and the scope for alternative policies to be put to the electorate and, very importantly, to be responded to by the main contenders in an election campaign ought to be encouraged in the interests of the public. This would not be achieved by reducing the resources available overall in election campaigns. It is not a question of 'fairness' to the parties but of the interests of the nation.

The need to broaden and open up political debate at election time must surely be a compelling argument for easing the access of parties to the public. This objective would not be furthered by imposing limits on the amount the parties may spend on election campaigns, and it is for this reason that I would oppose such a measure. Nor would the objective be furthered by banning other organization from participating in the policy debate, possibly by promoting other parties. Such a ban could damp down public debate. We ought to be looking at ways of easing and widening rather than reducing access to the voters. This could be achieved by making additional resources available to the parties, either by the provision of money, earmarked for election campaigns if need be, or of additional assistance 'in kind'. This, I suggest, is the approach we need to take to the financing of election campaigns.

CONCLUSION

I have considered only a narrow part of the wide subject of political finance in this chapter. But my conclusions about the reasons why it is important are equally relevant to other issues of principle that arise, such as methods of funding party activity in the policy-making and parliamentary sphere. I am not particularly concerned about fairness to the parties for the parties' sake, but rather about the public interest in having well-informed, well-considered decisions made by voters at election time, by MPs going through the lobbies and by ministers and opposition members at their desks.

NOTES AND REFERENCES

1 The authoritative works on this topic are: K. Ewing, *The Funding of Political Parties in Britain* (1987); H. F. Rawlings, *Law and the Electoral Process* (1988); and R. J. Clayton (ed.), *Parker's Conduct of Parliamentary Elections* (1990). See also: *Report of the Committee on Financial Aid to Political Parties* (the Houghton Report) (1976), Cmnd. 6601; and the report of the Hansard Society Commission upon the financing of political parties, *Paying for Politics* (1981).
2 Representation of the People (Variation of Limits of Candidates' Election Expenses) Order 1991 (S.I. 1991 951).
3 *Tronoh Mines case* [1952] 1 All ER 697.
4 MORI, *The State of the Nation* (1991).
5 Hansard Society Commission on Election Campaigns (the Chataway Commission), *Election Campaigns: Agenda for Change* (1991).
6 Home Office Memorandum, 1918 in HC 32-II, p. 14, quoted in H. F. Rawlings, *Law and the Electoral Process* (1988), p. 122.
7 H. F. Rawlings, *Law and the Electoral Process* (1988), pp. 122–124.
8 K. Ewing, *The Funding of Political Parties in Britain* (1987), Ch. 2.
9 Trade Union Act 1984, section 12.
10 See: Ewing, *The Funding of Political Parties*, p. 183.
11 M. Pinto-Duschinsky, 'Trends in British Party Funding 1983–1987', *Parliamentary Affairs*, **42** (1989), 197–212; see also submission to the Hansard Society Commission on Election Campaigns (1991), 'Fair election and party finance in Britain: is there a case for reform?'
12 M. Pinto-Duschinsky, 'Trends in British Party Funding', *Parliamentary Affairs*, **42** (1988), 197–212.
13 D. Butler and D. Kavanagh, *The British General Election of 1987* (1988), Table 8.4.
14 M. Pinto-Duschinsky, 'Fair Elections and Party Finance in Britain: Is There a Case for Reform?' Evidence to the Hansard Society Commission on Election Campaigns (1991).

15 [1952] 1 All ER 697.
16 For further discussion of this see: Hansard Society Commission on Election Campaigns, *Election Campaigns: Agenda for Change* (1991), paras 65–77.
17 See: M. Pinto-Duschinsky, 'Fair Elections and Party Finance in Britain: Is There a Case for Reform?', evidence to the Hansard Society Commission on Election Campaigns (1991).
18 *Report of the Committee on Financial Aid to Political Parties*, Cmd. 6601 (1976).
19 *Paying for Politics. The Report of the Commission upon the Financing of Political Parties* (1981).
20 Ewing, *The Funding of Political Parties*, p. 182.
21 J. Rawls, *A Theory of Justice* (1972), p. 227.
22 Ewing, *The Funding of Political Parties*, p. 184.
23 D. Marquand, *The Unprincipled Society* (1988).

9

Does Britain Need Proportional Representation?

PHILIP NORTON

Pressure for a new electoral system is not new. The Electoral Reform Society is a long-standing advocate of change. So too is the Liberal, now the Social and Liberal Democratic, Party. However, electoral reform has become more prominent on the agenda of political debate in recent years. The two general elections of 1974 provided a significant spur to reform. The attraction of change was notable among, but not exclusive to, those of the political centre and centre-right. The third successive Conservative victory in the general election of 1987 appeared to induce a new willingness on the part of many on the left to contemplate constitutional reform, encompassing *inter alia* a Bill of Rights and a new electoral system. Since the present system no longer appeared capable of offering what they expected of it, they were prepared to consider a different system. Support for change thus came to span the political spectrum. Those of the centre and left coalesced in 1988 with the formation of Charter '88.[1] By 1991, support for the introduction of a system of proportional representation (PR) appeared to be gaining in popular support. A MORI poll for the Rowntree Trust found that 50 per cent of respondents supported PR.[2] For proponents, it began to be seen as an idea whose time had come. My purpose in this chapter is to challenge the case for proportional representation in Britain. I propose to focus on the principal arguments advanced by proponents of change and also to consider the extent of popular support claimed for it. Before doing so, some preliminary observations are in order for the purposes of clarification.

The current debate is hindered rather than helped by the observation that Britain does not have a system of 'proportional representation' but that many other countries do. This is often compounded by the assumption that the systems of other countries are sufficiently similar to be considered as part of a coherent family group. This is most apparent in the discussion of elections to the European Parliament. The elections are often presented in dichotomized terms: the UK (except in Northern Ireland) does not employ PR, the other member states do. What is often overlooked is that there are many types of electoral systems (the number devised, mostly on paper, runs into hundreds). Other member states of the European Community do not have 'a' system of PR. They employ different systems. When advocates of PR point out that newly emerging democracies in Europe are employing PR systems, they fail to note that the systems being adopted are not necessarily the systems they favour for the UK. Even within the EC, only two member states (Ireland and Germany) employ electoral systems that find significant support among UK electoral reformers.

Furthermore, of the systems on offer, many are not – either in design or effect – strictly proportional. The use of thresholds (a party having to receive a stipulated percentage of votes to be eligible for parliamentary representation) and of multi-member constituencies at sub-national level produces distortions. Only three countries – Ireland, Malta and (for the Senate) Australia – use the single transferable vote (STV) method for national elections. Under STV, both Ireland and Malta have experienced elections in which one party has won a majority of seats with a minority of the votes cast. STV is the system most favoured by UK reformers. The argument is thus not as dichotomized, as starkly drawn, as reformers imply. The debate essentially is one of whether or not we want to replace our existing system with a more proportional one, and, if so, which of the electoral systems on offer is preferable. Few, if any, are problem-free. None which can offer precise proportionality (such as a national list system) is among those proffered by reformers.

WHAT WE EXPECT OF THE SYSTEM

Should the UK introduce one of the, often inaptly named, systems of PR? In answering, my starting point is not the electoral system itself. That has relevance only in the context of the British polity and what Britons expect of their system of government. What do they expect of it?

Society requires government, and in democratic countries electors look to government that derives from political authority. Political authority concerns the persisting and pervasive relationships between governors and governed and it rests on the twin pillars of effectiveness and consent. 'An organisation that cannot effectively influence the society around it is not', declares Richard Rose, 'a government. A government that acts without the consent of the governed is not a government as we like to think of it in the Western world'.[3] To be effective, a government has to be able to organize the complex maze of institutions that constitutes the modern state and to raise and allocate resources to meet its commitments of public policy. It is also essential that it maintain elite and popular support. As Rose notes, the two are clearly interrelated, for the success of public policy requires the co-operation of affected citizens.

British political culture has largely facilitated the maintenance of effectiveness and consent. That culture has favoured a strong executive but one bounded by, and accountable to, the political community. Over time, the executive has changed, from the monarch to a prime minister-in-cabinet; the political community has evolved, from a small elite to a mass electorate; as the concept of representation has gained currency, the method of selecting the executive has changed (from the hereditary principle to a method of indirect and partial election and now one of direct and partial election); but what has not changed has been the basic relationship between governors and governed. And central to that relationship has been, and remains, Parliament.

Parliament is the central mediating body between governors and governed, facilitating effectiveness by allowing government to govern (Parliament itself has never, on any continuous basis, been part of government) while at the same time maintaining consent by fulfilling, and being seen to fulfil, its essential role of representing to government the grievances of citizens, ensuring an adequate response to those grievances, and providing the bounds within which government may operate.

Parliament has played a vital, often not fully appreciated, balancing role. It is a complex role and it is a delicate one. If Parliament injects itself too much into the making of public policy, it risks jeopardizing effectiveness (making it difficult for government to govern); if it does not involve itself at all, it risks jeopardizing consent, appearing too much as a body for the 'rubber stamping' of measures emanating from government. At times, it has been difficult to sustain that balance, but overall it has achieved it. Recent years have demonstrated the capacity of Parliament to be more effective in that role than hitherto; and, indeed, the potential to move more towards the ideal inherent, but never realized in practice, in the Westminster model of government.[4]

Parliament remains the core institution in maintaining political authority and one (crucially, given its centrality) that has largely retained public support. The same MORI poll in 1991 that has been so heavily utilized by reformers found that 59 per cent of respondents believed that Parliament was doing a good job; less than 10 per cent deemed it to be doing a bad job. It was a finding in line with surveys of earlier decades.[5] And, within the context of citizen–Parliament relations, the representation of individual constituents has become even more central, occupying more time and receiving significant popular support.[6]

My opening contention, therefore, is that one should tread warily in contemplating any significant change that may threaten the maintenance of that essential and delicate balance between effectiveness and consent.

It is, I think, plausible to contend that our present electoral system *facilitates* the maintenance of this balance. I put it no higher than that. It is not a causal factor, given that this essential balance existed before the electoral system developed in the form that we now know it. But it facilitates that balance, allowing for a form of election, however imperfect, of the executive, while at the same time favouring – I use no stronger a term, since I accept that it is by no means certain to produce such a result – the return of a government with an overall majority.

Equally importantly, as Karl Popper has emphasized, reflecting another facet of consent, it provides a relatively effective means of removing a party from office. One party can be removed from office and replaced by another. Election day constitutes, in Popper's words, a Day of Judgement. 'A democracy needs parties that are more sensitive . . . and, if possible, constantly on the alert. Only in this way can they be induced to be self-critical. As things stand, an inclination to self-criticism after an electoral defeat is far more pronounced in countries with a two-party system than in those where there are several parties.'[7] One party is allowed to govern while being constantly aware that it may be turned out by the electors. The capacity to be turned out by the electors, clearly and by a popularly accepted process, is at the heart of Popper's theory of democracy.

I concur with Popper's argument. This is not to assert that Britain has a perfect system. It is, however, to assert a prima-facie case for the present system. If it is to be changed, it is incumbent upon those who wish to change it to demonstrate, clearly and unequivocally, (1) that change is necessary and (2) that, in the context of this argument, a system based on PR (or near-PR) is the form of change that is desirable. To demonstrate that the present system is unacceptable is not to prove that an electoral system based on PR is necessarily what should replace it. This is a point often missed by reformers. Their argument tends to be 'the present system is wrong, therefore we need PR', whereas the logical sequence of argument should be 'our present system is wrong, we need change, that change might be a system of PR'. It is always possible to argue that some change other than PR is desirable.

The case the reformers need to argue is more complex than is perhaps realized, and it is up to those who advocate change, especially a particular type of change, to prove their case. That case is not proven.

Indeed, my contention is that it is flawed and threatens the maintenance of effectiveness and consent. I cannot prove that beyond a reasonable doubt. I do not need to. It is sufficient for my purposes to demonstrate that the threat is clearly there, to an extent that makes the introduction of a new electoral system potentially dangerous to the health of the body politic.

Let me concentrate on the case for PR. As will be clear from the foregoing, I believe it fails on two grounds: first, that the arguments it advances are inherently flawed and, second, that it threatens the twin pillars of effectiveness and consent on which rest the edifice of our political system. Without those pillars, the system lacks stability. Let me demonstrate both points by dealing with the principal arguments advanced by proponents of PR: that it would produce a fairer electoral system and that it would put an end to 'adversary politics', and hence policy discontinuity, in British political life.

A FAIRER SYSTEM?

Would the introduction of PR provide a more equitable and just electoral system? Though this is the stronger of the two arguments, the answer nonetheless is 'not necessarily'.

The contention that our present plurality, first-past-the-post system is unfair and that a PR system is fair is not sustainable. This is not to deny that there are problems with our present system. What it is to deny is that the introduction of a system of PR would be unquestionably fair. PR systems have features and consequences that are not necessarily equitable and just. How unfair they are will vary depending upon the system and the polity in which it exists. What we have to discuss, therefore, is not a choice between a palpably unfair and a palpably fair electoral system but a choice between systems with their own elements of unfairness.

A PR system may produce fairness at the individual level of electing an MP but not necessarily at the aggregate level of choosing a government. By this, I mean that an individual's vote would count in electing the MP – or MPs – of that individual's choice (though the difference between no effect and contributing towards the election of one's third or fourth choice may not be considered overwhelming), but the problem arises in selecting the government. If (and it can only be an if) present voting patterns were to be maintained under a new electoral system, then no party would be returned with an overall majority of seats. The result would either be a minority single-party government or a coalition government. Minority governments offer the prospect of instability and, likely but not certainly, short periods in office. Coalition government offers the possibility of two significant unfairnesses.

Firstly, unless the parties have made clear at an election what other parties they would join with in government and on what terms, then a coalition government will result from post-election horse-trading. The result is a government that has received no definitive support in the polling booths. If party A, contesting the election alone on a particular manifesto, wins 40 per cent of the votes cast, and party B, contesting the election on the same basis, wins 20 per cent, and the two parties agree – after the results are in – to form a coalition on the basis of policies cobbled together quickly, does that new government ($a + b$) nonetheless enjoy the support of 60 per cent (40 + 20 per cent) of the voters? It does not. Forty per cent of voters voted for party A, 20 per cent for party B, and 0 per cent for A + B. Hence, rather than enhancing consent for the political system – by producing a fairer, more legitimate electoral system – PR could actually jeopardize the very consent that reformers crave.

There is an allied problem, deriving from Popper's theory of democracy. A coalition may produce irresponsibility in terms of electoral accountability. If two or more parties form a coalition, one may be identified more closely with a particular policy than another. Indeed, one may distance itself from the rest. Which parties can the electorate hold responsible for past coalition actions?

Our own history provides an occasional brief glimpse of what could be the rule rather than the exception. The minority Labour government of James Callaghan (1976–1979) demonstrated a capacity for survival, but little else.[8] It led a hand-to-mouth existence in terms of getting measures passed and, to survive a confidence vote in 1977, agreed to a pact with the parliamentary Liberal Party.[9] The measures agreed by the two sides constituted no coherent programme and did not necessarily enjoy the support of the two parliamentary parties. The government proved unable to deliver majorities for the introduction of a system of PR for direct elections to the European Parliament and to the proposed Scottish and Welsh Assemblies. (There was a majority of 183 against PR for the Scottish Assembly and one of 97 against PR for the European Parliament.) The pact was unpopular with the Tribune Group of Labour MPs and with a substantial number of Liberal Party activists and was brought to an end in 1978. There was no one body at the subsequent general election that electors could hold responsible for the policies of that particular period.

Secondly, the absence of an overall majority for any one party would place a premium on the support of one or more parties holding the balance of power. Hence, there is the potential for a third party, possibly one of the smallest, being in government on an almost indefinite basis. The Free Democrats in West Germany are frequently, and justifiably, offered as a good example. Though they have at times had difficulty in achieving much in excess of the 5 per cent threshold of votes cast, they have held cabinet posts for all but four years since the West German constitution was approved.

Instead of a system that favours disproportionately the largest single party, one has instead a system that favours disproportionately one of the smaller parties. Where is the fairness in that? Our plural system may not be unambiguously fair, but it is questionable whether a system based on PR would necessarily, or to any great extent, be fairer.

AN END TO 'ADVERSARY POLITICS'?

The second principal argument advanced by proponents of PR is that it would rid us of adversary politics, the product of a two-party battle for the all-or-nothing spoils of a general election victory, and the intrinsic feature of adversarianism: policy discontinuity.[10]

This argument derives from a number of assumptions: first, and most apparent, that the electoral system encourages adversary politics, one party coming into office and reversing the policies of its predecessors; second, that there is a consensual, or centrist, electorate in Britain, the views of electors grouping round the centre of the ideological spectrum; and third, that a centre-coalition government would result from the introduction of PR, capable of ensuring continuity in public policy.

All three assumptions are open to question. It is doubtful whether we have adversary politics in substance, as opposed to rhetoric. The language of politics is, indeed, adversarial and sometimes strident, exemplified by prime minister's question time in the House of Commons. However, the substance tends to be consensual rather than adversarial. Parliament proceeds on the basis of a degree of consensus between the parties; without it, parliamentary business would largely grind to a halt. Most bills are passed without a division. Of those that are contested on second reading, many cannot be classified as adversary bills in a manner analogous to money bills (in other words, exclusively adversary in nature); one study of bills in the 1970 and 1985 sessions found that only one in seven (12 out of 87) could be classified as controversial.[11]

The most significant study undertaken on the subject, that by Richard Rose in *Do Parties Make a Difference?*, concluded that the most appropriate model was not that of adversary politics but rather what Rose termed a moving consensus.[12] One party comes into office, absorbs much of what its predecessor has done (policy reversals are the exception rather than the norm) and then shapes a new political agenda, that agenda influencing the opponent party. Even with the radicalism of the Thatcher government returned in 1979, there were significant continuities, the rhetoric increasingly exceeding the substance of policy changes. Cash limits and monetarism do not have their roots in a Conservative government.

This is not to deny that there are significant shifts and discontinuities in public policy. Some are the product of a new party entering office, as indeed is variously the case with new governments returned to office under PR systems. But the most significant are the product of external pressures, governments having to respond to international, economic, military or environmental crises. And the capacity of political parties to affect economic trends, as Rose found, is limited. They can make some difference, but not a great deal – a finding recently reinforced by the PSI study *Britain in 2010*. The effect of market or interventionist policies on economic performance, particularly on economic growth as measured by gross domestic product, 'does not seem likely to be as great as is commonly supposed'.[13] There is little empirical evidence to bear out one of the principal assumptions made by the reformers. What *Adversary Politics and Electoral Reform* offers us, in the British context, is essentially a hollow model.

This is borne out when we consider another of the assumptions: that there is a politically centrist electorate. The electorate tends to penalize divided and extreme parties but there is little evidence that it is centrist on particular issues. Reformers confuse the ideological centre with the electoral centre. The two are different and do not always coincide. On some issues, a plurality of electors veer to the left (support for a national health service, for example), on others to the right (capital punishment, immigration).[14] Appearances to the contrary notwithstanding, government and Parliament will be more centrist on some issues than the electorate, especially in recognizing and abiding by rules of due process.

Furthermore, the argument advanced by reformers is based, in part, on a false premise: namely, that issues are amenable to some consensual, or compromise, solution. Many issues are not. Policy-makers are faced with mutually exclusive options. You either have the death penalty or you do not. Attempts at a compromise in the 1950s (retaining the death penalty for particular categories of murder) proved largely untenable and for anyone opposed in principle to the death penalty were not acceptable. There is no *via media*: you cannot half-hang someone. Similarly with nuclear weapons: either you retain them or you do not.[15]

The final assumption – that there would be a centre-coalition government capable of ensuring policy continuity – is also contestable. A government, regardless of its structure and composition, can be blown off course by external pressures. That is borne out by experience elsewhere. Nor is there any guarantee that a centre-coalition government would be Britain's lot. It is one of several possible outcomes under a new electoral system. The others, assuming no major shifts in voting behaviour, would be minority government or weak coalition government.[16] Neither would necessarily be conducive to maintaining, let alone enhancing, effectiveness and consent. And even the prospect of a centre-coalition government in office for the foreseeable future (necessary for the purposes of ensuring policy continuity) is not obviously an uncontested benefit. It produces a second party that is likely to enjoy the status almost of a permanent 'out' party. Prolonged exclusion from government, especially if the party enjoys substantial support, may undermine consent and generate tensions in the political system. Indeed, the tensions seen as being generated by our present system – excluding a third party enjoying in the region of 20 per cent of the national poll and, for more than a decade now, the second largest party – would be exacerbated under the situation that reformers posit as the ideal.

We thus have a thesis which, stripped to its essentials, does not carry the weight claimed for it. It is largely unsubstantiated and, indeed, in part contradictory. We are told, as we have seen, that the ideal would be to have a centre-coalition government capable of ensuring policy continuity. We are also told that PR (or certain types of PR systems – those proposed for the UK) would encourage more independent parliamentarians, free of the rigid party constraints that are ascribed to our existing party system. 'Distinguished independents have a much better chance of election.'[17] That itself is questionable. Much depends on the particular electoral system. But, if one accepts the proposition that it would have the effect claimed, how is one to square greater parliamentary independence with policy continuity? If MPs are to ensure continuity in policy, and vote accordingly, and consistently, how are they to demonstrate independence of government? The conundrum is, admittedly, an academic one, for the most likely outcome is high party cohesion (not independence), with MPs having to vote together in order to support the policies agreed by their leaders in consultation with the other parties to the coalition. Party cohesion is a feature of countries employing the PR systems favoured by UK reformers. In the German Bundestag, that cohesion is not only strong but getting stronger, the government since 1970 suffering far fewer defeats at the hands of parliamentarians than the government in the UK.[18] So much for the potential of 'distinguished independents'.

The case advanced for PR is thus flawed, derived as it is from false assumptions and, in part, sloppy reasoning. It is also dangerous. It raises expectations that cannot be met. There will not be a revitalization of the political system, with a more independent Parliament and enhanced consent. The reality will not match the expectations raised and, as such, will constitute a significant threat to support for the political system.

It is, as I outlined at the beginning, incumbent on the proponents of change to make a case for change, and to put the case for change beyond any reasonable doubt. In terms of the substance of the argument, they have clearly failed. But what of the support for change? Regardless of the merits of the case, has not the electorate been won over to the need for change? Again, the position is not quite what the reformers pretend.

AN IDEA WHOSE TIME HAS COME?

The case for PR has, it is claimed, gained ground, to the point where it now enjoys popular support. When questioned about demanding PR as the price of support in a hung Parliament, even though PR was not supported by the two main parties, SLD leader Paddy Ashdown claimed that the demand would have legitimacy because PR enjoyed popular support.[19] A MORI poll carried out in March 1991 found, as we have already noted, that 50 per cent of respondents supported the introduction of PR in Britain. In conjunction with larger majorities for other reforms, such as the introduction of a Bill of Rights, the findings were trumpeted by supporters of change – especially signatories of Charter '88 – as demonstrating clear support for a new constitution. 'Voters', declared Dunleavy and Weir, 'are fast becoming disillusioned with the monopolies of power produced by two-party politics'; there was, they claimed, a 'new public mood', with the survey demonstrating a loss of faith in the governing system.[20]

The rhetoric, again, does not quite match the reality. Only one in four respondents actually expressed a preference for coalition government. Although 50 per cent expressed a preference for PR, an almost identical proportion (49 per cent) expressed a preference for one party to gain an overall majority and form a government after the next election. And, perhaps most telling of all, responses to other questions demonstrated that support for PR is neither deep nor well-informed. Of the 50 per cent of respondents favouring PR, less than half (23 per cent) 'strongly supported' its introduction; the rest (27 per cent) 'tended to support' it. When asked how much they felt they knew about PR, only one in 20 (5 per cent) claimed they knew a 'great deal', and 25 per cent claimed they knew 'a fair amount'. Fifty-eight per cent of respondents knew 'just a little' or 'hardly anything at all'; 10 per cent admitted they had never heard of it.[21] In short, seven out of ten respondents know very little, if anything, about the subject. Given that some respondents may have wished to hide their ignorance, the proportion may be even higher. This is hardly a substantial base on which to rest a claim for legitimacy in demanding PR.

CONCLUSION

If a system of PR is introduced in the UK, it will come in on the basis of poor argument and ignorance. The case for change has not been made, other than at a fairly superficial level. Popular support exists on the basis of a general (and admitted) ignorance of the subject, with an absence of popular support for some of the likely consequences. The faults of the existing electoral system are not as great as critics claim, the attractions of PR not quite what they make them out to be.

Proponents of PR raise expectations that cannot be met. It is necessary for the health of the political system that their claims are challenged and exposed for what they are. Only then can the real problems – the substantive social and economic problems – facing Britain be addressed. PR is not a solution to those problems. It is a distraction.

NOTES AND REFERENCES

1 See: P. Norton, 'In Defence of the Constitution', in P. Norton (ed.), *New Directions in British Politics?* (Aldershot: Edward Elgar, 1991), pp. 146–153.
2 See especially: P. Dunleavy and S. Weir, 'Ignore the People at your Peril', *The Independent*, 25 April 1991.
3 R. Rose, 'Ungovernability: Is There Fire behind the Smoke?', *Political Studies*, 27 (1979), 353.
4 See: P. Norton, 'The Norton View', in D. Judge (ed.), *The Politics of Parliamentary Reform* (London: Heinemann, 1983), pp. 54–69; and P. Norton, *Parliament in Perspective* (Hull: Hull University Press, 1987).
5 See, e.g., Granada Television, *The State of the Nation* (Manchester: Granada TV, 1973), p. 201; and P. Kellner, 'Who Runs Britain?', *Sunday Times*, 18 September 1977.
6 See: B. Cain, J. Ferejohn and M. Fiorina, *The Personal Vote* (Cambridge, Mass.: Harvard University Press, 1987); J. W. Marsh, 'The House of Commons: Representational Changes', in P. Norton (ed.), *Parliament in the 1980s* (Oxford: Basil Blackwell, 1985), pp. 69–93; P. Norton, ' "Dear Minister . . ." The Importance of MP-to-Minister Correspondence', *Parliamentary Affairs*, 35 (1982), 59–72; and P. Norton and D. Wood, 'Constituency Service by Members of Parliament: Does It Contribute to a Personal Vote?' *Parliamentary Affairs*, 43 (1990), 196–208.
7 Sir K. Popper, 'The Open Society and its Enemies Revisited', *The Economist*, 23 April 1988, p. 28.
8 The 1974–1979 Labour government slipped into minority status in the House of

Commons in April 1976 following by-election losses and the defection of John Stonehouse.
9 See: A. Michie and S. Hoggart, *The Pact* (London: Quartet, 1978). See also: P. Norton, 'The Liberal Party in Parliament', in V. Bogdanor (ed.), *Liberal Party Politics* (Oxford: Oxford University Press, 1983), pp. 167–169.
10 The principal work advancing this thesis is S. E. Finer (ed.), *Adversary Politics and Electoral Reform* (London: Wigram, 1975).
11 Research undertaken by E. C. Page. See: P. Norton, 'Public Legislation', in M. Rush (ed.), *Parliament and Pressure Politics* (Oxford: Oxford University Press, 1990), p. 210, n. 11.
12 R. Rose, *Do Parties Make a Difference?*, 2nd edn (London: Macmillan, 1984).
13 J. Northcott *et al.*, *Britain in 2010: The PSI Report* (London: Policy Studies Institute, 1991), pp. 329–330.
14 See: I. Crewe and B. Sarlvik, 'Popular Attitudes and Electoral Strategy', in Z. Layton-Henry (ed.), *Conservative Party Politics* (London: Macmillan, 1980), pp. 244–275.
15 See: J. A. Chandler, 'The Plurality Vote: A Reappraisal', *Political Studies*, **30** (1982), 87–94.
16 P. Norton, *The Constitution in Flux* (Oxford: Basil Blackwell, 1982), pp. 239–240.
17 'Fair Voting is Safer', *ER Leaflet No. 40* (London: Electoral Reform Society, n.d.).
18 See: T. Saalfeld, 'The West German Bundestag after 40 Years: The Role of Parliament in a "Party Democracy" ', in P. Norton (ed.), *Parliaments in Western Europe* (London: Frank Cass, 1990), pp. 68–89, especially Table 1, p. 74, and, in the same volume, P. Norton, 'Parliament in the United Kingdom: Balancing Effectiveness and Consent', pp. 10–31.
19 BBC Television, 'On the Record', Sunday, 5 May 1991.
20 P. Dunleavy and S. Weir, 'Ignore the People at your Peril', *The Independent*, 25 April 1991.
21 *British Public Opinion*, **14** (1991), 7.

10

Judicial Independence in Britain: Challenges Real and Threats Imagined

GAVIN DREWRY

The existence of a judiciary that operates independently of and is protected against improper pressure by the executive is universally regarded in developed democracies as a bulwark of both representative government and the rule of law. This is certainly the case in Britain, notwithstanding the absence both of a codified separation of powers and of a Bill of Rights, and the tardy development of anything remotely resembling a developed system of administrative law. In an age of 'big government' and executive domination of the House of Commons (underpinned by an electoral system whose fairness is widely disputed), the courts seem to some people to offer the only possible check upon the excesses of elective dictatorship and of large-scale, imperfectly accountable public bureaucracies: this view has been implicit, and sometimes explicit, in the debate that has been rumbling on since the mid-1970s about whether Britain should either enact its own Bill of Rights or incorporate the European Convention on Human Rights into domestic law. It should be noted, however, that other observers take no comfort at all from the prospect of non-elected, non-accountable and socially unrepresentative judges – however 'independent' they may be – purporting to check the actions of elected politicians and their officials. The judicial process, according to this view, can never be a substitute for the political process.[1]

This chapter proceeds from the premise that an independent judiciary (the meaning of the term is considered below) is a goal worth fighting hard for; but it goes on to argue that there has in some quarters been a degree of over-zealousness, potentially detrimental to the credibility of the judges themselves, in protesting too much about imagined threats – threats which may reflect nothing more sinister than concern about securing adequate public accountability for increasingly expensive legal services, including those provided through the medium of the courts.

Judicial independence is such a familiar part of British vocabulary that for most of the time Britons probably give very little thought to it. It has melted into the landscape of political and constitutional discourse. However, discerning readers of British newspapers in the last year or two may have noticed that the phrase 'judicial independence' has recently enjoyed a much higher profile than that to which it has hitherto been accustomed. Recent events have also demonstrated a tendency to use the expression rhetorically, without sufficient thought to what it really means.

This was particularly evident in the aftermath of publication in January 1989 of the Lord Chancellor's three Green Papers on legal services and the legal professions – in particular the one entitled *The Work and Organisation of the Legal Profession*,[2] which proposed relaxing the barristers' long-established monopoly of advocacy in the higher courts, and introducing a new system for licensing advocates. A lay-dominated advisory committee (a reconstituted version of the Advisory Committee on Legal Education, now to become the Advisory Committee on Education and Conduct), would advise the Lord Chancellor 'on the education, qualifications and training of advocates appropriate for each of the various courts. The Lord Chancellor should be required to consult the judiciary before reaching decisions as a result of advice tendered by the Advisory Committee, although the final decision would be for him'.[3]

It confronted the cherished autonomy of the bodies representing the branches of the legal professions, thus:

> Professional bodies whose members wish to offer advisory and advocacy services will be required to submit their proposed codes of conduct for the endorsement of the Advisory Committee whose role it will be to ensure that such codes of conduct embody the approved principles . . . The Government proposes that the Lord Chancellor should prescribe by statutory instrument the principles which must be embodied in these codes . . . The Government is not prepared to leave it to the legal professions to settle the principles which these codes should adopt because they will be of great importance both to the administration of justice and to the public.[4]

Hereupon, many leading members of the Bar, and senior judges, went on record as saying, often in rather extravagant language, that all this posed a gross threat to judicial independence and the rule of law. In the Lords debate on the Green Papers,[5] the Lord Chief Justice, Lord

Lane, attacked the new advisory committee procedure as a movement towards executive control over the judiciary, adding for good measure: 'Oppression does not stand on the doorstep with a toothbrush moustache and a swastika armband'.[6] Lord Donaldson, Master of the Rolls, said that, if necessary, he would tell the government to 'Get your tanks off my lawn'.[7] Former Lord Chancellor, Lord Hailsham, said that he was 'shocked' by the prospective threat posed to judicial independence:

> It is proposed in the Green Paper that a member of the executive, advised by an advisory committee which is staffed secretarially by his own department and composed of a majority of persons unqualified in the law, shall be in command of the qualifications, the ethics and the statutory framework within which the right to practise is exercised. That same member of the executive is to be in command of the whole of that apparatus. Where are we going if that is to remain the case?[8]

Part of the answer to Lord Hailsham's rhetorical question is that we are going less far than was originally envisaged because the government watered down various aspects of its scheme in response to some of the objections raised. The clauses in the Courts and Legal Services Bill relating to rights of advocacy provided in effect that before final approval of the rules by the Lord Chancellor, the four most senior judges[9] must also give approval; but a schedule to the Bill said that any such 'designated judge' who declines to approve would be publicly identified, along with his reasons for dissenting;[10] in theory, this could render the judges' veto subject to judicial review in the courts. The judges remained less than satisfied with this and other aspects of the package, but the language of their opposition was much more muted than that used in the earlier debate on the Green Papers. Perhaps it was realized that judicial independence can more plausibly be defended if the judges themselves refrain from descending too noisily into the parliamentary arena.

The bemused observer, brought up in a culture where (in deference to the British model of judicial independence) judicial utterances are seldom contradicted save by other judges, was left wondering if the proposals in their original form really did pose such a serious threat to the constitutional order. Or was hyperbole of the kind just cited from judges and lawyers (and there is plenty more where that came from) simply a self-interested knee-jerk response on the part of an articulate professional pressure group which is very well represented, perhaps over-represented, in Parliament?[11]

At least two other examples come to mind where controversy has arisen over supposed threats to judicial independence. The first is a continuing saga about the management of magistrates' courts. The Justices' Clerks Society and the Magistrates' Association have expressed anxiety about the implications for the independence of magistrates posed by the Home Office's Scrutiny Report (the Le Vay Report) on Magistrates' Courts, published in 1989, which proposed setting up an independent management agency to improve efficiency.[12] Secondly, in a very different context, we have the continuing debate about sentencing policy – where the success of public policy requires co-operation from the judiciary, but where respect for judicial independence is considered to require that ministers express their views on the subject in oblique language. The Lord Chief Justice has strongly resisted any encroachment by the executive into areas hitherto regarded as a matter solely for the courts and has opposed the oft-mooted proposal for some kind of sentencing council. To quote Frances Gibbs: 'he has always resisted attempts by officials to draw him into discussion on [sentencing] policy; indeed he was recently reported to have left the room during a private Home Office seminar for those involved in the criminal justice system when sentencing came up.'[13] This is in rather striking contrast to the episode a few years ago when *Time Out* was the grateful recipient of a leaked memorandum relating to an interview between Lord Donaldson and the newly appointed permanent secretary to the Department of Employment, Michael Quinlan, who apparently wanted some advice about industrial law reform. The wrath of the establishment fell upon the leaker rather than upon the judge.[14] However, there is evidence in the archives of the Lord Chancellor's Department that suggests that this episode is far from unique.[15] It can of course be argued that this kind of dialogue between judges and administrators should be welcomed rather than condemned; but the judges cannot blame critics for commenting adversely upon episodes of this kind given that they themselves get so worked up about their independence from the executive. Moreover, present attitudes encourage judges and civil servants to converse covertly, even furtively, rather than openly – a fact which further inflames outsiders' suspicions.

What then is the meaning of this familiar phrase 'judicial independence', in defence of which so many strong words have been uttered?

JUDICIAL INDEPENDENCE

It must be noted at the outset that the notion of judicial independence is linked to other concepts, in particular those of impartiality and neutrality. We must be careful not to confuse them.

Independence has to do with the absence of improper external pressures and with the capacity of judges to resist such pressures without fear of penalty. Insofar as the concept is historically bound up with the constitutional doctrine of separation of powers (and several of the critics of the Mackay Green Papers expressly alluded to that doctrine) the 'improper pressures' referred to are principally those that may emanate from the executive and from Parliament. However, the realities of modern corporatist government demand a wider definition. To quote Simon Shetreet:

> Independence of the judiciary has normally been thought of as freedom from interference by the Executive or Legislature in the exercise of the judicial function . . . In modern times, with the steady growth of the corporate giants, it is of the utmost importance that the independence of the judiciary from business or corporate interests should also be secured. In short, independence of the judiciary implies not only that a judge should be free from governmental and political pressure and political entanglements but also that he should be removed from financial or business entanglements likely to affect, or rather *to seem to affect him* [see below], in the exercise of his judicial functions (my emphasis).[16]

Then we have the related, but quite distinct, concept of *impartiality* which, to quote John Bell, 'involves the judge listening to each side with equal attention, and coming to a decision on the argument, irrespective of his personal views about the litigants' – this being the essence of the phrase, 'equality before the law'.[17] *Neutrality* requires that 'whatever his personal beliefs, the judge should seek to give effect to the common values of the community, rather than any sectional system of values to which he may adhere'.[18] Bell goes on to note that, while there may be some connection between the ideas of impartiality and neutrality, 'there is no reason why the reputation of judges for being willing to listen to all sections of the community should necessarily depend on them adopting a politically neutral position'.[19]

At this point it should be noted that all these concepts have a subjective as well as an objective quality. It is crucial for the authority of the courts and for the legitimacy of the processes by which justice is administered, that people *believe* in the independence, the impartiality and the neutrality of judges. And it is in this subjective dimension of the topic that the boundaries between these logically quite different concepts are apt to become blurred. One can readily understand, for instance, how a perception – justified or not – on the part of, for example, trade unionists, ethnic minorities and women that the judicial process, operated almost exclusively by middle-class white males, is working in a partial way, and to their detriment, might also foster doubts about the claims of judges to being politically neutral.

This in turn may well encourage a belief that judges whose political neutrality is suspect *might* be less independent, in the sense of being immune from outside political influences, than they like to pretend. This muddying of definitional waters has been a feature of political rhetoric about judges; for instance, in the context of the debates in the early 1970s about the role of the Heath government's National Industrial Relations Court, and of the more recent controversies about the desirability or otherwise of introducing a Bill of Rights.

Meanwhile, the link between independence and impartiality is the basis of an interesting account of judicial independence, in W.A. Robson's pioneering *Justice and Administrative Law*. Robson starts from the premiss that impartiality is a fundamental prerequisite of justice. He then proceeds to argue that such impartiality requires an independent judiciary, noting that, in Britain, independence has come to be associated with security of tenure:

> Whether or not the decisions of a judge bring satisfaction or anger to the Prime Minister and his colleagues, or to the Lord Chancellor, he cannot be dismissed at will. His tenure is for life, or until retirement, subject only to good behaviour. His salary is fixed and paid out of the Consolidated Fund in order that it may not be subject to that running fire of criticism in Parliament to which all the ordinary items of budgetary expenditure are liable. His conduct cannot even be discussed in Parliament save on a substantive motion for an address for removal from office: an extreme step to be taken only in the event of impropriety of the gravest kind. The judiciary is, in effect, part of the public service of the Crown. But a judge is not 'employed' in the sense that a civil servant is employed. He fills a public office, which is by no means the same thing; and part of his independence consists in the fact that no one can give him orders as to the manner in which he is to perform his work.[20]

However, Robson also makes the important point that tenure is not a *logical* prerequisite of independence: 'judges might be appointed for a set term of years . . . and administrative officials might be appointed for life subject only to good behaviour, and no immediate change might be perceptible in the method of carrying out their duties'.[21] The importance of tenure for judicial independence is psychological: unlike the administrator, the judge

> can displease an indefinite number of persons an indefinite number of times without any personal consequences ensuing

to himself, providing only that he remains sane and does not commit one of those enormities which constitute misconduct . . . The independence of the judge is . . . of essential importance in so far as it enables the judge to adopt a particular attitude of mind towards the questions which come before him for decision. He can, in short, determine the case before him without fear that adverse results or material reward will accrue to him according to whether the decision does or does not meet with the approval of other persons.[22]

Writing more recently,[23] Rodney Brazier has suggested four prerequisites for judicial independence:

1 Judicial appointments and promotions should not be subject to uncontrolled ministerial patronage.
2 Judges should be free from improper attempts by ministers, MPs or peers to influence the results of cases still under adjudication.
3 Judicial salaries should not be reduced.
4 Judges should not be removed from office unfairly or without reason.

He goes on to argue that existing arrangements broadly satisfy the last three conditions – but he argues that there are serious problems with the first. His article is, in essence, a critique of the Lord Chancellor's exercise of patronage, of the secrecy surrounding the operation of the Lord Chancellor's Department and of the absence of satisfactory machinery to secure public accountability for legal services. Brazier calls for the creation of a new 'Department of Law' (thus carefully avoiding the provocative term 'Ministry of Justice').

THE OFFICE OF THE LORD CHANCELLOR

In theory the main custodian of judicial independence in England is that peculiar constitutional animal, the Lord Chancellor, who guards the frontier between government, the judiciary and Parliament, being himself a member of all three branches; a minister who presides, nowadays, over a large departmental empire of about 11,000 civil servants, with an annual budget that approaches £1 billion. In recent years, that empire has absorbed, and become increasingly absorbed by, the familiar watchwords of Thatcherite public administration: efficiency, effectiveness and economy; value for money; market forces; contracting out public services; Raynerism; the Financial Management Initiative, and so on. This, as we shall see, raises issues that are highly germane to the subject of this chapter.[24]

But meanwhile the Lord Chancellor remains, constitutionally, a member both of the executive and of the judiciary. And the supposed importance of retaining the Lord Chancellor's position as constitutional link-man between the two branches of government, in order to safeguard judicial independence, was stressed by Lord Chancellor Birkenhead, in an essay published in 1922:

> if they are totally severed there will disappear with them any controlling or suggestive force exterior to the Judges themselves, and it is difficult to believe that there is no necessity for the existence of such a personality, imbued on the one hand with legal ideas and habits of thought, and aware on the other of the problems which engage the attention of the executive government. In the absence of such a person the judiciary and the executive are likely enough to drift asunder to the point of a violent separation, followed by a still more violent and disastrous collision.[25]

Later Lord Schuster, the permanent secretary of the Department throughout the interwar years, was to refer in a departmental memorandum to the need for 'some link or buffer' between executive and judiciary;[26] later still, his successor, Sir Albert Napier,[27] used the metaphor of a constitutional 'hinge' to describe the Lord Chancellor's position. This remains the conventional wisdom of today: thus Sir Nicolas Browne-Wilkinson, Vice-Chancellor of the Supreme Court (and so destined, coincidentally, to become one of the four 'designated judges' of the Courts and Legal Services Bill), in a public lecture delivered at Lincoln's Inn in November 1987,[28] referred to the unique constitutional position of the Lord Chancellor as providing 'a flexible and efficient means to transmit the needs of the legal system to the executive and to Parliament'. Lord Mackay himself quoted the above passage from Lord Birkenhead's essay, with evident approval, in his recent Earl Grey Public Lecture.[29]

This takes us back to those debates on the 1989 Green Paper, 'tanks on the lawn', 'swastika armbands' and all that. A degree of creative tension between the different branches of government is arguably a healthy and inevitable feature of mature democracy, but this sort of language, directed by senior judges at the minister responsible for the judiciary, and himself a judge *ex officio*, suggests that the buffer may have broken, that the hinge badly needs oiling and that something may have gone wrong with Sir Nicolas Browne-Wilkinson's 'flexible and effective' means of transmission.

GAVIN DREWRY

THE LORD CHANCELLOR: PROBLEMS AT THE CONSTITUTIONAL VORTEX

The Lord Chancellor does have one advantage denied to his ministerial colleagues: he is required to be an expert in the main subject of his department's business. But his multiple role in superintending/appointing the judiciary, safeguarding its independence from executive interference, and answering to Parliament for the machinery of justice, entails a heroic piece of stagecraft, one which requires in turn a massive suspension of disbelief on the part of the spectator.

The main criticisms are well known. First, it has long been a matter for adverse comment that the Lord Chancellor does not sit in the Commons; the Attorney General (who has no power to command the officials of the Lord Chancellor's Department and has a job that is quite different from that of the Lord Chancellor) has until recently deputized for him. He acted 'as a courier between the Commons and the Lord Chancellor – and indeed as a courier who rarely brings any reply'.[30] Secondly, his relations with the judiciary are highly secretive, and the manner in which his powers of discipline, patronage and promotion are exercised has given rise to intermittent concern. Robert Stevens has culled some lurid episodes that bear upon this in his trawl of the files of the Lord Chancellor's Department, cited earlier.[31]

Let us pause to consider just one aspect of this: the removal of members of the higher judiciary on a formal address – something that has not actually happened since 1830.[32] Paterson and Bates have pointed out that no Scottish or English judge has ever actually been removed in modern times. Not, they rather cryptically suggest, 'because there have not been any unfit or incapable judges during that time' but because:

> The perceived importance of the separation of powers and the independence of the judiciary is such that successive Lord Chancellors and Lord Presidents have preferred to put pressure – sometimes very strong pressure – on judges to resign rather than to invoke more formal measures. Since 1890 there have been at least 15 instances where judges of the superior courts in the United Kingdom have been the subject of strong pressures or inducements to resign, ostensibly on the grounds of ill-health which they were reluctant to face up to or incapable of recognising.[33]

And, they go on:

> The problem with such an approach is not just the secrecy with which it is pursued but that it provides no overt support for the democratic principle that public officials who are entrusted

with considerable powers should be held accountable for the exercise of these powers.

There is a third area of difficulty, perhaps the trickiest of all. The Justice report on the Administration of the Courts (published in 1986 and considered more fully below) looked at the problem of how best to handle public complaints against judges. The report says that some members of the Committee believe that the increasing tendency for public authorities to be involved in litigation will make it 'increasingly difficult for the public to accept that judges are independent when the head of the judiciary, who is responsible for their behaviour, is also a leading member of the government'. One solution, they suggest, would be to restrict the role of the Lord Chancellor to being head of the judiciary and Speaker of the House of Lords – which 'would be a logical solution if as some have suggested, a Ministry of Justice is set up, with its departmental Minister in the House of Commons'. This possibility is tentatively mooted but the report stops short of making a positive recommendation along these lines.

THE SPECTRE OF EXECUTIVE CONTROL: DEBATE ABOUT A MINISTRY OF JUSTICE

Others have not been so reticent. Since the Haldane Report on the Machinery of Government in 1918[34] there have been various proposals from various sources for a rejigging of ministerial responsibilities for the machinery of justice and for the establishment of some kind of Ministry of Justice.[35] Some recent variants of this have surfaced in policy documents from the former Alliance parties[36] and from the Labour Party, which, in its 1990 policy review document, has called for a new Department of Legal Administration;[37] Brazier, as we have seen, takes a similar position. There has been little consistency in the proposals put forward – and indeed the ground has shifted over the years. Since the 1940s, for example, changes in the arrangements for judicial business in the House of Lords have made it much harder for Lord Chancellors to find time to sit judicially. And since the early 1970s the Lord Chancellor's Department has grown from a tiny domain concerned mainly with judicial patronage, into a major spending department with about 11,000 civil servants, responsible for administering a major public service.

One common ingredient in these proposals has been that the Minister of Justice should sit in and be accountable to the House of Commons. Another common factor has been that whenever the phrase 'Ministry of Justice' has been mentioned there has been an almost audible shudder of horror from the judges about the supposed threat such a development would pose to their independence. Lord Chancellor Hailsham (while claiming, himself, to be a Minister of Justice[38]) made clear his own fierce resistance to developments of this kind: he said of the Alliance's proposal for a new Department of Justice that such a move would be 'constitutionally very dangerous' and a menace to the independence of the judiciary.[39]

Since Lord Hailsham's departure from the office of Lord Chancellor, the spectre of executive inroads into judicial independence has been raised in a new context – and with a new villain in the shape of Lord Chancellor Mackay, an outsider to the cosy traditions of the English Inns of Court and a proponent of a utilitarian-Thatcherite outlook on the machinery of justice, very different to that of his predecessor. Lord Mackay is also the author of those three famous Green Papers discussed earlier.

THE BROWNE-WILKINSON THESIS

However, this part of the story begins in the Hailsham era, and not so much with the Green Papers themselves as with the cult of efficiency and economy that has been such a feature of the Thatcher years. The Lord Chancellor's Department, like every other department in Whitehall, has become subject to the new disciplines of Raynerism and the Financial Management Initiative (FMI). The Civil Justice Review (initiated by Lord Hailsham),[40] the reorganization of legal aid and the Green Papers are all products of this.

Sir Nicolas (now Lord) Browne-Wilkinson, then Vice-Chancellor of the Supreme Court, foreshadowed some of the anxieties articulated by the judges in the context of the Green Paper debates in his 1987 public lecture, cited earlier.[41] Writing before the Green Paper debates but anticipating, in measured language, some of the shriller protests of his judicial colleagues, Sir Nicolas identified several developments in the last 30 years or so that, in his view, posed a threat to the continuing independence of the administration of justice.

He noted, for instance, the post-1971 shift in the administrative control of the courts from judges to civil servants in a Lord Chancellor's Department that has undergone a considerable expansion since the Second World War. Noting that the theoretical distinction between administrative and judicial functions is not so easy to maintain in practice as some might like to pretend, he suggested that this has 'given rise to stresses between the judiciary and the administrators as to their different functions'.[42] The administrative listing of cases for trial is a notoriously vexed illustration of this point. There has recently been a running saga over the exclusion of the Parliamentary Commissioner from reviewing alleged maladministration on the part of court staff who, although they are civil servants, act, at least theoretically, under the instruction of judges.[43] Sir Nicolas pointed to worrying deficiencies in the command structure, in that there is no machinery for resolving disputes between judges and administrators, short of the Lord Chancellor himself.[44]

The point on which he laid greatest stress has to do with the recent development of 'financial management' and 'value for money' disciplines relating to public expenditure, and their application to the Lord Chancellor's Department:

> the requirements of judicial independence make the Lord Chancellor's Department wholly different from any other department of state. It is not for the executive alone to determine what should be the policy objectives of the courts. It is not for the executive alone to determine whether or not a particular judicial procedure provides 'value for money'. Justice is not capable of being measured out by an accountant's computer . . . [U]nder our constitution it is for the judge to determine what is just, and what is not just, subject always to legislation passed by Parliament. As a result of such policy being applied to the Lord Chancellor's Department, that department is being required to formulate policy and to make determinations as to 'value for money' according to financial yardsticks and without, for the most part, even consulting the judges.[45]

Thus, said Sir Nicolas:

> The Lord Chancellor's own position, representing as he does simultaneously both the independent judiciary and the interests of government, is becoming more and more difficult, since the price to be paid for obtaining funds for the administration of justice is dependent on satisfying the Treasury that any particular course represents, in their terms, value for money.[46]

His department is forced by the demands for financial economy to move more and more into areas which the judges have traditionally considered to be their exclusive preserve.

While conceding that 'there is no justification for a claim that the legal system has a greater right to public funds than, for example, the National Health Service or education',[47] he went on to argue that, while the fixing of the total budget must be a political act, judges must, in the interests of judicial independence, be involved in the preparation of the estimates and in the allocation of the budget once it has been voted by Parliament. By the same token, judges should be more involved in the formulation of legal policy. Sir Nicolas concluded, first, that the dual role of the Lord Chancellor should continue; secondly, that 'there should be a collegiate body of judges charged with responsibility for taking policy decisions on behalf of judges': funded by the Lord Chancellor's Department but accountable to the Lord Chancellor for its expenditure of those funds.[48]

Even if we accept Sir Nicolas's diagnosis it is hard to see how the latter proposal could be made to work in practice. Consultation is one thing, 'responsibility' is very much another. Lord Mackay in the Earl Grey public lecture referred to earlier[49] seems implicitly to reject this plea for direct judicial involvement, certainly in respect of funding matters, while at the same time defending his own position as a minister in the House of Lords:

> The House of Commons is not itself a policy-making body. In such a system, the judicature needs a minister to act as its friend at court [an interesting phrase], who can compete on equal terms – so far as differences in size permit – with other spending departments for a share of the public money. The intensity of political conflict in the House of Commons also makes it desirable, in our system, that the judiciary should not become directly involved in the politically charged process of obtaining resources. The Lord Chancellor serves to insulate them from that process.

So now we have the metaphor of 'insulation' to set alongside those noted earlier, such as the 'buffer' and the 'hinge'.

We have already noted the colourful language used by senior judges in the context of the debates on the 1989 Green Papers. The issues were aptly summarized in an *Observer* article, published soon after the Lords debate, which noted the unbridgeable gap

> between those who believe that legal services (which are largely paid for out of the Exchequer) should be subjected to empirical tests of efficiency and accessibility, and those who believe that the present disposition of the English legal system was brought down from Sinai by the framers of the Revolution Settlement and should not be tampered with by outsiders.[50]

Readers may by now have begun to suspect, quite correctly, that the author of this chapter is emphatically in the former category. A legal system exists to provide a service to the public. Judges seem sometimes to forget that they are paid public servants and to give the impression that defending their constitutional fortress against the theoretical possibility of attack takes priority both over quality of service and value for money. An independent judiciary seems all too often to be depicted as a self-evidently admirable end in itself rather than as a means to an end.

The same tendency on the part of judges to close ranks and to rail, sometimes in intemperate language, against any attempts to impose even a modicum of external quality control, has bedevilled the debate about accountability for legal services, to which I now turn.

PARLIAMENT, JUDICIAL INDEPENDENCE AND THE DIVISION BETWEEN 'JUDICIAL' AND 'ADMINISTRATIVE' FUNCTIONS

Here we take it for granted from the outset that the machinery of justice is a part (albeit a peculiar part) of the apparatus of government, and that the administration of justice is an important public service (as well as being an expensive one, subsidized by the taxpayer). This may seem so obvious as hardly to be worth saying, but it seems that some lawyers do sometimes need to be reminded of it (witness the debates on the Green Papers). The 1986 Justice report, *The Administration of the Courts*, put it thus:

> The courts exist for the benefit of the public and provide, and should be seen to provide, a public service, as much as, say, the National Health Service. We would like to see a wider recognition of this fact. The customer in the law courts may not always be right but it is he or she, and not the judges or lawyers, for whom the service is provided.[51]

Opening the Commons debate in July 1979 on motions to establish a new system of departmentally related select committees, Norman St John-Stevas rejected a proposal by the Procedure Committee[52] that the Home Affairs Committee should undertake scrutiny both of the Lord Chancellor's Department and the Law Officers' Department. In his speech (prompted, as it has since been made clear, by Lord Hailsham) St John-Stevas spoke of the threat to the independence of the judiciary that might arise

> if a select committee were to investigate such matters as the appointment and conduct of the judiciary and its part in legal administration, or matters such as confidential communications between the judiciary and the Lord Chancellor and the responsibility of the Law Officers with regard to prosecutions and civil proceedings.[53]

He added that the Lord Chancellor's functions are all 'deeply interwoven with judicial matters'. But, as several Members pointed out, it simply is not true to suggest that judicial independence is threatened by committee investigations into the administration of, for instance, legal aid (or for that matter the Public Record Office). It seems clear that the Procedure Committee never envisaged the Home Affairs Committee looking at judicial activity as such.

Both the Home Affairs Committee and the Liaison Committee pressed the government to change its mind. In the meantime, Lord Hailsham voluntarily gave evidence to the Home Affairs Committee both in its Prisons inquiry and its Remands in Custody inquiry, and the British constitution apparently remains more or less intact; the English and Scottish Law Officers have also given evidence to the Committee. In any case, the Lord Chancellor's Department has always been answerable to the Public Accounts Committee.[54]

Lord St John of Fawsley has since explained that the exclusion was a matter of tactics rather than principle,[55] but John Wheeler, chairman of the Home Affairs Committee, has broadly accepted the Hailsham line, arguing that 'to some extent the lack of direct monitoring of the Lord Chancellor's Department has been justified by the need to preserve judicial independence'.[56] At the end of 1991 there was a change of heart and the remit of the Home Affairs Committee was extended to cover the LCD. But the original conclusion was just one of many instances of a widespread tendency to be very protective – arguably over-protective – towards the judiciary when it comes to public accountability. Another is to be found in the 1980 Justice Report, cited earlier.[57]

THE JUSTICE REPORT ON THE ADMINISTRATION OF THE COURTS

The Committee that produced this report was set up, under the chairmanship of John Macdonald QC, to inquire into the machinery for dealing with public complaints about the administration of the courts. The inquiry excluded consideration of complaints about the merits of courts' decisions (in respect of which there is often a right of appeal), and time and time again the report comes back to the need to preserve judicial independence by separating 'administrative' matters from 'judicial' ones – a division that Sir Nicolas Browne-Wilkinson (see above) has acknowledged to be highly problematical.

Thus the report discusses the role of the Parliamentary Commissioner for Administration who in 1984 reached a concordat with the Lord Chancellor's Department about the location of the boundary line between 'administrative' and 'judicial' (a matter best left, the Justice Committee argues, in another part of the report, to the 'common sense' of experienced LCD officials), since when 'the number of complaints involving the Department has risen'. The 1984 agreement subsequently broke down following the Lord Chancellor's Department's obtaining counsel's opinion to the effect that court staff supplied by the LCD but working under the instructions of judges did not come within the purview of the Parliamentary Commissioner Act 1967: and the Select Committee on the PCA took evidence on the subject from both Lord Hailsham and Lord Mackay.[58] The Lord Chancellor subsequently agreed to bring his Department within the purview of the PCA by way of a new clause in the Courts and Legal Services Bill.

The Committee also notes the rather startling fact that, in dealing with complaints by disgruntled litigants, the Lord Chancellor's Department's refusal to accept responsibility for administrative actions carried out on the instructions of a judge has meant that only 5 per cent of complaints are accepted for consideration. It says, with some understatement, that it is not surprising if such a low take-up rate gives rise to 'some lack of confidence' in the system.[59]

In fact, the Committee – in common with so many other people – became preoccupied with the issue of judicial independence to a point where it virtually lost sight of any legitimate claims of public accountability. At one point it considered the objections that might be raised to extending the powers of the PCA to include investigations of judicial behaviour, a change favoured by some members of the Committee. One objection, it said, 'is that, as the Ombudsman reports to the House of Commons, this would *encourage MPs to pry into the affairs of the judiciary*' (my emphasis).[60] But this objection was then promptly rejected on the grounds that the PCA is an independent officer who 'would only investigate a complaint if he were satisfied that it was serious', and, the Report continues, 'if a serious complaint is made, it would seem better that it should be investigated by an independent person of the standing of the Ombudsman than for it to become *the subject of ill-informed speculation in Parliament*', (my emphasis).[61] So much for parliamentary accountability: no wonder parliamentary discussion *is* sometimes ill-informed, given the prevalence of this kind of thinking.

CONCLUSIONS

Judicial independence is, as William Robson argued, an important precondition for impartiality (a necessary condition, though not a sufficient one); both attributes have a subjective as well as an objective dimension. This writer does not dispute for one moment that issues like judicial patronage, salaries, removal from office are of historical importance, and he shares much of the concern of Brazier and others about the defects in the present departmental arrangements pertaining to the administration of justice, and about the secrecy and lack of accountability pertaining thereto. We should also recognize that the judges – notably Sir Nicolas Browne-Wilkinson – have a point when they say that the terms of their old partnership with the Lord Chancellor, acting traditionally as a constitutional 'buffer' in defence of their independence, have altered significantly, and probably irreversibly, as the LCD has become more and more like any other large spending department, imbued with the tough managerial values of the Thatcher era and fighting its corner with other departments for scarce public resources.

But in any case, the subject goes far wider than the traditional boundaries of judicial independence set out in standard textbooks on constitutional law. The formal buttresses of judicial independence – removal only on an address, salaries directly chargeable to the Consolidated Fund and so on – are virtually worthless if the self-professed independence and impartiality of judges are doubted by those whom the courts are there to serve. An emphasis upon the impartial quality of the judicial process, with the justification of independence recognized as being its role in underpinning impartiality and a recognition of the subjective quality of these attributes, brings much more sharply into play a number of issues that might be regarded as peripheral if we were confining ourselves to the issue of whether judges really are manipulated by the executive – issues such as the method of appointment and the judges' social/educational backgrounds.

It is quite possible (as United States presidents have sometimes found to their surprise) for judges who owe their offices to political patronage to display robust independence once they are in post. The proclaimed end of a political spoils system (from the late 1920s) in Britain is commonly regarded as having been an important watershed in enhancing the *perceived* impartiality of the judiciary – though there is no evidence that judges appointed in the 1920s were any more or less 'partial' than their successors. Indeed, because of the secretiveness of the Lord Chancellor's Department and the cliquiness of the Bar there is not a lot of evidence of any kind relating to judicial appointments, promotions, and so on: a booklet on the subject of appointments produced by the LCD is a singularly unrevealing document.[62]

Can the public, whose taxes pay judicial salaries, be blamed if it, and its elected representatives, sometimes wonder what the profession has to hide? Similarly, judges have been inclined to scoff at the notion that their impartiality might somehow be compromised by the narrow exclusiveness of their social and educational backgrounds. Perhaps they are right; but secretiveness is the enemy of informed discussion, and in any case they surely cannot blame people for musing upon the implications of, for instance, the Bar's long-held monopoly of judicial appointments and of the almost total absence of women and people of minority ethnic groups from the professional Bench.

Public perceptions of the judiciary, and confidence in the judicial process itself, must surely be influenced for the worse by their exclusiveness, their defensiveness, their complacency[63] and their propensity to attack their critics with stridently expressed constitutional platitudes in lieu of reasoned argument – the Green Paper debates are a case in point. The problem is exacerbated by lack of parliamentary accountability and by the secrecy surrounding matters pertaining to judicial appointments. The Courts and Legal Services Act 1990, with its emphasis on the interests of the consumers of legal services, is in principle to be welcomed rather than rudely dismissed as a threat to judicial independence. The latter, as defined earlier in this chapter, remains an important constitutional principle, but discussion of it cannot be conducted without due regard to far wider issues relating to the judges and the judicial process – and to the nature and funding of legal services in a modern democracy.

NOTES AND REFERENCES

The original version of this chapter was delivered as a seminar paper in the Department of Politics at the University of Hull (November 1989); a later version was delivered as a public lecture at the Centre for British Constitutional Law and History, King's College London, in February 1990. Preparation of the final version of the chapter has taken grateful account of comments and suggestions made on those two occasions. Several paragraphs of the chapter also appeared in my inaugural lecture, 'Never Mind the Administration, Feel the Justice', delivered at Royal Holloway and Bedford New College on 3 May 1990. An earlier version was published in P. Norton (ed.), *New Directions in British Politics* (Edward Elgar, 1991).

1 Notably J. A. G. Griffith, 'The Political Constitution', *Modern Law Review*, 42 (1979), 1–21.
2 Cm 570 (1989).
3 *Ibid.*, paragraph 5.13.
4 *Ibid.*, paragraphs 4.11–4.12.
5 *House of Lord Debates*, vol. 505, c. 1307–1480.
6 *Ibid.*, c. 1331.
7 *Ibid.*, c. 1369.
8 *Ibid.*, c. 1333.
9 The Lord Chief Justice, the Master of the Rolls, the Vice-Chancellor of the Supreme Court, the President of the Family Division.
10 Schedule 4, para. 11.
11 The judges are directly represented in Parliament by the Law Lords. During the Lords' Second Reading debate on the Courts and Legal Services Bill (*House of*

Lords Debates, 19 December 1989, c. 154), Baroness Phillips noted that of 36 peers who had put their names down to speak, 28 had been trained as lawyers. In the Commons about 100 MPs are lawyers, two-thirds of them barristers.

12 ' "Efficiency Role" for New Magistrates' Courts Agency', *The Times*, 20 July 1989; see also the editorial in *New Law Journal*, 28 July 1989, p. 1029; and J. Davis, 'A Water-Tight Case for Court Overhaul', *The Times*, 26 September 1989.
13 *The Times*, 5 February 1990.
14 See R. Pyper, 'Sarah Tisdall, Ian Willmore, and the Civil Servants' Right to Leak', *Political Quarterly*, 56 (1985), 72–81 and the editorial comment; 'Secrets, Moles, Ministers and Judges', *Public Law* (1984), 177.
15 R. Stevens, 'The Independence of the Judiciary: The View from the Lord Chancellor's Office', *Oxford Journal of Legal Studies*, 8 (1988), 222–248.
16 S. Shetreet, *Judges on Trial* (Amsterdam: North-Holland, 1975) pp. 17–19.
17 J. Bell, *Policy Arguments in Judicial Decisions* (Oxford: Clarendon Press, 1983) p. 4; cf. W.A. Robson, *Justice and Administrative Law*, 3rd edn (London: Stevens, 1951) p. 369.
18 Bell, *Policy Arguments*, p. 4.
19 *Ibid.*.
20 Robson, *Justice and Administrative Law*, pp. 43–44.
21 *Ibid.*, p. 45.
22 *Ibid.*, pp. 46 and 48.
23 R. Brazier, 'Government and the Law: Ministerial Responsibility for Legal Affairs', *Public Law* (1989), pp. 64–94, at 74.
24 There is a large literature on the office of the Lord Chancellor: an excellent bibliography can be found in P. Polden, *Guide to the Records of the Lord Chancellor's Department* (London: HMSO, 1988).
25 Viscount Birkenhead, *Points of View*, Vol. 1 (London: Hodder and Stoughton, 1922) ch. 4.
26 Public Records Office, file LC02 3630.
27 Public Records Office, file T162 877/E48680, 1944.
28 Sir N. Browne-Wilkinson, 'The Independence of the Judiciary in the 1980s', *Public Law* (1988), 44–57, at 45.
29 Lord Mackay, 'The Role of the Lord Chancellor in the Administration of Justice', Earl Grey Lecture, University of Newcastle, 24 February 1990.
30 Brazier, 'Government and the Law', p. 68. After the 1992 election a junior Commons minister was appointed to act for the Lord Chancellor.
31 Stevens, 'The Independence of the Judiciary'.
32 Shetreet, *Judges on Trial*, pp. 143–144.
33 A. Paterson and St John Bates, *The Legal System of Scotland*, 2nd edn (Edinburgh: Green, 1986) p. 172.
34 Cd. 9230, 1918, Ch. X.
35 See: G. Drewry, 'Lord Haldane's Ministry of Justice – Stillborn or Strangled at Birth?', *Public Administration*, 61 (1983), 396–414; and 'The Debate about a Ministry of Justice – A Joad-Eye's View', *Public Law* (1987) 502–509.
36 'Government, Law and Justice: The Case for a Ministry of Justice', *Alliance Papers No. 1* (London: SDP/Liberal Alliance, 1986).
37 *Looking to the Future* (London: Labour Party, 1990), p. 40.
38 Fourth Report from the Select Committee on Home Affairs, *The Prison Service*,

Session 1980–81, HC 412 (London: HMSO, 1981) Evidence, QQ 995–996.
39 *The Guardian*, 26 May 1986.
40 *Report of the Review Body on Civil Justice*, Cm. 394 (1988).
41 Browne-Wilkinson, 'The Independence of the Judiciary in the 1980s'.
42 *Ibid.*, p. 46.
43 See n. 58 below. Also the Parliamentary Commissioner for Administration, *Annual Report for 1988*, 1988–89, HC 301, para. 60, and Justice Report, *The Administration of the Courts* (London: Justice, 1986), paras. 2.20–2.24, 3.7–3.9 and Appendix D.
44 Browne-Wilkinson, 'The Independence of the Judiciary in the 1980s', p. 47.
45 *Ibid.*, pp. 48–49.
46 *Ibid.*, p. 50.
47 *Ibid.*, pp. 53–54.
48 *Ibid.*, p. 56.
49 Mackay, 'The Role of the Lord Chancellor in the Administration of Justice'.
50 L. Mark, *The Observer*, 9 April 1989.
51 Justice Report, para. 3.1.
52 First Report, 1977–78, HC 588, para. 5.24.
53 *House of Commons Debates*, 25 June 1979, c. 35ff.
54 For a recent instance, see Sir Derek Oulton's evidence to the Public Accounts Committee, 9 April 1986, 1985–86, HC 182.
55 Second Report from the Select Committee on Procedure, *The Working of the Select Committee System*, Session 1989–90, HC 19–II (London: HMSO, 1990), para. 742.
56 Letter to *The Times*, 16 February 1989.
57 Justice Report, *The Administration of the Courts*.
58 Evidence of Lord Hailsham, 31 March 1987, 1986–87, HC 284–ii; evidence of Lord Mackay, 26 January 1989, 1988–89, HC 159.
59 Justice Report, *The Administration of the Courts*, para. 3.7.
60 *Ibid.*, para. 4.14.
61 *Ibid.*
62 *Judicial Appointments: The Lord Chancellor's Policies and Procedures* (London: Lord Chancellor's Department, 1986).
63 The recent record in relation to the courts' reluctance to face up to past mistakes in respect of gross miscarriages of justice might be cited under both the last two headings.

11

By Law Established: The Church of England and its Place in the Constitution

DOMINIC GRANT

INTRODUCTION

The startling diminution in the importance attached by many constitutional commentators to the Church of England is an indication of the extent to which it has slipped from the mainstream of constitutional study. Yet it remains a rich field: the continued operation of some sixteenth-century statutes makes it a showcase for the institutional preference for change by evolution rather than innovation.

Texts which do examine the Church's position tend to be lacking in one or more areas. Those which discuss the practical consequences of Establishment generally fail to provide a sufficient account of its structural basis, and vice versa. In this chapter a more 'holistic' approach will be offered, combining an account of the Anglican Church's structure and relevant aspects of its historical origins with an examination of the modern interaction of Church and State. In keeping with this spirit of 'holism', the spiritual aspect of the Church will not be ignored.

The study is written from a perspective of Church of England membership; apologies are offered in advance for any lapses in impartiality.

THE STRUCTURE OF THE CHURCH OF ENGLAND

> It is evident unto all men diligently reading holy Scripture and ancient Authors, that from the Apostles' time there have been these Orders of Ministers in Christ's Church; Bishops, Priests, and Deacons.[1]

Thus a three-tier ordained ministry exists within the Church of England: a deacon may not preside over the Eucharistic Prayer, pronounce Absolution, or bless; and only a bishop may ordain, confirm the baptized, or consecrate land. But the distinction also has a bearing on the allocation of administrative powers and duties in the Church. Many clergy promotions are made on the basis of administrative skills as well as pastoral ability.

The structure of Church government is highly complex. In addition to a hierarchy of individual members of the clergy, there are synods and assemblies at various levels with a membership comprising both ordained and lay people. The two systems are not mutually exclusive in their spheres of operation, but it will be convenient to study them separately.

The most basic unit in the Church is the parish. Day-to-day running of the parish church rests largely with the parish priest ('the incumbent'), who is normally appointed by the bishop after consultation with representatives of the congregation. The incumbent may also appoint one or (occasionally) more deacons or assistant priests[2] to facilitate the parochial administration and the provision of worship and pastoral care.

Parishes are grouped into deaneries, and one of the parish priests will serve also, at the pleasure of the bishop, as rural dean. Few specific duties are attached to this position, although the rural dean may assist liaison between parishes, and provide a priest to act as a locum on occasion.

A group of deaneries, and the parishes therein, will fall under the supervision of the archdeacon. Again, this is an appointment made by the bishop, and is of considerable importance. He is normally kept abreast of important church affairs down to parish level, making a formal visitation at least once a year, although some of his duties may be delegated to the rural deans. The archdeacon is also an important figure in the ecclesiastical courts system.

As has been seen, the bishop holds, in addition to the pastoral responsibilities inherent in the cure of souls, a very great authority in the life of the local churches. He may make formal visitations in his diocese (although the disciplinary aspect of this is now virtually obsolete); he too has an important ecclesiastical jurisdiction. Bishops are appointed by the Crown; the procedure for appointment is described elsewhere (see p. 176).

There are in fact two kinds of bishop: the diocesan and the suffragan. The relationship between the two is similar to that between parish priest and 'curate': the suffragan (if indeed the diocesan bishop chooses to appoint one) assists his diocesan superior in the exercise of his episcopal responsibilities. The diocese of London is a special case: as well as the diocesan Bishop of London and the suffragan Bishop of Fulham, there are four 'area bishops'.[3] These enjoy within their respective areas (which correspond geographically to archdeaconries) a greater degree of autonomy than the suffragan, but are by no means independent of the diocesan bishop.

The Archbishops of York and Canterbury are both diocesan bishops; in addition they exercise jurisdiction over their respective provinces and are to be obeyed by the other diocesan bishops. The Archbishop of Canterbury, as inheritor of the ancient see of Saint Augustine, is Primate of All England and is looked to as president of the worldwide Anglican communion.

Also of note is the cathedral dean and chapter. Much of its work consists of the upkeep of and provision of services of worship in the cathedral; it also participates in the appointment of a new bishop to the see. The dean is appointed by the Crown; the chapter is made up of canons appointed either by the Crown or by the bishop.

We turn now to study the various assemblies which play a part in Church government. Each parish church has an electoral roll[4] whose members meet annually to choose churchwardens (normally two) and elect a parochial church council. The office of churchwarden has lost much of its historical significance, but remains an important link between the lay people of the parish and their bishop.[5] The purpose of the parochial church council is to act in co-operation with the incumbent in the running of the church; it has a number of mandatory responsibilities (such as dealing with the finances and maintaining the church buildings); beyond these it provides vital lay involvement in parish church administration.

Deanery synods were introduced as part of the reorganization of Church government brought about by the Synodical Government Measure 1969. Their main function is discussion rather than the making or implementation of policy; their membership (drawn from every parish in the deanery) is between 50 and 150, comprising a House of Clergy and a House of Laity.

Diocesan synods consist of a House of Bishops (including suffragans), a House of Clergy and a House of Laity. The latter two Houses are elected by their deanery synod counterparts. Whilst it too is largely deliberative, the diocesan synod enjoys a good deal more authority than the deanery synod: it administers diocesan finances and constitutes influential committees. Also, in the continuing debate over female ordination, it is the dioceses which are currently being asked to vote for or against the introduction of women priests; their decisions will be crucial.

The most ancient organ of ecclesiastical government has now become anomalous and virtually powerless. The Convocations of the Provinces of York and Canterbury each consist of an Upper House (all diocesan bishops plus some suffragans) and a Lower House of cathedral deans, archdeacons, provosts (representatives of diocesan clergy and cathedral chapters) and representatives of the universities and religious communities. There is no lay presence.

Up until the twentieth century, the provincial convocations together were the Church's legislative body.[6] In 1919, however, and at the request of both convocations, Parliament passed the Church of England Assembly (Powers) Act. This gave statutory recognition to the new National Assembly of the Church of England (or Church Assembly), transferring to it the legislative powers of the convocations. Resolutions of the convocations may now be a persuasive contribution to ecclesiastical debates, but are without legal effect.

The Church Assembly was renamed General Synod in 1970, and comprises the Houses of Bishops, Clergy, and Laity. Membership of the Houses of Bishops and Clergy is the same as that of the Upper and Lower Houses respectively of the two convocations; elections to the House of Laity occur every five years at deanery level. As well as debating and passing legislative measures for parliamentary approval (see p. 178) the General Synod frequently commissions and considers influential and controversial reports.

It remains to study the management of the Church of England's finances. Churchgoers' offerings, even if they were sufficient to fund their church, would surely vary widely between areas; a system therefore exists to ensure both the payment of fair stipends to all clergy and the continued provision of funds for the work of the Anglican Church as a whole.

Each parish church is assessed yearly to determine the level of its 'diocesan quota', a payment into diocesan funds. Each diocese is in turn assessed for a contribution towards expenses incurred by General Synod. The diocese also receives money from the Church Commissioners (discussed below), enabling it to augment the incomes of the diocesan clergy so that stipend levels are met.

The Church Commissioners were created in 1948 by the statutory merger of Queen Anne's Bounty with the Ecclesiastical Commissioners. Queen Anne's Bounty was a body established by Letters Patent in 1704; its purpose was to restore to Church use the 'first-fruits and tenths', that part of ecclesiastical incomes which had been (and until 1926 continued to be) paid to the Crown.[7] The Ecclesiastical Commissioners were established by statute in 1836 to regulate episcopal incomes and manage much Church property. Today the Church Commissioners have a variety of powers; they frequently devise schemes to alter parish boundaries, create new parishes, and amalgamate existing ones into 'team ministries'. As well as ecclesiastical figures, the Commissioners include numerous parliamentary and other office-holders, thus providing a noteworthy manifestation of the legal ties between Church and State.

The idea that the Anglican Church is financially supported by the State is, however, a popular misconception. The compulsory payment to the Church of tithes on the income of certain land was curbed by the Tithe Acts 1936 and 1951, and was replaced by a system of redemption stock and annuities. All remaining liabilities thereunder will be extinguished by 1996.[8]

The nexus between the State and the Church of England will be examined more closely in a later part of this chapter; first, however, it is necessary to study aspects of the Church's historical basis. This will be an extremely selective account: the focus will be the Reformation under Henry VIII, yet even this will not be dealt with in full. The criterion throughout will be relevance to a discussion of the Church's position in the constitution today. When Ian Paisley warns that unity with Rome would dethrone the Queen, or when George Carey's use of the term 'heresy' (in relation to opposition to women's ordination) is denounced as not only questionable but unconstitutional, it is important to have a historically grounded understanding of the reasons.

THE HISTORICAL BASIS OF THE ESTABLISHED CHURCH

Throughout the medieval period, England had been dominated by the Catholic Church. The Church was among the principal landowners; her senior clergy occupied many of the Crown's highest offices; and even some of her lowest-ranking clerics were entitled to tithes and various other fees and offerings. In addition, the Church had been seen as the primary source of education and charity. Thus she claimed both authority and genuine respect in the temporal sphere, whilst of course holding the key to spiritual salvation.

It is hardly surprising, therefore, that the Church's influence pervaded every aspect of the nation's life. Indeed this arrangement was seen by successive sovereigns and their governments as potentially beneficial, for its doctrine of God-given kingship offered an incontrovertible justification of Crown authority in a pre-democratic state.

In practice, however, the relationship between Church and State had become increasingly fraught with difficulties. The English Church was merely a part of an organization which crossed national boundaries, whose officers swore primary allegiance to the Pope, and which was subject not to domestic laws but to the Church's own canon law. An uneasy compromise prevailed, by which the coexistence and universality of both canon law and common and statute law was accepted, and the king was permitted a significant though limited say in the life of the Church (the power to nominate, for example, to a vacant see rested in him if the pope chose not to appoint the new bishop).[9] Nevertheless, the tension between nationalism and papal theocracy became ever more difficult to suppress, and finally surfaced in the events surrounding the Henrician Reformation.

Henry VIII found himself presiding over an increasingly bitter debate as to the boundaries of State and Church jurisdictions. Powerful members of the laity had become disenchanted with clerical pretensions, not least because of the known and potentially hostile influence of the King of Spain over the Pope. The death of Richard Hunne whilst in the Bishop of London's prison awaiting trial for alleged heresy[10] brought this antagonism to the fore, and when the King himself was drawn into the conflict, the days of papal power in England became numbered.

It was Wolsey's inability to resolve the question of the King's marriage which finally demonstrated the incompatibility of the two hierarchies. Wolsey's position of power was unique: he had become Chancellor in 1515 and papal *legatus a latere*[11] in 1518, and therefore seemed ideally qualified to achieve the desired dissolution of Henry's marriage to Catherine of Aragon. He was permitted in 1529 to set up a commission to consider the matter; but he failed to win from Rome full jurisdiction to decide it, and in August that year it was taken out of his hands by the Pope. Wolsey was toppled by his irreconcilable responsibilities to King and to Pope, and his downfall heralded that of the Roman Church in England. Whether to resolve the particular matter of his proposed 'divorce' or to put an end to the wider conflict, Henry now saw that spiritual authority must be annexed to the Crown. With the minds of Englishmen stirred by the success of the Lutheran Reformation in parts of Europe (Henry's condemnation of which, ironically, had earned him the title *Fidei Defensor*), the circumstances were ideal for action.

The attack was pragmatic. Initial parliamentary legislation sought merely to regulate and restrict certain clerical fees and privileges,[12] whilst the Court of King's Bench embarked upon a far more dramatic assault: an action against the whole clergy for breach of the fourteenth-century Praemunire Statute (an ancient assertion of the rights of the Crown in relation to ecclesiastical matters). The Convocations of Canterbury and York were granted a royal pardon only after paying huge fines and, more importantly, agreeing to recognize the King as the supreme head of the English Church. Slight ambiguity in the terms of this recognition allowed the clergy to assert that there were still limits to royal authority; nevertheless their reluctant concession and the continued threat of Praemunire allowed Parliament to continue its legislative assault.

The most significant statutes passed by the Reformation Parliament were as follows:

1. The First Statute of Annates 1532.[13] This restrained the payment to Rome of annates, the income of bishops in the first year of their incumbency, and permitted the consecration of prelates even without the necessary papal bulls. Significantly, it also provided that the King and his subjects could legitimately continue 'to enjoy the sacraments, ceremonies and services of holy Church' even if the Pope should excommunicate them.[14] Keir[15] sees this statute as a bargaining chip in relations with Rome; indeed, the question of Henry's marriage had not been finally settled, and he was empowered to delay the Act's operation. Nevertheless, it is hard to see how the King, having thus nailed his colours to the mast, could have reached with the Pope any agreement sufficient to secure its indefinite suspension.

2. The Ecclesiastical Appeals Act 1532.[16] This recognized the coexistence of spiritual and temporal jurisdictions within the realm, but placed both under the supreme headship of the King. It thus restructured the ecclesiastical jurisdiction, in particular ousting that of Rome itself as a court of appeal.

3. The Submission of the Clergy Act 1533.[17] This Act was largely declaratory of concessions already made by the convocations. It necessitated royal assent to any new legislation by the Church, and subjected existing canon law to review by the King with a commission of 32 (comprising 16 clergymen and 16 parliamentarians).

4. The Second Statute of Annates 1533.[18] As well as renewing the 1532 Annates Act, this ousted the Pope's power to nominate to vacant bishoprics, building upon the procedure which had been followed on those occasions when this power had been delegated to the King[19] (hence the Statute Law Revision Act 1948 gives this statute the new short title 'the Appointment of Bishops Act').

5. The Act of Supremacy 1534.[20] This Act, merely declaratory in form, placed the King as 'the only supreme head in earth of the Church of England' and endowed him with all powers relating thereto, including that of correction of heresy (and thus formulation of doctrine).

Subsequently there was imposed on all subjects an oath of obedience to the exclusive authority of the King under God, and of allegiance to the settlement of succession brought about by his marriage to Anne Boleyn.

A distinction has already been alluded to between the Lutheran and Henrician Reformation movements. The former was predominantly a doctrinal revolution, with increases in State power occurring only in response to this. Henry, on the other hand, sought only to sever the cords of papal authority. Aside from this, his theological standpoint was almost identical to that of Rome. It was vital for him, having cultivated an atmosphere in which matters ecclesiastical could legitimately be called into question, to take a firm hold of the Church's teaching; hence the provisions of the Act of Supremacy.

Nevertheless, theological change had become inevitable. Protestant doctrinal trends came to the fore during the reign of Edward VI (one notable innovation being clergy marriage); this period also saw the increasing confidence of Parliament and the Council in exercising the royal supremacy 'in the King's name'.[21] In contrast, his successor, Queen Mary, was determined to restore the Church to its pre-Reformation state, and repealed many of the Henrician and Edwardian statutes. She failed, however, to rescind the title of 'supreme head', and her efforts ultimately served to underline the continuing hostility of the ruling classes towards the papacy.

Elizabeth I was less concerned with theological debate than with achieving political stability. She quickly reversed the Marian trend with the Act of Supremacy 1558, which confirmed the exclusive ecclesiastical authority of the Crown, and the Act of Uniformity 1558, which revived the ritual and doctrine contained in the 1552 Prayer Book, originally issued under Edward VI. But the Elizabethan settlement envisaged uniformity as nothing more than an artificial expression of a united 'nation at prayer', and diverse theological viewpoints were allowed to develop under its aegis. These different viewpoints frequently vied for predominance, but their advocates were largely content to remain within the national Church.

The constitutional crisis of the seventeenth century was religious as well as political. The eventual victory of the parliamentarians and the accession of William and Mary guaranteed the exclusion of papal influence over the Crown, and confirmed that the sovereign's power over the Church was one which could be exercised through Parliament alone. It was enacted[22] that the monarch must be in communion with the national Church, and must on accession solemnly declare adherence to Protestantism and the Protestant succession.

A further effect of the constitutional upheaval was to encourage certain movements to leave the Church of England. Nonconformism for some considerable time entailed great disadvantages: it was not until the 1820s, for example, that the Test Acts (which excluded non-Anglicans from Parliament) began to be repealed. Religious pluralism was recognizable in fact long before it was acceptable in the eyes of the constitution; and now that the Anglican Church is only one of many, which the individual may choose primarily for its doctrines and way of worship,[23] its enshrined constitutional position is a potential source of embarrassment.

We come now to a consideration of the practical and procedural implications of history's legacy to the Church of England.

THE CONTEMPORARY CHURCH–STATE RELATIONSHIP

The Anglican Church in the closing years of the twentieth century is in a strange position. Its members appear on the whole to be concerned more with informal ecumenical co-operation than with remaining a drily formalized 'nation at prayer'. At the same time, however, the ceremonial enthronement in April 1991 of George Carey as Archbishop of Canterbury, and the nomination a few weeks previously of David Hope as Bishop of London,[24] provided a well-publicized reminder of the Church of England's unique constitutional position.

The procedure for choosing a new diocesan bishop is still governed by the Appointment of Bishops Act 1533, although further provisions (both legislative and conventional) have been added. The diocese sets up a Vacancy in See Committee[25] which may recommend appropriate names; more important, however, is the Church's Crown Appointments Commission, which is free to disregard the diocesan committee's advice. The Commission will eventually reach a shortlist of two names to be forwarded to the prime minister; he may recommend either candidate to the Queen or may ask for further names. The identity of the successful candidate is normally made public as soon as he has been recommended to the Queen, although the appointment procedure is at this stage only half-complete.

The Queen now sends a *congé d'élire* (licence to elect) to the dean and chapter of the relevant cathedral, together with a letter missive giving the name of the person whom they are to elect to the bishopric. If the Crown's nominee is not elected within 12 days, the appointment may instead be made by letters patent.[26] Thereafter the election must be confirmed by the provincial vicar general, a judicial officer. Objections are permissible only on the grounds of mistaken identity or defect in the election. Having taken the requisite oaths, the nominee is deemed to be the new bishop (although he has yet to be enthroned in his cathedral church and may not even have been consecrated bishop). It should be noted that there is less State involvement in the appointment of suffragan bishops (governed by the Suffragan Bishops Act 1534). The diocesan bishop chooses two names to be sent directly to the Queen, who appoints one of them.[27]

The procedure for the appointment of diocesan bishops has occasioned some criticism. Objectors complain of the intolerability of a system whereby a political figure is able to determine who will occupy the higher echelons of the Anglican Church – a body to which the nominator may not even belong.[28] It can be readily seen that the system is a natural product of the historical basis of the Church's Establishment and the general transfer of Crown powers to ministers and Parliament. It may even be argued that, if England were still a predominantly single-Church nation, there could be no objection to it. But in the light of contemporary religious diversity and of the perceived secularization of politics, it is indeed difficult to defend in theory the present procedure. In practice, however, there appears to be a broad consensus among leading churchmen that it works well enough. An Archbishops' Commission in 1964 advised that 'the present system of Crown appointments to ecclesiastical offices . . . is preferable to any of the more radically different systems that have been suggested'.[29] Whereas the prime minister ultimately chooses the bishop, it should be borne in mind that it is a Church body which provides the shortlist. Further, it is believed that as a matter of etiquette the prime minister will choose the first-named candidate. Nevertheless, it is rumoured that on a number of occasions Margaret Thatcher declined to nominate the Church's preferred candidate – two notable cases being the appointments of Graham Leonard to London in 1981[30] and George Carey to Canterbury in 1990.[31] It is similarly said that she came to see the appointments of John Habgood to York and David Jenkins to Durham as political mistakes.

There was an attempt in 1984 to alter the episcopal appointments procedure by replacing the process of election and confirmation with the sending of letters patent by the Crown to the provincial archbishop. However, the proposed measure was rejected by Parliament. It seems indeed strange that the ritual election, whose outcome is always a foregone conclusion, should still survive; the prayers for guidance which precede it may even appear offensive to some. A possible justification emerged in the events surrounding the election of George Carey on 6 March 1991. He had angered many by accusing those who opposed the idea of women priests of 'a most serious heresy' (later amended to the less emotive term 'theological error'). Fr Peter Geldard, chairman of the General Synod's Catholic Group, said of the election:

> It still has a value and this is a classic case in point. If some people want to express concern, it is the only opportunity they have.[32]

The force of this argument is, however, somewhat diminished by the fact that the precise election results are never disclosed.

Twenty-six bishops have seats in the House of Lords, and are known as the Lords Spiritual.[33] They occupy the cross-benches, and although entitled to speak and vote, they usually refrain from doing so. In addition, Church of England clergy are among the classes of people disqualified from election to the House of Commons. The theory behind this bar is that priests are represented in Parliament by their bishops; this theory may be criticized on the grounds that not every diocesan bishop is a member of the Lords Spiritual.[34] The automatic peerages of (certain) Anglican bishops are themselves a target for criticism in a contemporary multi-faith society; it is only by ministerial grace, for example, that a peerage was granted to the last chief rabbi, Lord Jakobovits.

It is a source of frustration to many that the Church of England does not have legislative independence over its own affairs. A measure which has been passed by the General Synod must be approved by Parliament before it may receive the royal assent; parliamentary approval is signified by a favourable resolution in each House. Not every proposed measure is supported by Parliament,[35] but the Synod's Legislative Committee liaises with Parliament's Joint Ecclesiastical Committee in order to minimize the risk of conflict by withdrawing unpromising measures (a measure which reaches Parliament may be withdrawn but not amended). In addition to passing measures, the Synod may legislate by canon. Royal assent is still required,[36] but the proposed canon need not be laid before Parliament. The disadvantage of this method is that canons bind only members of the ecclesiastical hierarchy, and lack the statutory authority of measures. Canons also require a more complex legislative process within Synod.

There are numerous other discernible legal consequences of the Anglican Church's constitutional position, from the jurisdiction of the Privy Council to hear appeals from the ecclesiastical courts[37] to the right to be married in one's parish church.[38] Equally noteworthy, however, is the informal aspect of the Church–State relationship. It is, of course, against the interests of every political party to alienate the members of any major religious movement, but the Church of England's Established status leads to an even greater prominence being given to any of its perceived differences with the government of the day. *Faith in the City*, a report issued in 1985 by a Church-sponsored commission, occasioned such a clash by criticizing the effect of government policy on poorer urban areas:

> To affirm the importance of wealth creation – as we do – is not enough . . . What seems to be lacking at present is an adequate appreciation of the importance of the distributive consequences . . . of national economic policies.[39]

The government's response to this and other Church criticisms has been to reprimand churchmen for meddling in politics. Indeed, Margaret Thatcher in particular seems to have opposed any form of prophetic role for the Church: she was apparently furious at Archbishop Robert Runcie's sermon at the Thanksgiving Service after the Falklands War, for he preached about the need for reconciliation. Under the premiership of John Major, however, the government's tone appears to have mellowed; although a victory parade and service of thanksgiving did take place to commemorate the end of the Gulf War, the prime minister was reportedly more wary than his predecessor of the dangers of triumphalism. Meanwhile the claim by the Bishop of Durham that such a service would be 'obscene' was attacked more by clerics than by politicians.[40]

It should not be thought that the Church is unanimous in claiming a right to speak out on political issues: there are many in its ranks who feel simply that 'the Church's job is to get souls into Heaven'.[41] But assuming that the Christian Church as a whole does possess such a right, it is submitted that the Established Anglican denomination in particular has almost a duty, as part of the state framework, to do so if it perceives contravention of God's will.

Nevertheless there are many who feel that this role could be more successfully fulfilled by a disestablished Church of England.[42] Indeed, disestablishment seems to offer a remedy for all the alleged inadequacies discussed in this section. It is to the disestablishment debate that we now turn.

ARGUMENTS ABOUT DISESTABLISHMENT

> 1. On the day after the expiration of six months, or such extended period as Her Majesty may fix by Order in Council, not being more than twelve months after the passing of this Act, the Church of England, shall cease to be established by law, and no person shall, after the passing of this Act, be appointed or nominated by Her Majesty or any person, by virtue of any existing right of patronage, to any ecclesiastical office in the Church of England.[43]

This was the bulk of a private member's bill introduced in 1988 by Tony Benn, who although not a member of the Church has described himself as 'a serious student of the teachings of Jesus'.[44] Among its supporters was Eric Heffer, who was a practising Anglican. The bill came five years after an address by Benn in which he urged the mounting of a national campaign for disestablishment;[45] the bill failed, and the campaign has never had the breadth of support necessary for it to succeed. Nevertheless his arguments, and those of other commentators, deserve closer scrutiny.

As a preliminary to a discussion of the contemporary debate, the changing nature of the disestablishment question should be noted. Its political importance was far greater in the period *c.* 1820–1920; this was due largely to the divisive effects of a single national Church with a continued need for Nonconformist emancipation.[46] Indeed Lord Hailsham[47] considers that the Liberal Party's strength during this period was partly attributable to its 'represent[ation of] organised nonconformity in religion against the Church by law established'. The whole matter began to fade from the limelight as Nonconformists' disabilities were removed, although in 1920 the Anglican Church in Wales was indeed disestablished by the Welsh Church Act 1914 (the coming into force of which was delayed by the First World War).[48] This concession was made largely as a result of the sheer strength of Nonconformist churches in Wales.

Over the last few decades the growth of other religions (rather than denominations) has rekindled the debate. The claimed inadequacy of the blasphemy laws in the row over Salman Rushdie's novel *The Satanic Verses* has in particular led to a feeling in some quarters of dissatisfaction with the State's apparent endorsement of one faith and mere toleration of others.[49] Indeed, in a society in which the Islamic community is growing in number and influence whilst the Church of England must struggle even to prevent attendances falling, the Establishment link does appear anachronistic.

There are, however, two further strands of argument in favour of disestablishment which relate more closely to the Church itself, and it is to these that we now turn. The first looks to the essential nature and characteristics of the Church, while the second warns of the practical dangers of Establishment. Different critics give varying degrees of prominence to these propositions.

The central thrust of Benn's argument is that the constitutional position of Anglicanism 'necessarily involves a subtle corruption of the spirit of the Church'. He laments political control over Church legislation and episcopal appointments, and sees in the ties between Church and State a strong disincentive against the calling into question of political policies by ecclesiastical persons. He claims that even if this disincentive can be overcome, the Church's authority is diminished by its being seen as beholden to the very object of its criticism. He advocates a form of 'liberation theology',[50] with disestablishment a necessary condition thereof.

Benn's position has been undermined somewhat by the occasional but highly provocative criticism of the government by leading churchmen during the 1980s. Another weakness is his tendency to see political commentary as the Church's primary role – a somewhat limited view which, it is respectfully suggested, may hinge upon his stance of admiration for but non-membership of the Christian Church. Nevertheless, other aspects of his argument are persuasive: he is keen to point out that the government which ultimately controls the Church of England is elected by members of all faiths and none, and he demonstrates the absurdity of having the Queen 'change her denomination' when in Scotland.

Bishop Mark Santer espouses an argument which is based not so much on the political silencing of the Church of England as on the obscuration of its rightful nature. For him, the Church's subjection to Christ is clouded by constitutional complications; its State-imposed shackles must be broken in order to restore it to its apostolic nature. He fears that its lack of autonomy will leave it lacking in integrity, and severely disadvantaged in any ecumenical ventures.

In response to this view, it may be said that the Anglican Church has happily *not* been at a disadvantage in interdenominational dialogue; the wider Church's respect for it was made evident by the unprecedented degree of participation in the Archbishop of Canterbury's enthronement service by dignitaries from a host of other denominations. Still, the argument is reminiscent of a powerful assertion by Bishop Hensley Henson in 1933: 'Whether the State be, as generally in the past, friendly, or, as not improbably in the future, hostile, the subordination of the spiritual society to the secular power is intrinsically wrong.'[51]

A defence of the Anglican Church's position which is pragmatic and practical rather than intuitive and theoretical is offered by such commentators as Clifford Longley[52] and Sir Owen Chadwick.[53] They highlight its historically cohesive role in society, and its existence for the benefit of the whole nation (not just its own members). The Archbishop of York, John Habgood, expands upon these ideas in his concept of 'folk religion'.[54] In essence the claim is that the mere existence of an Established Church induces more people to profess adherence thereto. It is even claimed that in certain areas the vicar will be welcome at virtually every door, simply as a result of Establishment. Meanwhile a related phenomenon, 'state religion', is said to ensure a Christian input to government.[55]

This argument presents great difficulties to the Christian commentator. On the one hand, it may fairly be said that it is unjust as regards other denominations and arrogant as regards atheists and members of other religions; such egocentricity is considered by most to be distinctly un-Anglican. On the other hand, if true, it means that disestablishment would block off an important route into the fellowship of the Church as a whole (while those who question the level of commitment of such proselytes could similarly be accused of arrogance).

Thus there is value in the arguments both of those who seek to disestablish the Anglican Church and of those who defend it. The concept of a Church subjugated by State power is indeed repugnant, but, as has been seen, the practical reality of the situation is very different. The Church of England has not been afraid to express publicly doubt concerning governmental wisdom; further, it appears not to have lost sight of its identity as a part of Christ's Church, and has been able without handicap to engage in meaningful co-operation and dialogue with other denominations and faiths. The system may not be ideal, but it works well enough for the Church. Governments, too, appear to find criticism from the Church no more difficult to sustain than, say, murmurings from the House of Lords. The British constitution is notorious for its atrophy in all but cases of urgent necessity; major change to the Church–State relationship is therefore unlikely.

CONCLUSION

The Established Church is a product of our constitutional history. Its special position in law has enabled it to inherit a fine tradition of music, art, architecture and liturgy, of which many of its members are justifiably proud. Its doctrine and practice is enshrined within a legal framework denied to other Churches. It is an organ of the State, permitted generally to take the initiative in its internal affairs, but subject ultimately to the Queen-in-Parliament.

The Church of England is also a part of the single 'holy, catholic and apostolic Church' referred to in the Nicene Creed. It must look to Jesus Christ as its founder and supreme governor; all that it does, it must do for his sake.

In the rarefied atmosphere of constitutional practice, the Anglican Church's continuing mission may be obscured by the formalized nature of its position as the State religion. In the parish church on a Sunday morning, however, it is more likely to be the ecclesiastical authority of the State that is forgotten. It is submitted that greater attention needs to be paid by all interested parties to both these aspects of the Anglican Church's life, for the next decade is likely to be a time of tremendous change. Anglicans are participating in the international 'Decade of Evangelism' under the leadership of a primate who appears uniquely qualified within the Anglican tradition to appeal to the unchurched masses; at the same time, there is a very real danger of a split within the Church's ranks if the ordination of women is approved at the final vote in 1992. It may well be that the Church of England will want, need, or be forced to change its constitutional position. Any decision as to how and when to do so ought, as far as possible, to be taken on an informed basis by all its members.

NOTES AND REFERENCES

1 The opening words of the Preface to the Ordinal, *Book of Common Prayer* (1662).
2 Assistant priests are normally called 'curates', although this term in fact means one with cure of souls in the parish (i.e. the parish priest and the bishop).
3 The Bishops of Edmonton, Kensington, Stepney, and Willesden. Such a scheme may be devised in any diocese: Dioceses Measure 1978 (No. 1) s. 11.
4 Inclusion on the Electoral Roll is not automatic, but any person who is over 16, baptized, and an Anglican resident in the parish or habitually worshipping in its church is entitled to be included.
5 See: E. Garth Moore, *Introduction to English Canon Law* (2nd edn, 1985), pp. 36–37.
6 Royal assent to its Acts was required after the Submission of the Clergy Act 1533. See p. 174.
7 Before 1533, the recipient had been the Pope. See p. 174.
8 Moore, *Introduction to English Canon Law*, p. 108.
9 D.L. Keir, *Constitutional History of Modern Britain since 1485* (9th edn, 1969), p. 51.
10 *Ibid.*, p. 55.
11 This was a papal appointment made only occasionally, granting local ecclesiastical authority superior even to that of the archbishop.
12 G.R. Elton, *The Tudor Constitution* (2nd edn, 1982), p. 255.
13 *Ibid.*, p. 350.
14 He in fact did so in the latter half of the next year.
15 Keir, *Constitutional History of Great Britain since 1485*, p. 62.
16 *Ibid.*, p. 353.
17 *Ibid.*, p. 348.
18 *Ibid.*, pp. 358–360.
19 It thus set in place the machinery still used today for episcopal appointments. See pp. 176–177.
20 Elton, *The Tudor Constitution*, pp. 364–365.
21 This was due, of course, to Edward VI's minority.
22 Bill of Rights 1688 s. 1; Act of Settlement 1700 ss. 2, 3.
23 Although, as can be seen from contemporary synodical debates, these remain highly varied within the Church of England.
24 He was enthroned on 14 September 1991.
25 Vacancy in See Committees Regulation 1977.
26 In such circumstances the dean and chapter would, until its abolition in 1967, have been criminally liable for a praemunire offence.
27 The appointment (not the nominees) may require prior synodical approval: Dioceses Measure 1978 (No. 1), s. 18.
28 A Roman Catholic may not, however, exercise this power: Roman Catholic Relief Act 1829.
29 Quoted by D. Nicholls (ed.), *Church and State in Britain since 1820* (1967), p. 7.
30 Reported by Tony Benn, 'A Case for the Disestablishment of the Church of England', in D. Reeves (ed.), *The Church and the State* (1984), p. 67.

31 Reported by Clifford Longley, *The Times*, 8 April 1991.
32 Quoted in *The Times*, 4 March 1991.
33 These are the two archbishops and the bishops of Durham, London and Winchester plus the 21 longest-serving diocesan bishops.
34 This is because new dioceses have from time to time been created without appertinent peerage rights.
35 Consider, for example, the 1984 proposal to change the episcopal appointments procedure: p. 177.
36 Submission of the Clergy Act 1533: p. 174.
37 A result of the Ecclesiastical Appeals Act 1532: p. 174.
38 See, for example, *R.* v. *James* [1850] 3 Car. and Kir. 167.
39 *Faith in the City: Report of the Archbishop of Canterbury's Commission on Urban Priority Areas*, para. 9.28. This is merely one example of the criticisms made by the report.
40 *The Times*, 4 March 1991.
41 The words are those of Brian Masters, Bishop of Edmonton.
42 Not least because it would avert a situation whereby the Queen-in-Parliament is in effect condemned by the Queen-in-the-Church.
43 English Church Bill 1988.
44 Quoted in *The Times*, 3 March 1983.
45 *Ibid*. He reproduces his argument under the title 'A Case for the Disestablishment of the Church of England', in D. Reeves (ed.), *The Church and the State* (1984).
46 See generally: Nicholls, *Church and State in Britain since 1820*.
47 Lord Hailsham *The Dilemma of Democracy* (1978), Ch. VI.
48 It is interesting to compare this Act, which runs to 39 sections and 5 schedules, with Benn's English Church Bill, a mere 12 lines in length.
49 *R.* v. *Lemon* [1979] 1 All ER 898, in which the House of Lords confirmed the continued operation of the offence of blasphemy in relation to the beliefs of the State religion, remains authoritative.
50 That is, a doctrine which recognizes the Church's authority to denounce and indeed work to overthrow oppressive political policies.
51 Quoted in Nicholls, *Church and State*, p. 210.
52 *The Times*, 16 September 1985.
53 *Report of the Archbishops' Commission on Church and State* (1970) – of which Chadwick was the chairman.
54 See generally: John Habgood, *Church and Nation in a Secular Age* (1983).
55 Indeed, the Speaker's Chaplain is greatly respected by parliamentarians of various religious persuasions.

Index

Abdication, *see* Monarchy
Administrative law, 65–78, 61
   duty to give reasons, 70–72
   order 53, 66–68, 71, 72–74
   reform, 70–76
   tribunals, 70
Andrew, Prince, 4, 9
Anne, Princess, 4
Armstrong, Sir Robert, 7, 89
Ashdown, Paddy, 113, 114, 145
Asquith, Herbert, 36
Attlee, Clement, 35, 84

Bagehot, Walter, 3, 11, 14–19, 22, 24, 26
Baldwin, Stanley, 6, 35, 79, 82, 83, 84
Beatrix, Queen, 4
Benn, Tony, 6, 11, 12, 87, 179, 180
Blake, Lord, 36–38
British Broadcasting Corporation, 127
Browne-Wilkinson, Sir Nicolas, 155, 158–161, 162, 163

Cabinet, 14–31, 87
   collective responsibility, 17
   committees, 20–22
   see also Prime minister
Callaghan, James, 6, 35, 39, 89, 141
Campbell-Bannerman, Sir Henry, 36
Carey, George, 170, 172, 176, 177
Chamberlain, Neville, 36, 84
Charles, Prince, 5, 9, 10
Church of England, 4, 10, 83, 84, 168–184
   legal basis of establishment, 172–176
   proposal for disestablishment, 179–182
   structure, 168–172
Churchill, Sir Winston, 3, 35, 36, 82, 83, 87
Civil service, 24–26
Commonwealth, 3, 4
Conservative Party, 32–39, 50, 51
   constitutional ideology, 51–59, 79–91
   leadership rules, 33–35

INDEX

Constitutional monarchy, 2, 3
  see also Monarchy
Crossman, Richard, 6, 19, 24, 40

Diana, Princess, 9
Diplock, Lord, 66
Disraeli, Benjamin, 22, 32, 79, 83, 86
Donaldson, Lord, 150, 151
Douglas-Home, Sir Alec, 33

Eden, Sir Anthony, 36
Edward VIII, King, 4, 10
Election campaigns, 120–135
  broadcasting, 126, 127
  constituency expenditure, 120–123, 127–134
  deposit, 122, 123
  party income, 123–134
Elizabeth II, Queen, 1, 3, 5
  see also Monarchy
Emergency powers, 59
European Communities, 39, 81, 113, 137, 141
European Convention on Human Rights, 122, 128, 148
European public law, 69, 71, 73

Falklands war, 88, 179
Foot, Michael, 86

George V, King, 1, 3, 5

George VI, King, 1, 3, 4, 10
Gladstone, William, 1, 20, 22, 32

Hailsham, Lord (formerly Quintin Hogg), 7, 36–38, 79, 82, 87, 150, 158, 161, 162, 163, 180
Hamilton, William, 12
Heath, Edward, 5, 6, 35, 81, 85–89, 153
Henry VIII, King, 4
Heseltine, Michael, 34, 35, 37, 39, 88
Hewart, Lord, 65, 67
Hogg, Quintin, see Hailsham
House of Commons, 5, 6, 15, 16, 142, 157, 160, 178
  select committees, 48
  see also Parliament
House of Lords, 1, 4, 84, 157, 160, 177
  see also Parliament
Howe, Sir Geoffrey, 33, 34, 85
Hughes, Simon, 7, 8
Hurd, Douglas, 35

Independent Broadcasting Authority, 127
Ingham, Bernard, 23

Jennings, Sir Ivor, 1, 2, 7
Joseph, Sir Keith, 8, 88
Judiciary, 148–167
  independence, 151–154

INDEX

Kinnock, Neil, 39, 115

Labour Party, 34, 38, 45, 79, 80, 87, 89, 92, 157
Lane, Lord, 68, 150
Liberal Democrats, *see* Social and Liberal Democrats
Liberal Party, 34, 38, 89, 180
   merger with SDP, 92–119
Lloyd George, David, 36, 84
Low, Sir Sidney, 7

MacDonald, Ramsay, 35, 36, 84
Mackintosh, John, 6, 19, 40
Maclennan, Robert, 92, 94–96, 100, 103–108, 110, 112
Macmillan, Harold, 36
Maine, Sir Henry, 79
Major, John, 2, 5, 6, 8, 35, 38, 86, 179
Margaret, Princess, 4
Margrethe II, Queen, 4
Meyer, Sir Anthony, 33
Monarchy, 1–13
   abdication, 5, 10
   and the Church of England, 176
   Commonwealth, 3, 4
   Crown finance, 7, 8
   and the prime minister, 5, 6, 19, 38
   royal prerogatives, 5–7
Monopolies and Mergers Commission, 48–51, 53, 60, 71
Morrison, Herbert, 45, 80

Nationalization legislation, 42–64
No-confidence motion (in the Commons), 6, 36, 37

Order, 53
   see also Administrative law
Owen, David, 94, 95, 111–114

Park, John James, 14–17, 22, 24, 26, 27
Parliament, 11, 16, 17, 26, 74, 156, 157, 161, 178
   and nationalized industries, 48
   proposal for fixed term, 7
   see also House of Commons; House of Lords
Peel, Sir Robert, 18
Political parties, 79–119
   and finance, *see* election campaigns
   see also Conservative Party; Labour Party; Proportional representation; Social and Liberal Democrats
Powell, Enoch, 81
Prime minister, 5–7, 14–27, 32–40, 153
   proposal for prime minister's department, 25, 26
   see also Cabinet
Privatization legislation, 42–64
Proportional representation, 5, 136–147

Regency, 5

189

Reid, Lord, 66
Robson, William, 43, 153, 163

St John-Stevas, Norman (later Lord St John), 36–38, 49, 161, 162
Scarman, Lord, 67, 75, 76
Select committees, *see* House of Commons
Social and Liberal Democrats, 80, 92–119, 157
Steel, David, 94, 97, 99, 100, 105, 109, 111, 112

Tebbit, Norman, 86

Thatcher, Sir Denis, 33
Thatcher, Margaret, 2, 5, 6, 18, 20–27, 32–40, 81, 85–89, 109, 114, 154, 158, 164, 177, 178
Tribunals, *see* Administrative law

Victoria, Queen, 6, 9

Wade, Sir William, 69
Williams, Shirley, 95, 100, 104, 105
Wilson, Harold, 6, 35, 39, 81
Woolf, Lord Justice, 67, 71